BEHIND THE BOARDROOM DOOR

Books by Robert Kirk Mueller

Effective Management Through Probability Controls
Risk, Survival and Power
The Innovation Ethic
Board Life: Realities of Being a Corporate Director
Buzzwords: A Guide to the Language of Leadership
Metadevelopment: Beyond the Bottom Line
New Directions for Directors
Career Conflict: Management's Inelegant Dysfunction
Board Compass: What It Means to Be a Director in a Changing World
The Incompleat Board: The Unfolding of Corporate Governance
Board Score: How to Judge Boardworthiness

BEHIND THE BOARDROOM DOOR

Robert Kirk Mueller

Illustrated by
Robert Manley

Crown Publishers, Inc.   New York

Grateful acknowledgment is hereby made for the use of excerpted materials as follows:

Board Life: Realities of Being a Corporate Director by Robert Kirk Mueller, copyright © 1974 by Amacom, a division of American Management Associations, New York. All rights reserved. Reprinted by permission of the publisher.

The Incompleat Board: The Unfolding of Corporate Governance, copyright © 1981 by D. C. Heath and Company, Lexington Books, Lexington, Massachusetts. All rights reserved. Reprinted by permission of the publisher.

Published by Crown Publishers, Inc., One Park Avenue, New York, New York 10016, and simultaneously in Canada by General Publishing Company Limited
Manufactured in the United States of America
Library of Congress Cataloging in Publication Data
Mueller, Robert Kirk.
    Behind the boardroom door.

    Includes index.
    1. Directors of corporations.   I. Title.
HD2745.M79   1984   658.4'22   83-25173
ISBN: 0-517-55255-8

Book design by Leonard Henderson

10 9 8 7 6 5 4 3 2 1

First Edition

Contents

Acknowledgments

Numerous thankworthy persons are among the several hundred fellow directors and trustees with whom I have served over the years in the ranks of advisory boards, councils, statutory boards, and trusteeships. A few turkeys, yes, but mainly eagles as far as ethics, élan, eminence, and empressement are concerned.

The nonfictional actors in the boardplays recalled in these chapters could well riposte with spoor from my own ploys, peccadillos, and eccentricities—both conscious and unconscious. But I can claim some board squatter's writes in undertaking *Behind the Boardroom Door.*

Saying grace to all those unidentified contributors to whom acknowledgment is due rightfully ends with a special open thanks to Alma Triner. She suggested the less serious approach to the boardroom and was my guide in many manuscript improvements. James O. Wade, my editor, provided order to my "war stories." I am indebted to Jim for encouragement, suggestions, and incisive editing of the book.

Lincoln, Massachusetts   Robert Kirk Mueller

BEHIND THE BOARDROOM DOOR

1

Entering the Boardroom

Caveat Lector (and Would-be Director)

Managers manage; directors govern. I have written five books on corporate governance—that body of lore dealing with how members of boards of directors *should* behave and what they are *supposed* to accomplish. But this book is largely concerned with what really goes on in that corporate crypt known as the boardroom. This is an insider's collection of "war stories." It begins with a cautionary note and goes on to give some advice about survival in the corporate briarpatch of governance.

If you are thinking about the rewards that come with a seat on a board of, say, a good-sized corporation, or even one of modest dimensions, consider this first:

- In 1978 more total years of prison time were assessed against corporate officials, including directors, under the Sherman & Clayton antitrust statutes than during the preceding eighty-nine years of the act's existence. Winds of change are howling at the boardroom door.
- Corporate gadflys—legal, government, and academic analysts and journalists—are attacking director performance. They fail to stress the good side, the potential, and means for improving director service.

1

- Problems of board responsibility, inactivity, abuse of power, and dereliction of duty are more than can be dealt with by public opinion or by regulatory or legal reform. An understanding of human frailty and the novel side of directorship is essential. In reality, corrective action must come from directors themselves.

Yes, there is trouble in ample measure at the very top. But there is no shortage of volunteers, even though the road to the boardroom may be a great deal more difficult than aspirants can imagine.

In the Beginning

The boardroom door first opened for me in 1942 through an invitation to join the Western Massachusetts Advisory Board of Liberty Mutual Insurance Company in Springfield, Massachusetts. The dominant qualification for membership was holding a responsible position in a company buying insurance. No fiduciary aspects or fees were involved. Compared to the current "due-diligence-do-something" boardroom climate, the nature of this advisory role was that of just sitting around the stove. Our participation consisted of listening to senior executives of the company extol their regional plans while we enjoyed one another's company and a splendid lunch several times a year.

This is where I first learned the best thing to hold on to in the boardroom is each other. I also learned never to delay the end of a board meeting nor the beginning of the lunch hour. Thinking back on the experience, I've decided the only thing wrong with accomplishing nothing at a board meeting is that you never know when you are finished.

My next admission to a boardroom was in the 1950s through the simple device of forming my own corporation. Since the first role of a director is to legitimatize a corporation—all companies must have directors—three of us ("Bud" Harrison Lyman, Esquire, an attorney; Ralph Hansen, a marketing executive and inventor; and I) registered a Massachusetts corporation—Line and Staff, Inc.—and elected ourselves directors. This smallish enterprise created, manufactured, and marketed "clever" self-help aids for business—essentially studio-card printed communications. As chairman and CEO, I saw that our board meetings paralleled those of typical closely held corporations. Boardroom mates were close friends and we convened only because the law says you have to have a directorate. We were not young enough to know everything, so our enterprise flamed out in three years as competition reacted and sales plummeted. Collapse was triggered when two of the directors were relocated geographically.

Lessons learned: (a) never do anything for the first time, (b) at some time in the life cycle of virtually every corporation its ability to succeed in spite of the board runs out, and (c) there are more buzzards than carcasses.

Curtain Raisers

My first industrial boardroom experience came along in 1952 with selection as president and election as director of Shawinigan Resins Corporation in Indian Orchard, Massachusetts. I never knew what governance was until I was elected to this board. Then, of course, it was too late. The company was a joint venture between Shawinigan Chemicals Ltd., a Canadian company, and Monsanto. The mission was to develop, manufacture, and market polyvinyl butyral—a plastic safety-glass interlayer. The board was made up of insiders from the parental owners and served primarily to increase the effectiveness of the management. This meant that shortages and losses were divided equally between the Canadians and the Americans.

The initial business concept was sound. The Canadians furnished a patented process and source of vinyl acetate monomer, which was a prime raw material. Monsanto furnished a plant site, management, and a marketing organization which had served the safety-glass market since the early automotive days of isinglass curtains for the Model T and later cellulose nitrate safety glass during the celluloid-collar period. The new interlayer replaced these acetate and nitrate plastics, which some of us remember as producing brown spot deterioration and bubble formation in roadster windshields of the Roaring Twenties.

One of the tough boardroom problems inherent in this fifty-fifty venture was the ever-present threat of stalemate, particularly over price of raw materials purchased only from the Canadians. Resolution of this key matter always escalated to a bargaining session between a private American chairman (which I had since become) and a Canadian chairman. This would be duly ratified by the daughter company's board made up of captives from each joint-venture company. Such formal action came after a long cocktail party and sumptuous dinner preceding the next day's board meeting. This rather raucous event occurred annually at time of purchase-contract signing. The captive directors' attitude was understandable—eat, drink, and be merry, for tomorrow we may be retroactive. It was here that I gained great admiration for Canadian consumption and respect for age, particularly when it is bottled.

My directorship of eleven years' duration with Shawinigan Resins Corporation saw the successful development of a high-technology growth company, albeit not directly a publicly owned entity. Here I learned: (a) anytime things appear to be going smoothly you haven't got the right information, (b) the board is an ingenious device for recognizing individual performance without individual responsibility, (c) strategies develop most easily from big backlogs, (d) the company's share of the market is really lower than you think, (e) the number of competitors never declines, (f) only mediocre directors are always at their best, and (g) if you have been to enough board meetings over a long period of time, the meetings become more important than the issues.

More boardroom doors opened for me in the sixties, primarily because of fallout from volunteer activities on councils and boards of professional societies, trade associations, editorial groups, and not-for-profit institutions. It is true that half of life's experiences are below average in satisfaction, but as a boardroom buff I can say from these exposures that there is no substitute for genuine lack of preparation for directorship. The process for director selection is imperfect. It is a mix of who's-who and who-knows-whom. The latter criterion prevails; if you have to tell other board members about your distinguished background, you don't have one.

The volunteer, advisory-board, and council route to the star chamber is perhaps the best development track into the corporate boardroom. Recognizing that "men of principle outnumber men of honor" on most boards of directors, the aspiring director should be aware that internal harmony is more valued in most boardrooms than effectiveness. This may be one reason women and minorities are so poorly represented. When a firm becomes large, widely held publicly, and professionally managed, the board role tilts toward its socially oriented trustee or stewardship function whereby it represents *all* owners and the society in which the corporation exists. Mobil Corporation, Mead Corporation, and Connecticut General Life Insurance Company are examples of such corporations.

Financial Intermediaries

Thanks primarily to old college blue-and-gold ties from my graduate school, the University of Michigan, and my position in a For-

tune 500 company, I was elected in 1965 to the board of
Massachusetts Mutual Life Insurance Company. I had been a
director and executive committee member of the Valley Bank and
Trust Company of Springfield, Massachusetts, since 1958 and
served with some insurance company executives who were also on
the bank board. This helped, of course, with the cross-check recruiting practice most often used for director nominations. While
explicit criteria for boardworthiness, if applied, were never re-

vealed to me, insurance and banking are regulated industries. Thus their boards have rather special requirements for directorship.

Bank boards are a very special species. Directors rarely *think* in bank board meetings. They sit together and talk through the standard agenda drill specified by the bewildering web of federal and state statutes and regulations from the comptroller of the currency, the FDIC, and the Federal Reserve Board. The directors receive information from the management, adjudicate, and compromise. But they seldom can think or create anything in the highly regulated inner sanctum in which they govern. Troubled times are changing this relative state of immobility. Still, you would be surprised to see how many bank directors drive off in their Mercedeses to get advice from stockbrokers who rode to work on the bus.

Some lessons learned over twenty-four years in bank boardrooms cast an interesting light on accountability and functions of directors:

- A higher level of performance and behavior is expected of a bank director than of a business corporate director.
- Those who think they know it all are very annoying to those who do.
- Bank directors take an oath of office; business corporation directors do not.
- Bank directors have residence and citizenship requirements; their peers in business may but often do not.
- Fees are a function of meeting frequency and not results of board action.
- Investment bankers cannot serve as bank directors but can serve on business corporate boards.
- Regulations require bank directors to approve loans, but, so far, they don't require directors to approve loans that cover the interest on the initial loans.
- The most difficult thing in the boardroom is to know how to do a thing and to watch—without commenting—a fellow director doing it wrong.
- A bank director may be removed from office for unsound practices with recited statutory liability for damages resulting from willful violation of the law; only vague, if any, procedures like these appear in typical business corporation codes.

- At board meetings the one unmatched asset is the ability to yawn with your mouth closed.
- Some directors will believe anything if it is whispered to them.
- Trivial matters take up more time because we know more about them than important matters. Trivial matters are handled early in the agenda. Important matters either are never resolved or are sorted out at the end of the agenda, when there is insufficient time for full discussion.
- If you explain you were late for the board meeting because you had car trouble, the next meeting you *will* have car trouble.

These early years on bank and insurance company boards, advisory councils, and a small high-tech company board taught me that board meetings are no substitute for progress; that anyone who thinks there is some good in every director hasn't met enough of them; and that when it is not necessary to make a decision, it is necessary *not* to make a decision. My most enlightening boardroom experience, however, came in 1961.

Big Business Board Debut

Nineteen-sixty-one was the year the DNA genetic code was broken by Watson and Crick, Kennedy ordered the Bay of Pigs invasion, the Berlin Wall was erected, and Vostok I, the Russian-manned spaceship, first circled the earth. My election to the Monsanto board amid these profound world events was little noticed except by my family. They pointed out that people are elected to boards not by what they can do but by what people think they can do.

This comparatively shallow event in the scheme of world affairs came at a time when an inside director could serve without drawing much SEC or public attention. It did, however, bring forth a flush of attention from insurance and real estate agents, stockbrokers, investment advisers, credit card purveyors, Cadillac dealers, charitable institutions, political and alumni fund raisers, Jehovah's Witnesses, environmental activist groups, burglars, landscape services, septic tank installers, driveway surfacers, tax shelter experts, airline frequent-traveler clubs, and private-aircraft peddlers.

The first director practice that I had to learn in this career of company board membership was that it takes rare talent for a director—particularly an inside director—to appreciate the difference between running a company and seeing that it is well run. You have to buy more flyswatters and fewer sledgehammers.

It is sort of like stopping going out with the girls and devoting your attention to studying Freud. One has to keep monthly board issues separate from daily operating executive problems. As our oldest outside director told me at my first board meeting, "I leave my problems in the boardroom. . . . I have another set at home."

The other revelation was the full realization of the limits of impact of an inside director, who advises but mostly consents in his company's boardroom—except in instances when he is also the chief executive officer. There is no way to soar into independent governance decision-making with the outside-director eagles when you are an inside turkey daily reporting to your boss who is CEO and of course is also on the same board.

Directorship on the multinational Monsanto board afforded an unusually global view, because I was the parent board-level housemother for Monsanto's eighty-seven overseas subsidiary, associated, and affiliated companies. These were second-, third-, and fourth-tier corporations in which Monsanto owned anywhere from less than 10 percent to 50 percent and on up to 100 percent of the equity. Most directors, except where required by local law, were captive company executives.

It was here that I first learned about European labor participation in the boardroom. Swedish boards have more women in the boardroom than any other country. Women directors hold more than 10 percent of Swedish board seats. I also found out about "corporate transparency" and the Dutch "guilder complex" in which the parliament requires disclosure on salary structures and honoraria paid company directors.

One gimmick we learned from the Japanese was how to uncouple a director. The Japanese have a proverb—*Ebi odoredemo kawa wo idezu* ("Though the shrimp may jump about he will not leave the river"). When Japanese go to work for a company, they expect—and the company expects—that they will be there until retirement. In return for such allegiance, the company behaves like a father-protector to its employees and officers. Benefits include housing, low-interest loans, welfare services, inexpensive meals, transportation, vacations, and ceremonial allowances for marriage, for children, and burial costs of nearby relatives.

In Japan, with employment assured up to the normal retirement age, firing is not a practical means of shedding an executive. Instead he is elected—promoted—to the board, where he is no longer legally an employee and *can* be fired. We have an American phrase which covers this maneuver: "percussive sublimation."

The British practice on directorial perquisites was probably best stated by James Callaghan, who said that "directors' boardrooms are the top people's National Assistance Board [i.e., unemployment offices], only they are better upholstered."

In May 1982 the American Law Institute held its fifty-ninth annual meeting in Philadelphia to discuss its Tentative Draft No. 1 of "Restatements" devoted to clarifying the law on the governance and structure of the business corporation. This 425-page document was the outcome of several years of legal and philosophical noodling by experts in this ineffable domain of corporate governance. The recommendations for good corporate practice were aimed at the director who has a "significant relationship" with the senior executives of a corporation if, among other things, he is employed by the corporation or was employed within two preceding years. The newly proposed principles of corporate governance deemphasize the distinction between inside and outside directors in favor of the critical distinction between "directors who have a significant economic or professional relationship with senior executives and directors who do not."

These significant relationships of "inside directors" may be cause for reviewing or otherwise acting on matters in which the director may be or has been involved. The senior executives may be protégés or subordinates of the chief executive, or insiders who often receive continuing payments from the corporation that are partly discretionary—stock options, bonuses, or other benefits. Such emoluments are subject to action by the board on which the recipient sits. To quote H. L. Mencken, this makes the insider director like the "law student who marks his own examination papers."

Among other problems of large publicly held corporations addressed by the American Law Institute are (a) the board nominating itself, then congratulating its elected directors in its annual report, thus functioning as a self-perpetuating oligarchy; (b) holding management accountable for performance and how to monitor this; (c) relationships between directors, management, shareholders, and the company itself; (d) "tenure" on the board; and (e) separation of chairmanship of the board from the CEO role. A better check-and-balance system is being called for, but it will be some time before any consensus of legal and business leaders is attained.

So much for my own valuable directorship experience on the multinational corporate circuit. This has been further enriched in serving on the Arthur D. Little, Inc., board and its various overseas subsidiaries and in consulting with boards of directors of foreign and United States clients.

Boardroom Axioms

Some say anyone who accepts election to a publicly owned United States company board doesn't know enough about the exposure and liabilities to be qualified. But for those who do seek and/or accept an invitation to join a board, the following "axioms" may help.

- No matter how much of a dividend is declared by a board of directors or how significant an acquisition, divestiture, or merger may be, some of the shareowners won't like it.
- No matter how trivial a capital expenditure or investment may be, it is always possible to build it up to a major expansion as far as competition is concerned.
- Emeritus directors will attend all meetings regardless of the weather, the agenda, or the inconvenience. There will be the same old faces but a lot of new teeth.
- The less important or younger you are on a board of directors, the more you will be missed if you don't show up for a meeting. Some directors have to be stuck with committee work.
- Scope of board action is greatest when knowledge is least complete. Scope of board action is the least when knowledge is the greatest.
- Advisory boards tend to accomplish very little unless the chairman of the statutory board or the CEO is very careful about the care and feeding of advisers. Otherwise, advisory

directors get together to renew acquaintances, exchange
business gossip, and redirect their hostilities and hurt feelings.

- When all is said and done in the boardroom there is more
  said than done.
- When you get a chance to join a board, don't rush it. Keep
  calm, check your lawyer, spouse, and minister. Ask good
  questions like "What can I bring to the board?" Don't
  mention fees or perks.
- If you don't know who is to blame for inaction on the
  board, you are!
- Keep a diary of your disinterested, unaffiliated, independent, objective, nonpartisan (to use the SEC terms of ven-
  ery) positions on controversial board matters. Try to soar
  with the SEC eagles rather than the captive turkeys who
  also have the actual or perceived conflict-of-interest and
  hierarchical burdens to bear.
- Three boardroom crises occur with the owners of closely
  held corporations: (a) the crisis of letting go, (b) the crisis of
  reorganization, and (c) the crisis of succession—the dynas-
  tic tendency.
- A continuum of boardroom issues exists in closely held corporations. There is ceremony, matrimony, parsimony, acri-
  mony, and alimony. There is even palimony where
  cohabitation with certain in-the-family understandings
  exist in the boardroom without the legal entanglement
  which would be involved in a public corporation.
- There is good news and bad news in the boardroom. The
  bad news is that this year there will be more government
  intrusion, more regulation, and more directors sued and
  put in jail than last year.
- The good news is that this year's board problems are going
  to be less than next year's problems. The issues to be faced
  in the boardroom during the eighties will be even more
  vexatious than those of the seventies.

High Hatiquette

The current social distinction attached to boardroom inhabitants
is transient. Public opinion polls in 1982 show corporate directors

in the United States only rank higher in public esteem than labor leaders and federal government officials. Despite this there has always been snob appeal about regents, viziers, governors, trustees, directors, and other actors on the stage of leadership.

If you happen to enjoy boardroom enshrinement—or imagine that you might—chances are you make sure others know of it, especially if they are from another country, another industry, another community or field of endeavor. The desire to join the elite, if not the elect, is a stirring force in the business world, which has its own extension ladders into this attic of the conventional business domain.

But there are all sorts of directors and director roles to aspire to, or avoid, depending on their appeal to you and on your morals, ethics, value system, intellectual bent, aspirations, bloodlines, central life interests, spouse pressures, economic interests, sense of social responsibilities, and age next birthday.

There is no hereditary or exclusive class of United States boardroom society, but a caste index might be as follows:

Exclusively Upper-Class (Concorde-ians and uppish private jet-setters)
   Directors of Fortune 100 industrial companies
   Directors of top financial intermediary companies
   Directors of top service companies
   Trustees and directors of major universities
   High-ranking military (retired) and former government officials
   International directors (e.g., *Aufsichtsrat* top-tier European governing boards)
   Directors or trustees of distinguished learned societies
   Trustees or directors of large churches and major hospitals
Infiltrated by Arrivistes (overly ambitious persons; upper-crust, often held together by their own dough)
   Controlling directors (SEC jargon for primary owners)
   Professional directors (no other employment)
   Minority directors (may move up if on prestigious board)
   Decorative directors
   Family directors
   Retired bureaucrat directors
Hopelessly Bourgeois (capitalists, social middle class)
   Functional directors (may be higher if topflight professionals)

Union or employee directors
Public directors
Founder directors (can move up if socially acceptable)
Directors of trade associations

Classless Society (relatively obscure roles)
  Inside directors (hired hands)
  Advisory directors
  Regional directors
  Surrogate directors
  Shadow directors
  Alternate directors
Untouchables
  Directors of privately held companies
  Emeritus directors
  Honorary directors
  Nepot directors
  Transvestite directors

History tailgates the current ranking of these director species. Whether you agree with the classification or not is unimportant. It racks up a set of gateways and paths to the boardroom. As P. T. Barnum might have said to the crowd of boardroom aspirants viewing this caste index, "This way to the ingress."

To begin with, learn to *look* important. Speak with assurance, sticking to generally accepted facts; avoid arguments; contrive to mingle with important people; before addressing someone you wish to impress, ferret out his or her remedies for current problems and advocate them staunchly. Above all, retain and develop your sense of humor if you yearn for a seat in the boardroom. The value of a sense of humor and a sense of detachment in maintaining emotional control cannot be overrated. In the boardroom of the eighties it may be that only he or she who laughs best will last.

2

I'm Okay—He's Not

It isn't so much what's on the table that matters as what's on the chairs.

WILLIAM SCHWENK GILBERT, English playwright

The psychodynamics behind the boardroom door set up some fascinating situations. Some of these are played out in the *Wall Street Journal, Fortune, Business Week, Forbes,* the *Economist,* and other business publications. A sprinkling of juicy headlines gives a keyhole view of some American boardroom interpersonal transactions.

- Clipped Wings: How Braniff Chief was Forced to Resign Under Fire

  WALL STREET JOURNAL
- Harvester Co. Slices 20% from Salaries of 16 Top Officers

  WALL STREET JOURNAL
- United Jersey Bank President, Chief Quits "For Personal Reasons"

  WALL STREET JOURNAL
- Two Dissidents Get Seats as Directors of Sorg Paper Co.

  WALL STREET JOURNAL
- Boardroom Rift over Nu-Swift Interim Account

  FINANCIAL TIMES
- Chairman of Policy-Setting Committee of ITT Austrian Subsidiary Involved in Scandal

  NEW YORK TIMES
- Five Star Loses Four Directors to Policy Disagreement

  DIRECTOR'S MONTHLY

Given these examples it is helpful to understand some alien-to-the-boardroom concepts and vocabulary which apply in this brief excursion into the ego state of the boardroom.

Out of the blue, in August 1982, I received the following letter request from an unknown person who apparently made a hobby out of playing on the self-esteem values of chairmen.

Dear Mr. Mueller,

I am a collector of business cards and I would like very much to add your card to my collection. As the chairman of the board of a major research company, I feel that your card would make an excellent addition to my collection. If you wish to donate your card to me, may I please ask that you mail it to me at this address.

Sincerely,
[name witheld]

After discussing this with our corporate counsel I figured the writer might be up to some misuse or abuse of possession of my business card, perhaps indicating personal friendship or acquaintance with the company, so I didn't respond. I've always wished I had let my vanity carry on with this unknown—probably harmless—guy who tried to get in correspondence with me.

To get back to the ego state of the boardroom, many directors feel themselves in the presence of true greatness the moment they close the boardroom door. One of my good friends has business cards made of each of the boards of directors on which he serves. He uses these cards variously to identify himself whenever such identity seems to give him a leg up on the occasion. Josh Billings commented on such boardroom ego in the mid-nineteenth century: "There's nothing that you and I make as many blunders about, and the world so few, as the actual amount of our own importance."

A director's brazen assurance in the boardroom flows from an ego state of mind, divided into three ego states, the cornerstone of transactional analysis (TA), which is a theory of personality, not a method of treatment.*

* For more on transactional analysis, see Eric Berne, *Games People Play* (1964), *Principles of Group Treatment* (1966), *Transactional Analysis in Psychotherapy* (1961), and *What Do You Say After You Say Hello?* (1972), all Grove Press, New York.

The boardroom, generally replete with "high intensity ego state" individuals—maybe even geriatric or blind at times—is the scene of considerable interpersonal gaming, group dynamics, and structural patterning. Human transactions and unconscious personal plans or scripts of individual directors are an integal part of boardroom activities when individuals function as members of a full board of directors. When we are on a board it is necessary to be sensitive to these psychodramas. Very few directors will admit, however, to the fact that they are acting in a boardroom play.

Ego States

When Oscar Levant remarked that he had given up reading books because "I find it takes my mind off myself" he expressed a familiar ego state or internalization of one of the three categories of coherent organizations of thought, feeling, and behavior. Levant's was the psychological state left over from childhood that reemerges in later life as the early, most intense feelings and needs are expressed. The child ego states are typically subdivided into adopted or natural states, depending on parental dominance or absence of such.

The second category is more popularly known as parental ego state. In this the mind set of the individual is borrowed from the parents' behavior in relation to the child, either punishing or nurturing. These clue into actual experience in childhood and with actual parents, according to psychodynamic theory. I can remember my mother teaching me the facts of life gradually—she started in with artificial flowers.

The third state of the ego is that of the objective and data-processing role of a mind attuned to external reality. This is manifest in adulthood and its mediation between the child and parent categories. This state is referred to as the adult ego state and, we hope, is representative of the boardroom condition. The only problem I see with every board member's being in this adult ego state is that there is no chance for advancement.

One measure of the adult ego state is when one begins to feel guilty about the sacrifices a spouse makes in the career climb of a typical person of distinction. An English business friend of mine, who was tapped from his top managing directorship to become chairman of a large multinational British conglomerate, inaugurated his administration by naming a newly launched petroleum tanker owned by the company after his wife. As he put it, somewhat drolly, at the christening ceremony: "I attribute my money, my position, and my accomplishments to my first wife, and my second wife to my money, my position, and my accomplishments."

Personality Structures

Given these three psychic states, parallels can be drawn between internal conflict and interpersonal behavior in that both have their origins in family interaction patterns. Whether a board is one big happy (or unhappy) family results, in part, from the relationships stemming from directors' individual states of mind as they join in the boardroom chorus to govern an institution—a chorus often rendered in several unsteady movements.

Analysis of boardroom play reveals mutual or individual isolation, conflicts, cooperation, or predominance within and between the personalities sitting in the boardroom chairs. No board of directors I know of would stand for such a structural analysis of its behavior behind the boardroom door. But no director ought to play the game unless he can recognize the *real* identity of the players.

The majority of boards have enough sophisticated, experienced, and well-educated directors who can comprehend the differences and interplay of personality with external, objective board dynamics in dealing with business problems. It is difficult to separate these two fields of play and to know which of the members of the board are totally objective, yet sufficiently subjective and empathetic to behave constructively and cause a correct decision to be made by the directorate. One New England board I'm familiar with is so contained and wound up in its own dynamics and oblivious of broader business problems, they just hope the South never gets the atom bomb.

Most directors have reached their adult ego state through experience, education, and inherent character attributes. Any formal or informal standards for director nomination have implicit requirements for maturity or "adultness" of personality. I well recall my first experience in the boardroom after election to a Fortune 500 company's board. I was being sized up as to my level of adultness and cool. When I arrived only one person said hello; when I left everyone said goodbye. I had apparently passed the peer test—or, on second thought, was it because they were glad to see me go?

Under the assumption that the board is populated by capable grown-ups, as distinct from a Junior Achievement model company board, there should be a minimum of adversarial personal interactions behind the boardroom door. But of course all boards aren't perfect in this respect. Consequently there does exist in every boardroom a ceaseless pattern of group processes, personal resistances, and reactions between directors. For example, I've noticed when directors arrive at a meeting at which there is some project or decision about which there is some doubt, the directors usually tend to shake hands.

Whether your board needs an analysis or not, there is merit in individual directors' being more personally aware of what really goes in the boardroom. One director friend expressed it this way: "The members of a board are supposed to think at a board meeting, the CEO is supposed to talk, and the chairman is supposed to keep the directors from talking and the CEO from thinking."

Games Directors Play—and How Kindly Chairmen Referee

Public faces behave differently in private places. Director faces are no exception. The state of mind and the personality shape the pattern of director behavior in the boardroom. This mind set is wrapped up in individual ego states. The result—directors often engage in ego games. These games are fascinating if you are aware of them. They usually occur only in the privacy of the boardroom. The games flush out personal beliefs, value systems, hidden agenda, emotional hang-ups, biases, human frailties, and political maneuverings.

One common thread in most director games is their well-defined, predictable outcomes despite any concealed motivations. Eric Berne called such transactions "a series of moves with a snare." Also the outcome usually has a dramatic quality about it. Histrionics accompanying a director's boardroom behavior often belie the ulterior nature of his or her position. The old maxim of raise your voice when your argument is weak also holds in boardroom games.

An effective chairman will recognize the games underway and play along or redirect the psychodrama. This steering can be toward more rational reckoning and realistic quality of the adult ego state of thinking and understanding. If the game is operating at the child's level of archaic fears or expectations, or the parent level of a prim, righteous, prejudicial mind set cluttered with preconceived ideas, the adroit chairman can often nudge deliberations toward the adult state of conscious reasoning. Pulling off such a shift in group behavior is the hallmark of good chairmanship. It requires an understanding of personalities, a shrewd sense of timing, and insight into the ulterior quality of the posturing and rhetoric.

Ego games do not abide by the bylaws, the rituals, or the pastimes normally present in the boardworld. An ego game is never candid. It is essentially a series of superficially plausible moves with some concealed motive and a planned payoff. Here are some disguised boardroom situations in which I have been involved in recent years where director ego states play ego games. The disguise is advisable, for the drama may be more of an inside story than an outside director should know (or tell) about the boardroom.

More often than not the sudden entry of the child comes as a shock when it happens on other occasions. It is not unusual for the child to pop up late in a board meeting when a particularly thorny problem surfaces requiring a lot of trade-offs of personal "stakes" or interests of individual directors. The board of International Investments Ltd.* had just decided to change its investment patterns in southern European countries. This meant partially abandoning the country where its founding had been the little acorn from which had grown the great oak of the corporation. It had been a painful discussion for all of the seven directors, four of whom were elder statesmen and immediate descendants of the founding families. The three younger directors, who were also related, though less directly, to the founding families, had attended graduate schools of business. An enlightened view of business strategy, the role of a board as distinct from management, and the issue of fiduciary responsibility of directors to *all* the shareowners had been inculcated in them. These matters troubled the younger members of the board. The issue before the board was a change in composition of membership through additional directors who would not be associated with the families holding sizable company ownership, although these families held only a small percentage of shares outstanding. One of the more eloquent of the younger directors expounded at great length on the social consciousness and fiduciary accountability of the incumbent directors, with no need to perturb the closed circle of board membership with outsiders. They wouldn't fit the image of the corporation and its great heritage, the election of more directors would indicate that there was a failing on the part of the board . . . all sorts of subjective arguments for maintaining the status quo were emotionally presented.

What was really behind this impassioned performance was the child role at work on "How could I ever explain this to my father?"—who had recently retired from the board at eighty years of age but whose influence still reigned. Other members of the board in their adult states understood this. The chairman intervened and decided to delay any board changes until the time was more opportune and a more conscious reasoning would prevail.

The child ego state was at play doubletime in another board crisis when the newly elected chairman of Imeroil Ltd.* was confronted by a challenge from one of his outside directors, who sought to bully the newly elected chairman into deference and submission

---

* These are not the real names of the companies.

on financial policy matters in which the chairman was less experienced. This not-so-subtle contest over who had the best financial
judgment took place over a nine-month period of stress. Arguments
took place on both significant policy and procedural decisions concerning the financial strategy of the corporation, particularly in the
area of foreign exchange risks. At first, this was a covert test of
wills. In some aspects, immature boardroom tactics and intuitive
verbal fencing began to occur openly in board meetings as the
"bully" and the chairman squared off repeatedly. The upshot was
that the dissident director saw that his warfare was now in the open
and his struggle for power was attracting insufficient support from
the other directors. He resigned because of "press of other duties."
The chairman had carefully played this hidden power struggle out
into the open board sessions in order to expose the lack of rapport.
Without overtly stating that this was a conflict of wills, he let the
challenger "hang" himself through realization that if push came to
shove on a board decision, the board would support the newly
elected chairman, who at the time was also the CEO.

Looking back on this series of events and knowing the actors involved, I recall that the defecting director had always had his way
during his successful business career. While his power tactics could
be considered flowing in part from the child ego state at work, he
also superimposed some of the parent in borrowing preconceived
ideas from his chairman-CEO role in his own company, where he
ruled with an iron hand and had a captive and docile board of
directors. The bully role had child emotional content.

The international twist to the games directors play took place
early in my association with the Transbay Corporation,* where I
was privileged to work with the board of directors on its expansion
into Latin America. The American president of the company was a
model of the ethical and professional marketing-type executive. He
carried the corporate flag overseas with great aplomb. As was the
custom, many of the trips abroad involved socializing with wives
and families of overseas staffs, government officials, suppliers, customers, and financial houses. Transbay worked up a major investment project in the $36 million range for a Brazilian factory near
Campinas. The economic evaluation, the country risk assessment,
and other elements of the project were favorable, and the project

---

* These are not the real names of the companies.

was up for consideration by the full board. The president had warmed up the outside directors over a period of about a year while the engineering and marketing work was done to support the appropriation request. The top management and the four inside members of the board had labored hard to support their chief's presentation. At the last minute the proposal was stricken from the board agenda and the president explained to his board that he and management had had second thoughts about the political stability of Brazil in the years ahead and therefore were deferring any further action. I later found out that this turning point in advocacy was triggered by and coincident with the president's trip to São Paulo about six weeks before the board meeting to check again on the local situation. His wife had been pinched on the Corcovado— or better said, she was pinched when they stopped off en route at Rio de Janeiro and took the aerial tram to the top of Hunchback Mountain.

The parent ego prejudice against foreigners was bruised when the primly righteous lady was admired and tweaked from behind by a Brazilian national. Perhaps her archaic child fears lay at the bottom? Apparently this was not the place a respectable Transbay Corporation should carry on its business, according to the president's reactive interpretation. The parent in the spouse overcame the adult in the president. Although the board never knew the real reasons for management's change of attitude, Brazil lost a major international investor. The company lost a window of opportunity to place its manufacturing in a growing if somewhat risky market. The company never recovered its enthusiasm for Brazil and still has not made a serious commitment there.*

In upper New York State I was attending a board meeting where the president, newly appointed following an outside search, was in high-gear discussion with his directors. Having been sought after and lured away from another chief executive position he was feeling his oats, and his manner was that of a lecturer to freshman students. The parent mind set was obvious in his preconceived ideas borrowed from his previous career. Over a period of several meetings he dealt with the board members in a condescending way as if they were in the child state of mind.

* In view of Brazil's economic situation today, this ill-timed tweak might well have been a message from the god of governance because the corporation saved millions it might otherwise have lost in a Brazilian operation.

The nonexecutive chairman was an understanding, wise old hand with the company and had been instrumental in getting the new CEO aboard. The outside board members were also quite adult in their personalities and understandings. They were attuned to the realities of the developing situation. The company was in dire need of firm, professional leadership. But the cocky new CEO went too far in imposing his parental ego state on the board at a meeting where forward strategy was debated. He became so adamant about his ideas that the chairman, sensing a near blowup, called for a recess. He took the CEO by the hand, walked him to a nearby lakeshore, and assumed the parent role long enough to tell the CEO he would have to accede to the board's position; otherwise, the outside directors would resign or replace him. This obviously shook the CEO, and to his credit he moved his mental set one notch forward to adult, where rational reckoning and logical decision-making took over, and, above all, acceptance of the reality of his position and tactics. A kindly and shrewd chairman can intervene effectively when director transaction states are in conflict or not congruent.

A most colorful director drama took place in South America last year. All three personality structures were in action amid the boardroom ceremonials which Latin cultures offer with such *elegancía*. The child, the parent, and the adult competed for airtime in this boardroom story, both in the actions and in the pantomime involved.

I was consulting for the chairman of a quasi-government-owned Latin American-based corporation. My colleagues had briefed me on the politically sensitive board situation, which resulted primarily from the character of the large natural-resource-oriented company. But I was unprepared for the boardplay and gaming that was to occur.

My task was to outline a new role for the directors. This addressed the conventional governance problems inherent in their multiproduct, far-flung national enterprise, which afforded employment to a great many citizens of this benevolently led nation.

I was ushered into a dimly lit, mahogany-paneled boardroom and seated at the head of the twenty-five-foot-long jacaranda table. Eight board members were seated at the table, which had a microphone in front of each director. A battery of an *ayudante de campo*, two translators, and three stenographers were positioned in seats against the walls. On my right was the bilingual, well-groomed chairman—the friendliest person in the room. On my left were two appropriately clad union representatives. There were five other men—a conservative-looking professor, two formally dressed executives of the company, a uniformed deputy minister of defense, and the fifth, who outshone us all. He was an air force general, right out of the movie stereotype. His uniform was magnificent, his hair and manner De Lorean. His display of medals required chest expansion, and his board-table carriage reminded me of an old maxim—when you're healthy you walk tall; when you've piles, you sit tall!

My tutorial was translated loudly and simultaneously from the sidelines; the mikes were superfluous. The contrapuntal effect of my English-spoken governance "truths" about conflicts of interest, insider dealings, social responsibility, and fiduciary duties, against the mellifluous Spanish version, made the session an unusually confusing one.

When I had finished, the gameplay began. The union leaders brought forth the "child" as they defended their constituents' point of view, which was dominated by a natural fear of any change and unrealistic expectations as to future gains for their members. The "parent" personality was clearly evident in the posturing of the government representatives, who were thinking about how difficult it would be to present any change to the political leaders who had appointed them to monitor (not change) the corporation. The adult game was skillfully played by the chairman, who marshaled the conversations and processed them gracefully to get members of the board to see the realistic need for change. It was masterful chairing of a crossfire of transactions going on between directors as they politely debated. The proposed change in the role of the board meant abandoning the past practice of overcontrol and stalemate on any issue that impinged on historical entitlements of the constituents—particularly workers' benefits and the vested interests of certain directors.

I learned more about the gameplay in a later, private session with the chairman. He indicated that the board had recorded the session and played the tapes for the executive committee of the board, which sorted out the issues and policy choices that were obscured by the games played on the day of my presentation.

Directors do behave differently than one might expect in the privacy of the boardroom. That's part of the mystique that shrouds boardrooms. The criteria and standards for boardworthiness are elusive, ineffable, subjective, or defiant of reason. The games directors play need to be recognized in this setting in order to understand how boards of directors actually carry out their functions. This gameplay is why a closed boardroom door is essential despite the activists' cry for "sunshine in the boardroom" in the form of more public disclosure of board affairs. The *in camera* nature of board deliberations obscures most of the petty faults and anachronisms and allows interpersonal relationships of directors to incubate and manifest their respective levels of child, parent, or adult. Trade-offs are made amid the rivalries of competing uncertain perspectives and interests. Conflict, tension, pacification, cooperation, cooptation, persuasion, bargaining, and maneuvering are involved in the games directors play. Adult chairmanship can referee these games and tactics to make a board more effective.

Bespoke Directorships

One of the most important targets of boardroom reformers is the process of recruiting directors. The charge is that directors are nominated only by the chairman, the chief executive officer, or a claque of directors, either members or outsiders. One of my favorite cartoons showed a typical businessmen's board of directors with an old unctuous one at the head of the table with his hands forming a steeple saying, "I'd like to think that you men would have voted me chairman even if I had only a teeny bit of stock."

The claim on boardroom seats often shows beforehand—that is, before the proxy votes are counted. A prearranged composition of the board is frequently custom-made to suit the interests of those in control, either in the boardroom or in the executive suite. This prearrangement is what the English lawyer Sir Julian Stafford Corbett called "a friendly reception for oneself." Those who are on boards get invited to join other boards. The process of nomination works through networking. Lord Boothby once commented on the lives of directors in the United Kingdom: "It has been said that if you have five directorships, its total effect is like having a permanent hot bath."

Bespoke directorships are a reality, and there is some abuse or lack of openness in many corporations' director recruitment process. The push for formalizing recruitment through formation of a nominating committee has come in the last ten years. In a recent directorship survey of 307 companies, 65 percent had nominating committees; 82 percent had outside directors. In a 1976 survey, only 8 percent of the cases of director election were indicated as a result of nominating committee candidacy. By 1982 this committee source of directors rose to over 45 percent, and I'm sure it's higher now—especially with the larger companies.

Some of the activists' proposals in the United States for formal change in the board regarding preordered, custom-made director nominations are (a) that nominations from shareholders should be solicited, (b) that the only manager on the nominating committee should be the chief executive officer (CEO) or (c) that all managers, including the CEO, should be excluded from the nominating committees, and (d) that every board should have a nominating committee. The thrust of these reform motions strike at cronyism, or as E. B. White had stated more elegantly: "It's easier for a man to be loyal to his club than to his planet." I have to agree with the activists that the use of a formal nominating committee of outside directors plus the chairman and chief executive officer is a much-needed innovation for many publicly held company boards.

The impact of activist pressure on closed, family-type boards can be great. I remember in 1979 when I was appearing on a conference panel in New York with a member of the top management of Johnson and Johnson. He gave a speech extolling the value of a company's having essentially inside directors. The next day's *Wall Street Journal* reported that Johnson and Johnson had added its first outside director at the behest of the activist groups pressuring the company. This event transpired without any prior knowledge of my fellow panelist and embarrassed him by exposing the fact that he was not an insider in his own company. Few managers who are not directors really know what goes on in their company's boardroom.

Summary

Perhaps the way to cope with the personality forces at work behind the boardroom door is by recognizing what Oscar Wilde epitomized: "Conscience makes egotists of us all." I have to admit in all good conscience that swiping a ball-point pen from a boardroom or hotel room is one of the most satisfying experiences a director can have. It feeds our acquisitive instinct, and since none of them work, you don't feel guilty afterward.

The ego state is a strong force to be recognized in every boardroom. If the boardworld is to resolve the problems that directors' interpersonal transactions cause in the boardroom and that are against the stockholders' interest, some understanding is required of the reality of the boardroom process. Otherwise, unworkable reforms may be imposed on the entire field of institutional governance. Self-examination by directors seems called for. Faults of other directors are like headlights on automobiles—they only seem more glaring than our own. The majority of us are subjective toward ourselves and objective toward all others—terribly objective sometimes. I call this the Garden of Eden syndrome. Since we live there we can't afford to be objective. The real task in the boardroom (and elsewhere) is to be objective toward ourselves and subjective toward others.

3

Character Armor

The principal foundations of all states are good laws and good arms; and there cannot be good laws where there are not good arms.

MACHIAVELLI, *The Prince*, XII

While it is obvious that many people have character who have nothing else, the whole life-style that a director assumes in order to live and act with a certain security makes up his or her character armor. The term "character armor" implies the shoring up or damming up of the individual's fragile sense of self-value without resorting to that esteem valve, the psychiatrist's office. Character armor keeps self-value safe from undermining by events and persons, an important attribute of an effective director. There is no more a role for a director who lacks self-confidence than there is for a shy drum major.

The practical problem is to get directors to understand this requirement of "good arms" and to learn how to gird themselves properly. Psychologists know that each person tends to close off his or her world and draw up a barrier in the process of growth and development. The developing "self" is the ego that Freud taught us to protect and respect. And Goethe pointed out that whatever liberates the spirit without giving us self-control is disastrous.

In order "to become a gentleman" in the eyes of English polite society, Mohandas K. Gandhi (in his late teens) spent hours practicing the arranging of his tie and hair and taking lessons in dance and music. Soon to become the Hindu spiritual leader, Gandhi was well endowed with character armor from his childhood days. He married at thirteen but wrote in his memoirs, "I see no moral argu-

ment in support of such a preposterously early marriage as mine."
Although it might be argued that sixty years of successful married
life followed this early marriage, it took G. K. Chesterton to provide the character-armor answer when he wrote that marriage was
an armed alliance against the outside world.

Wilhelm Reich introduced his phrase "character armor" to describe this self-protecting constraint as a form of self-bondage or
limitation of perception and action that each of us draws about us.
Directors, acting out their governance roles, draw their corporate
character armor about them, often presenting a stiff composure. Or
even a stuffy one at times, depending on how insecure the person
may be.

Ernest Becker, Pulitzer Prize winner and professor of cultural
anthropology at the University of California at Berkeley, observes
that character armor makes people remarkably unsympathetic to
points of view they have decided are not worth entertaining or are
too threatening to entertain.[*] This cuts off an individual from interpersonal relationships that might upset their world, even if the
upset comes in the form of kindness and love. There is fear that
compassionate relationships may destroy the armored person's
control.

I was asked to give a crash course in governance to the alumnae
organization of a Missouri-based college. It was clear from some
material sent to me by its chairperson (a) that the organization had
no explicitly stated purpose or objectives, (b) that there were no
criteria or standards for election to the board nor for performance
of incumbents, and (c) that the organization's implicit strategy
seemed to be based on bursts of frenzy devoted to a fund-raising
happening or some key event vaguely related to school affairs. I
presented these observations to the group, and after some emotional defense at first, the group settled down to plan some constructive action.

Three months later an example emerged from this exercise of the
value and impact character armor can have on a person's life. I was
at a social gathering where one of the alumnae directors happened
to be present.

I was accosted by an attractive blonde in her late forties marked

* Ernest Becker, *Angel in Armor: A Post-Freudian Perspective on the Nature of
Man* (New York: Free Press, 1969), pp. 82–84.

down to thirty-nine. She poured out her story in a most earnest way. Gloria was recovering from a recent divorce and admitted she had completely lost her self-confidence. She faced a forbidding world alone after being the wife of a prominent businessman in the community. Her fears about the effects of her shattered social position and the open question of what to do with her life had stripped her of the character armor she had worn unthinkingly as a spouse. She was embarrassingly grateful to me. She confessed that the analysis of the alumnae organization's ineffectiveness, its lack of purpose and objectives, and the process we used in correcting such drift were directly applicable to her personal situation. Her reward was in taking an analytical look at her own life, identifying the gaps and missing components, and plotting a new career for herself under new conditions of existence. Her bubbling enthusiasm filled me with surprised pleasure. Prodding an alumnae board of women directors to get their act together while at the same time providing a model for a divorcée to get her act going again is a trick I'm sure I would not attempt if I knew the situation.

It takes strength to stand exposed without character armor. Being open to the needs and influence of others is risky to one's sense of self-value and security. In the business world, humility and openness tend to decrease with every promotion; often they disappear completely upon election to the boardroom. Some directors inherit heavy character armor, although the Sukhomlinov effect can be observed in some outstanding directorships just as it is observed in war—victory goes to those armies whose leaders' uniforms are least impressive.

Directors of corporations, no matter how formidable, remote, or impersonal they may seem to those not privileged to enter the boardroom, are just as vulnerable to exposure without their personal character armor as any other human being. One fellow director whom I knew fairly well when I lived in Missouri served with me for three years on a board of directors of a medium-sized Midwestern enterprise in a service business. He had come from a wealthy family, and his scholastic record had been spotty. He got through prep school mainly because of parental contributions to a struggling Episcopal institution. His working career had been in the family business, where he quickly wound up as president. This seemed to be the recognition George needed, for he developed the firm rapidly and successfully. As a young CEO he was invited to join the board of directors of another company, where I had been serving for about two years. By this time George's character armor was formidable. He was replete with psychological shield, haughty helmet, and heritage halberd, and his behavior as a director was overly diligent, formal, and knightly. His preparation for board meetings was in fact impressive. We placed him on the nominating committee, where, alas, his self-protecting restraint of personal bondage showed up as typical of any insecure person.

The criteria for director nomination were flexible and included unwritten requirements, among which was a bachelor's degree. Never having completed college, George was unable to handle gracefully the discussion of candidates on this qualification point. His personal insecurity was masked under a brocade of rationalization. He was more stern in rejecting well-qualified candidates who had no formal college education than those of us who had been fortunate enough to qualify in this respect. The lesson is that once you are "in" you can blackball your potential peers on the basis that their admission would threaten your position. Or as Groucho Marx put it: "I wouldn't care to be a member of any club that would have me for a member."

I find that people who are more secure in their sense of self are more daring in their actions and are less rigidly armored. Conversely, those more constricted in what they can safely undertake or withstand will organize their perceptive actions and personality around a narrow theme. Psychologists have a name for this, "fetishization"; an individual establishes fetishes because he believes he has to protect himself against the world by narrowing down the world, shutting off experiences, and ignoring his own anxieties. The normal person bites off what he can chew and digest of life and no more. The well-adjusted person has the capacity to partialize the world for comfortable action.

Everyone has some character armor and is also somewhat a fetishist. When the situation is overwhelming we tend to focus on some restrained manageable area of things. In a board meeting the degree to which an agenda item is understood is inversely proportional to the amount of paperwork connected with it. This flight to the familiar is common when complexity or uncertainty lies ahead and trivial matters take up more time and attention because we know more about them than important matters.

From August 1968 until December 1973 I sat on the board of a small Swiss company in Zurich. It was a legal entity established mainly for tax and public relations purposes. The board had five members: one Swiss, one English, and three American. We met annually, and whenever necessary we met on paper and officially adjourned the meeting until we could rendezvous physically. One of the American directors was a retired executive vice-president of a Hartford bank. Charlie was hardly an internationalist, although his bank work had involved some modest overseas activity. He was a master of the single entendre. His contribution to the infrequent meetings was to come up with some trite aphorism like "Better to have had a fall than never to have been on a wall at all," or "If our ship ever does come in, there'll be a dock strike."

Whenever we had a real board matter to resolve, Charlie was a little right of where center was last week. He would draw on his bank experience of passing money from one hand to another until it finally disappears. His tales of "how we did it in Hartford" were the only things he knew. Europe frightened him, particularly Italy. Charlie was a flight-to-the-familiar prototype.

There is another tendency when we lack confidence in making a decision. If we cannot freely value everything nor freely weigh one qualification, say, of director nomination criteria against all other qualifications, we tend to give disproportionate value to certain characteristics which do not deserve such weight. A small area of consideration is inflated and given a higher value in the horizon of our perceptions and action. I remember in the early 1960s, in a board search for director replacements, a retired Navy commander surfaced as available and interested in directorships as the basis for a second career. He was in his early fifties and had an impressive service record, an erect bearing, worldly and social graces, and an attractive furbearing creature as his second wife. The commander and I hit it off well from the start. Based on my nomination, he was elected to the board of a $50 million company.

The commander proved to be a red tapeworm, the worst kind of bureaucrat I had ever encountered. This man's best friend was his dogma. His efforts to impose written rules and policies on the company, and essentially to close the system, were unreal. Those of us with operating experience found ourselves opposing him on every board decision, which he wanted to make according to a rulebook in his head, like Navy regulations, and everything had to be done

according to it. We finally uncorked the situation by subtly encouraging him not to stand for reelection. My follow-up with him
on a personal basis has been cozily received as he goes about his ordered existence rather successfully in other boardrooms. He should
have gone back to his former job in the Navy as anchorman.

Any area of secure concentration can be mastered, skillfully
manipulated, and used easily to justify oneself as to actions, sense of
self, or options taken. Directors are like everyone else in this regard. The boardroom is a jousting field with each member of the
board wearing his own character armor, distinguished by some em-
broidered silk coat of arms and colored scarf of his own personality
and style.

Change Agent

One key role of a director is to act as a change agent for the institution. In this role character armor plays an important part. The
role is not one of change for change's sake; it requires not only acting in crisis but initiating significant change in purpose, nature, or
strategic direction of the firm when such is warranted. Just because
you have a board doesn't mean the company is on the right course.
Directors must take sound initiatives.

The management and external forces should not be the only
sources of change in a corporation. Active directors can be a third
source to suggest and effect corporate change. Napoleon symbolized his governance creed in prescribing, "One must change one's
tactics every ten years if one wishes to maintain one's superiority."
If the management or environment doesn't force adaptive change
in a company, an active board of directors should.

The self-actualizing director role is easier to come by in smaller
entrepreneurial companies. Here the director may be the genius
inventor, the founder, or a person technically competent to create
new vectors of corporate strategy. Directors in such situations are
not bound by heritage, tradition, or necessity to maintain the status
quo. Rate of change is rapid in such growth situations. Entrepreneurial drive is 10 percent inspiration and 90 percent capital gains.
Directors may have different emphasis on evaluation, stewardship,
participation, or change-agent activity, depending on the stage of
existence or issues to be faced.

One of the most vexatious forms of change that directorates face from time to time is the challenge posed by drift in corporate purpose. When a company is formed its creators have a specific business purpose in mind. After time passes the founding purpose may have been served and the company may need to alter strategic direction, perhaps to cope with competition or different technology, or perhaps owners or managers become restive or bored. Directors may even have to face up to going out of business if the purpose has been served.

An interesting example of such basic change in purpose occurred a quarter century ago in the March of Dimes organization. The Salk poliomyelitis vaccine program was a major United States health project in the early 1950s. The March of Dimes board of directors faced a challenge as to the purpose of the entire effort. The March of Dimes was a thriving organization, successful in collecting money, and enjoying the esteem of scientists and physicians. The organization—with paid staff in all major cities—was suddenly faced with success of a dramatic order. The entire justification for the organization faced extinction. The March of Dimes succeeded in making a changeover from the polio target to the birth-defect target. The new mission has proved to be an equally laudable and publicly recognized contribution to the public health of the nation.

A board of directors may thus act as an agent of change. In doing so it may cope with several threats or influential factors. First, there tends to be a disorientation—a flight away from the familiar—and then the goal becomes that of creating the new purpose. Second, the relative capacity of the organization to unite, react, or interact is jeopardized.

Third, the organization tends to freeze and hang on to an obsolete role. There is a restriction of behavioral standards in favor of surviving organizational tasks along with a tightening of behavioral norms. The trouble with model directors in such situations is that they are no longer working models.

Fourth, the social franchise of the organization is threatened by radical loss of purpose. Public esteem for the institution is lowered. The March of Dimes was able to resurrect public sense of the value of its effort by successfully changing its purpose.

The boardroom task of deciding when imposed change is warranted is so complex that it takes high intelligence just to be undecided about this matter. The challenge calls for a closed boardroom door so that the board can wrestle with the trade-offs. The solution often involves changing the key actors in a corporate setup. When the character armor is removed in such difficult board sessions, some interesting human stories come out.

I had a poignant assignment last year in counseling a board chairman/chief executive officer who was one of two controlling owners of a fast-moving furniture company in New York State. The chairman, in his late forties, was gravely ill, and the president/chief operating officer, the other primary owner, was in a quandary about the future of the firm. The two of them had formed the company when they met a few years out of college. The chairman was the business brain and the president was the creative designer, who had the concept of a line of high-quality studio furniture that could be marketed by slick mail-order catalogues.

The company was a great success after fifteen years of struggle. It had gone public and was bursting with potential when tragedy struck the chairman in the form of a brain tumor. The board consisted of the two primary owners, their wives, and the corporate attorney. The problem was in facing the reality of management succession when the president was neither qualified to be nor interested in being chief executive. The business was in short-term financial trouble because of delayed decisions during the chairman's illness.

Through an intermediary, arrangements were made for me to counsel the two principals privately. The chairman was realistic about his inability to carry on. The president was equally realistic about his lack of the executive talent required to take over, but he confessed to me the real burden that obsessed him. His self-confidence was shattered. As a creative person he had little interest in managing his own (or the company's) affairs. He was deeply in debt, his life-style was admittedly improvident, and all his assets were in the one company. A further complication was that his wife was the chairman's sister.

This soap-opera situation was finally resolved by expanding the self-serving, incestuous board by adding three experienced businessmen who had professional experience as directors of growth companies. They had to bring in a professional chief executive from outside, decouple the chairman from the chief executive role, and divert the creative president to a research and development role with suitable title and income adequate to retain his talents. The company is back on track, profitably providing unique structures to support the body in various positions.

Armor Chinks and Checkered Careers

The ability of directors as individuals to adapt continually to new kinds of boardroom stimuli, the ability to change and grow, and the ability to shed old character armor and abandon fetishes are measures of true directorship. There is a basic psychological lesson here for members of a board.

The director who is armored and fetishized—and who isn't?—will be able to maneuver adequately in his role as a director only so long as his personal world is not too threatened. Normally, he or she will have been able, as a conscientious board member, to organize his personality around as broad or narrow a theme as he feels comfortable about. Our cognitive world is an adaptation from the real boardworld, selecting what goes along with the extent to which we have armored our character. The ability to shed old constraining armor is as important a can-opening exercise as setting the boardroom door ajar. To say it another way, while we may have had no bad habits, we should be willing to learn.

Boards as composite organizations need to open their governance systems in order to allow energy, value perceptions, interaction, and communications flow to and from the external environment and in order to adapt to a rapidly changing world. A closed boardroom door, implying a closed system of governance, is as vulnerable as a formidable set of character armor on an individual director.

The flexibility, or inflexibility, of an individual director in properly using and discarding character armor leads to successful and not-so-successful examples of board careers. Since I went on my first board of directors, in Massachusetts in 1942, there have been interesting examples of fellow directors girding, polishing, and shedding their character armor.

Probably the most vivid boardplay I was privy to occurred in a New York board experience in 1964. This not-for-profit international organization shall remain unnamed. The board of directors numbered twelve strong and sturdily armored male members—

bankers, company presidents, lawyers, a CPA, functional senior officers of several industrial organizations, in short, the majority types. The chairman-CEO was a distinguished businessman who was also adjunct professor of business management at a respected Eastern university. He spent little time in academia; most of his work was in consulting and in part-time leading of this prestigious organization. The relevance of the organization was threatened by international competition and a failure to keep current in the advisory services rendered. We were having so many meetings that the meetings became more important than the problems the meetings were supposed to solve.

As directors, we put the heat on the management over a period of several years. Our chairman's armor was superb for parade purposes but not for battle. Pressure for turnaround performance mounted. The chairman could no longer cope with the situation, and he began to react emotionally as his sinecure was threatened. This was particularly unnerving to him; his status and image as an intellectual leader in business management matters were under assault. After repeated efforts at board meetings to get full disclosure of actions underway, the board was faced with replacement of the chief executive. Since he also wore chairman-of-the-board armor, we had two coats of arms to penetrate.

I well remember the Armageddon board session. All twelve board members were present. By prearrangement, one of the senior directors moved the resignation of the chairman. Our leader, so threatened, refused to accept the motion. A verbal battle ensued which finally resulted in a written secret ballot cast and tabulated—eleven for forced resignation and one (his own) for support of the incumbent chairman-CEO.

Afterward, the behavior of the cast-out chairman caused much embarrassment. An investigation into expense accounts revealed irregularities which were never really clarified. The old philosopher's principle applied: "It is more shameful to distrust one's friends than to be deceived by them."

After this crisis behind the boardroom door, we carried on for several years with an interim chairman until the board faced the reality that the purpose of the organization had vanished. We more or less gracefully collapsed and deincorporated the institution.

In a different situation, another fellow board member proved to be an outright charlatan, an international scoundrel. He had an amazing South American coat of arms and suit of character armor. Actually, he was an Argentine, a technically trained businessman operating at the time in São Paulo, Brazil. The situation was a Brazilian joint venture with an American company, providing a license and know-how for the manufacture of thermosetting resins. Technology was transferred to a subsidiary company formed with this South American venturer, who operated the plant and built the business to a viable size, and to where his shining armor of partnership as an owner-director-manager could be shed safely. In 1958 he fled the company and country, taking with him the technical information and know-how learned as director and manager of the foreign venture. No patent protection was effective in Brazil at that time. The most upsetting part of the steal was the use of the goodwill and trade name of the Resinox resin product line, which he blithely used in his own factory setup in Argentina.

Only after this escapade did we naïve *norteamericano* directors investigate the character-reference armor of our former partner-director. An international checkout revealed we had been "taken" by a well-known professional character armor wearer, who changed suits of armor about every three to five years in Latin American industrial circles. The developmental state of the region made it possible for him to pass routine checkouts, and regrettably we had not taken the trouble to make a careful one.

Antitrust situations affecting boardrooms have been more in the news in recent years. The price-fixing convictions of senior executives in the electrical and paperboard industries have been well reported. It is almost impossible for anyone not acquainted with the individuals or boardrooms involved to appreciate the impact an indictment or conviction can make on our character armor. Two fellow directors of mine on separate boards were caught up in this legal assault on boardroom conduct.

The first occasion was in 1956 in connection with the board of a large institution. A fellow director was a senior officer of one of the large electrical products companies caught in price-fixing practice. My slightly overweight, sophisticated manager-type friend, an outstanding person of estimable personal integrity and character, was picked to reign over a division of the company where the violations occurred at several organizational levels below him.

The tension, stress, and time required in legal matters and court appearances wore my friend down visibly. He was so preoccupied that he became obsessed with the problem. While he was never indicted, some of his subordinates were. They were convicted and jailed. My colleague died from the strain a few years after the case was settled. His character armor had been pierced by his own conscience and response to the behavior of those with whom he had associated all his working career.

A second occasion was more recent, 1978 to be exact. A fellow director of a financial intermediary company was chief executive of a medium-sized conglomerate company that had acquired a small equipment parts firm, which was subsequently folded into the parent company as a captive subsidiary. My friend, a stolidly mature person, served for the record as chairman of the small acquired company, which remained as a legal subsidiary but functioned as an operating division. After acquisition, the acquired executives of the company were found guilty of engaging in price-fixing practices, which were rampant in that industry. Because my friend was legally accountable in the acquired firm, the judge sentenced him to a six-month jail sentence as an example to others. This shattered a promising career, forced retirement, and forced resignation from his own company and from our financial company board twenty-four hours before the proxy statement went to press. We could not afford to have a director with a criminal record as a member of our directorate.

One of the most poignant memories of this episode was when I arrived at an airport and saw my just-convicted friend waiting for the same plane I was booked on. He was dressed in work clothing, carried a duffel bag, and was a very forlorn figure. His wife and daughter had dropped him off at the airport. Unaccompanied, he was on his way to a prison in the South where nondangerous criminals were housed. He was glad to see me, but no words of consolation could soothe his shattered character armor. Nor has he recovered completely after returning to his civilian life as a retired chief executive.

Taking the rap is a risk all executives and directors assume with their roles. Character armor will not protect a director from circumstances beyond his control. The corrupt-practices series of convictions and investigations have reached behind many a boardroom door and penetrated many suits of director character armor.

Times have changed rapidly; ignorance of the law or regulations is no excuse for a director caught up in dubious practices.

A company I knew for a time, in the West, responded along with others in its industry to self-audit its practices on payoffs, kickbacks, and improper payments in connection with commercial activities. New top management and active outside board members uncovered improper payments traditionally made in dealing with Southern trade unions and supplier organizations. These low uses of high office practices were par for the course—and had been for thirty or forty years. This board decided voluntarily to reveal these violations to the Internal Revenue Service and to take remedial action in return for expected inaction on the part of the government. This initiative was successful but involved forced resignation of one inside director, who was in responsible charge of the subsidiary company division involved in the improper plant-level practices. In addition, the deposed director-executive was shifted in the parent organization to another remote assignment. His career upward was interrupted for years, and he recently took early retirement. The sad part is that the director-executive had inherited the "bad practices" division, and despite his own exemplary character he was held responsible by virtue of organizational accountability.

One last example of related chinks-in-character-armor situations concerns an interesting but very human value-system clash in the boardroom. Right out of college and employed by the now nonexistent Sinclair Oil Company, I watched a top-management succession problem being resolved strictly on a distaff character armor incident. The motherly but barren wife involved was a loyal sort who stuck with her husband through all of the trouble he wouldn't have had if he hadn't married her.

The executive vice-president, an inside director and heir apparent to the CEO-chairman spot, was a gregarious type and very friendly to technical persons newly employed. I guess it was because he had no children. Anyway, he became very friendly with me, and I warmed to his leadership and interest. When the time came for the incumbent CEO-chairman to retire, all bets were on my fifty-year-old mentor. But he was passed over. The reason, I found out many years later, was the character armor worn by his wife. When she attended a social meeting of the board—a fate worse than death for her—she "misbehaved." She was not totally and visibly enthralled with the company's boardroom behavioral basics and the hierarchy, and occasionally said so. The company lost an outstanding CEO candidate because his wife's armor plate clashed with the other directors' wives' comparable protective coating and alleged genuflection to the corporate culture.

Whatever personal thoughts we have about the existence or nonexistence of a protective personality shell around each boardroom inhabitant, I suggest that a key to effective corporate governance is the interpersonal relationship of the directors. Unfortunately, whenever we think we have found the key to this relationship, someone changes the lock. Any director who comes into the boardroom, voice first, may be merely displaying the good arms of his character armor. This may be only a shoring up of an individual fragile sense of self-value. We perceive such directors as able either to take it or leave it alone.

4

Star Wars:
The Proxy Rite

Two golden rules for an orchestra: "Start together and finish together. The public doesn't give a damn what goes on in between."

SIR THOMAS BEECHAM, Royal Philharmonic

Board of directors meetings are most always orchestrated carefully as to their start and their finish. The agenda and general plenary drill are standard, and a motion to adjourn is always in order. This stereotypical performance is especially true of the AGM—the annual general meeting—when the proxy votes are counted for election of directors. What really goes on in between proxy countings is the subject of this book.

Points for Future Peers

In connection with this my favorite boardroom guidebook is, alas, out of print. *How to Run a Bassoon Factory and Business for Pleasure* by the fictitious Mark Spade was originally published for the most part in *Punch*. It was recaptured thirty years ago in book form* after the sudden decease of Mr. Spade as the result of a disagreement with a foreman over a large adjustable wrench. This unfortunate happening was recorded as "a grievous loss to Bassoon-Manufacturing Circles, Bassoon-Playing Circles, and Small Circles. Few men went round in all of them so much."

Mr. Spade, at the time of his death, was engaged in a major work entitled "How to Avoid Running a Bassoon Factory in a Controlled Economy," which, had he lived, would have brought his philoso-

* Published by Hamish Hamilton, London, 1950, reprinted 1953.

phy of corporate governance up to date. As the record will show, Mark Spade not only put the bassoon on the map, but he contributed immensely to the theory and practice of corporate governance. While the facts show that Mr. Spade, at one time or another, left several wives and numerous children, his true mate was always the Queen of the Orchestra—the Royal Philharmonic in particular. And, as his biographer noted, "let the epitaph be a descending scale, staccato pianissimo, in the lowest register of the instrument he loved so well."

Anyway, Mark Spade's insight on annual shareholder meeting bears careful review. His analysis of the AGM points up that shareholders are not usually optimistic, that there is always a perfectly good reason why things have gone badly for which the board is not responsible, and that most shareholders live in such outlandish places that they can't come to the meeting anyhow.

The chairman's speech at the AGM, according to Spade, falls naturally into two halves: why things are as they are ("general incompetence, extravagance, stuff no good, manager bolted with cash, and don't know"), and the shape of things to come ("fundamental soundness of the position, drastic writing down of assets, investments shown at less than cost, conservative finance will bear fruit, etc."). The bad news is handled by noises about rapid improvement is useless to expect, recovery takes time, must reconcile ourselves to a difficult period, reorganization is underway, and so on.

Spade characterized the object of a board meeting as rather similar to that of the House of Lords. "It is intended to prevent any hothead who wants to do something from getting on and doing it. A good board working with proper skill can usually ensure that absolutely nothing is ever done at all."

Given this interpretation for what it is worth, it is helpful to examine the ploys a director may use at either a regular or the annual general meeting. Some of these devices have been recited previously but are brought up to date, given the rapid behavioral dynamics of the boardroom in the 1980s.

Rites of Passage

Many rituals reflect and dramatize our roles in real-life boardroom scenes or otherwise. This is particularly true of life-crisis rituals.

Rites are developed around birth, naming, weaning, first haircut, initiation, coming of age, marriage, childbirth, promotion, anniversaries, installations and inductions into offices or boardrooms, retirement, death, burial, and . . . annual general shareholder meetings! Persons, as a species, have an enormous curiosity about actions and events when persons, things, time, and space coalesce in human experience. These events become stories passed down through history. The tales become lore which in turn becomes ritualistic, causing formalization and standardization. This technique is most familiar in the fables of Aesop, La Fontaine, Thurber, and Uncle Remus. Tales behind the boardroom door are in the rudimentary lore stage, with a few fables falling out of the privacy of the boardroom and into the public domain.

But the earliest indication of ritual expressed in the human mind comes from Choukoutien, near Peking, at a time at least half a million years ago. Bodies of fifteen individuals were discovered by archaeologists in the period from 1926 to 1941. In a number of skulls the hole where the spinal cord runs had been enlarged. Interpretations are that at cannibalistic feasts, brains of the deceased were extracted by Peking Man—no doubt a practice to increase the wisdom of the elders and a forerunner to the well-known brain-picking technique of getting free advice from someone.

Whatever the ceremonial event, the ancient individuals participated in a group proceeding by observing certain rites or ritual. From the point of view of modern social dynamics, the attribute of ritualistic behavior is predictability. Board etiquette, for example, calls for certain ritualistic transactions.

Psychologists and group therapists call each unit of such ritualistic transactions a "stroke." It takes board chairmen at least seven strokes to get a board meeting underway. There are personal ho-ho-ho greetings before calling the meeting to order (stroke 1), the call to order (2), announcement that a quorum is present (3), reading of minutes of the last meeting (4), explanation as required of the agenda (5), passage of any statutory actions required to stay in business (6), and introduction of a substantive topic for board consideration (7).

One board chairman I know who dominates his board is quite an actor. He is a classy dresser, a lawyer who wears his hair departed down the middle. He waits until all directors are seated in the so-called nutty pine boardroom, which is elegantly furnished. Then he triumphantly enters, sniffs the air to see if anyone has been smoking, invariably orders the special ventilation fans turned on regardless of whether there have been any smokers, and proceeds to his thronelike seat at the head of a U-shaped table, with a communications panel and telephone setup that rivals Houston Control. He notes that there is a quorum present and proceeds ritualistically to go through the order of the day, never varying a flicker from the legal drill which the obsequious secretary of the corporation has carefully crafted.

When an annual meeting of a corporation gets underway in substance, the key event is the voting by proxy for the "stars" who have offered themselves up for election to the board. The proxy statement, sent out in advance of the meeting, with photographs of the candidates taken in more youthful times, provides the menu for voting. Because of the prearranged drill of proxy voting by mail, the voting is almost always ceremonial.

The telling issue in the boardroom is whether the body lives by rote and rite or by reason and right. No board, of course, functions solely by rote and rite. There must be some freedom or discretion in navigating from the boardroom in the same way that navigating by sea requires flexibility. But this intellectual deathtrap of rotelike existence does prevail in many boardrooms. Certainly it prevails at many annual general meetings, and it undercuts the crucial function of advancing the corporate governance process in the shareowners' interest.

I recall an annual general meeting of Monsanto, in St. Louis, twenty years ago. These affairs are always carefully planned events, with usherettes in Monsanto jackets ushering shareholders to their seats and elaborate exhibits and tours. Spouses of the directors are penned up in front rows, and the occasion always calls for a new hat at the minimum. The board sits on a dais, with the chairman flanked by the more senior directors. The script is well rehearsed. The corporate counsel labors for months in advance anticipating all conceivable questions which might come from the floor. An answer sheet is available for all directors. Most of the meeting is a show-and-tell affair, with movies displaying the CEO, for example, chumming unnaturally with union officials at some remote plant. New-product promotion is always included. After all the prepared stuff—proxy count, ratification of auditors, and other routine business—is over, including several canned speeches, the big moment comes when the meeting is open to shareowners.

On this particular occasion, after a relatively pedestrian performance that year, we were expecting shareholder unrest. When the chairman called for any questions from the floor there was a strained silence. Then, slowly, a distinguished gentleman rose in the audience and waited to be recognized. Meanwhile the secretary of the board, the public relations officer, and others were frantically trying to identify the questioner. He cleared his throat and began very deliberately. "This has not been a good performance year for the company or the industry," he said, and then paused for what seemed like ten seconds. "I just want to register my vote of appreciation as a shareholder to the management for getting us through this bad year." Then he sat down amid some delayed and scattered applause which adequately masked the otherwise audible combined sigh of relief of all of us on the directors' platform. Another AGM had passed and we were seated securely for at least one more year.

Ritualism does have a purpose. The Securities and Exchange Commission requires a proxy statement with details on the care and feeding of directors. Its motto seems to be that there's no substitute for lack of preparation. The proxy material required is becoming so detailed that it is not revealing. If any shareholder really reads the stuff he or she would wonder how the candidate has time to serve on the board, given the candidate's extensive, self-reinforcing qualifications.

The modern SEC prescription for the corporate household and its annual general meeting with shareowners has the following general "order of the day."

Proxy Statement Outline

1. An invitation sent well in advance to the shareholders, giving date, time, and place of the meeting, with but a mere hint or two about the agenda. It's rote-written, usually by the corporate secretary, in the stilted, impersonal style of a note "From the desk of ————." One is tempted to reply "Dear Desk" when responding to the AGM invitation.

2. Formal notice of the meeting with itemized agenda. There is an interesting subculture developing of AGM gadflys who enjoy shareholder happenings and come well prepared to rattle the cage of the chairman, if such is possible.

3. A proxy computer card for signature, voting, and return for tabulation. This always turns me off a bit, since the computerized card is so impersonal.

4. Proxy statement for the meeting. This sets forth the record date for determination of shareholders, conditions for executing votes by proxy, number of shares owned by any large factors, or other noteworthy facts concerning ownership.

5. Slate of directors nominated for election. Personal information, age, pictures of candidates, including nepotism references, if any (I always liked Robert Benchley's line on this—"The son-in-law also rises"), biographical data, service time as a director, other directorships, and share ownership. All are set forth in rogues'-gallery or person-wanted-poster style. In approving the text for the proxy, each director is required by the SEC to sign off on the representation, thus retaining the power to describe himself in the

way he sees himself. The aim of the candidate vignettes is to enhance the image of management and director competence—or at least dispel any thought of incompetence, defined as the lack of talent to compete at the bottom.

Proxy preparations can be interesting. At Macmillan, Inc., in the late 1960s, the directors were asked for the first time to furnish their résumés and photographs for proxy statement purposes. Mrs. Giles Whiting, venerable and matriarchal granddaughter of the founder, a director and major shareowner of Macmillan, did not respond immediately to the request. Belatedly, near the proxy due date, Alma Triner, who was the company officer in charge of the proxy preparations, heard from her secretary that a Mrs. Whiting was unexpectedly in the lobby and asking to see the vice-president in charge of the proxy. Ms. Triner had her quickly ushered in, carrying a twenty-inch-square suitably framed studio portrait of herself in 1920s evening dress. She asked if this picture would be acceptable for the proxy statement. With grace and political acumen, Ms. Triner accepted the portrait as most appropriate. The picture, cropped at the neck, proved to be the most attractive of the otherwise motley proxy gallery. It elicited "what a dish she must have been" comments from the staff. Incidentally, Mrs. Whiting was an active director until age ninety-one and expired at ninety-two.

6. Record of board committees' composition and activity, as well as the attendance record of each director. CEOs often scatter outside directors on the committees where they can do the least harm to the management plans.

7. Bylaw amendments, if any. The significance varies in inverse proportion to the number of bylaws understood by the average shareholder. The term comes from the Scottish local laws called byrlaws. Inhabitants of a district used to make laws for their own observance and appoint a neighbor called the byrlaw-man to carry out the pains and penalties.

8. Remuneration of, or any other transactions with, management and others. Annual aggregate direct remuneration exceeding a certain figure is listed for directors and offi-

cers. Deferred compensation is discussed. This is sort of a nothing vouchered, nothing gained record to discourage self-dealing and conflict-of-interest situations by exposing the annual take.

9. Transactions with principal stockholders, if any. A particularly interesting section is where there is buying, selling, or leasing between owners and the company. Reform always comes from the minority stockholders. No stockholder with four aces asks for a new deal.

The extent to which the federal regulators can carry out their oversight of the proxy rite is sometimes amazing. When Macmillan was in the process of acquiring a small gravure printing company, the SEC-required explanation in the proxy statement included the acquirer's estimate of "the value of the acquiree's stock five years after acquisition." The vice-president handling preparation of the proxy statement pointed out to the SEC that after acquisition there would be no separate shares to value for the acquired property. However, the SEC agent insisted that the forms be filled out with the requested information. The vice-president in desperation finally phoned the regional officer of the SEC to explain that it was nonsense to value nonexistent stock. He agreed with a sigh, and when asked why the commission pursued such a fantasy, he said candidly, "Well, it's because we're bureaucrats."

10. Selection of independent accountants. Nomination of financial auditors is required for vote by shareholders.

11. Shareholder proposals. With recent increased shareholder interest there has been an increase in suggestions and questions by shareholders for board consideration. The proxy solicits any such formal proposals. This is a corporate activist's favorite territory. Proposals to reduce the chairman's or CEO's compensation, to require cumulative voting, to boycott apartheid-tainted multinational companies, to put minorities on the board, to sell the company plane, to eliminate charitable contributions, and to adopt many other "good" ideas fall in this category.

12. Other business. This proxy item gives management an opportunity to identify any other items for the AGM. The
chairman is anxious to get through the AGM, so extra
items are not particularly welcome, in spite of their potential merit or legality—unless the company has an ex-
ceptionally good story to tell, question to answer, or
matter to promote.

There are always two kinds of shareholders at every AGM—
those who want to leave early and those who do not. Unlike invi-
tees to a party, these two types are not married to one another, but
the difference in meeting interest makes the handling of an AGM a
no-win proposition. A short meeting pleases the directors and some
shareowners. A long meeting pleases the retirees, who hold a few
shares and have plenty of time.

As Sir Thomas Beecham pointed out, the golden rule is to start
together and end together. Most annual general meetings accomplish that, but not a lot more.

5

Board Ways
and Means

Robert's Rules of Order

Each board of directors has its own drill, its own ways and means of confronting affairs. It was in 1876 that an eminent engineer took stock in his orderly mind of all the facts he had read, noted, and studied for years about such parliamentary conduct. It occurred to him that he could make good use of that interest by writing a book to systematize the procedure. His name was Henry Martyn Robert, and he called his book *Robert's Rules of Order.* In no time over a million copies were sold. While *Robert's Rules of Order* do limit creativity of groups, the rules force the chairman to take control and impose restrictions on the meeting process. We now know that participation is necessary to release the untapped supply of energy, ideas, and interest of individuals in a group. With social scientists turning their attention to group dynamics, boards of directors are beginning to struggle out from under the dead hand of habit, rote, ritual, and Mr. Robert's rules. No rain dance or other rite will do much more than put our problems behind us. What we have to do then is fight the solutions.

The parliamentary term "ways and means" has an active corporate governance meaning far beyond the conventional methodology of raising the supply of money for the current requirements of an institution. The chief justice of England set the pattern for government and corporations in 1628: "We have a maxim in the House of Commons . . . that old ways are the safest and surest ways." Walter Bagehot's description of Parliament as "nothing less than a big meeting of more or less idle people" adds to the perception of decision-making bodies as nonworking organizations sticking to historical drills and obsolete practices.

Auguste Detoeuf, retired chairman of Alsthom, a large electrical firm in France, had a view that "the board is the façade of the firm; but while fashion requires that façades of boutiques have few decorations and a great deal of light, one prefers most often to have a board made up of few luminaries and many decorations."* While chairman Detoeuf's pre–World War II version of a board is an anachronistic stereotype, it depicts the attention many boards focus on their star system of having celebrity directors who seldom add much to the basic work of a board except pomp and circumstance.

Through the Boardroom Keyhole

A survey conducted last year by Opinion Research Corporation on public attitudes toward business and fourteen other institutions involved interviews throughout the continental United States. Drawn from a probability sample of 1,054 people eighteen years of age or over, the perspective reflects what the public perceives goes on in corporation, bank, university, hospital, and church boardrooms and in the legislative chambers of our government at both federal and local levels.

- Overall, there has been an erosion of public trust and confidence in major institutions in our society since 1975, with large companies continuing to be held in relatively low esteem.
- Large companies continue to rank near the bottom of the list in terms of "high confidence." Only the boards of directors of large companies, the Congress, and the stock market rank lower in a broad spectrum of fifteen institu-

* Auguste Detoeuf, Propos de O. L. Barrenton Confiseur, Paris, SEDITAS (Société d'Editions et de Diffusion Tambourinaire Soiradel), 1947.

tions. Even more significantly, more people now express a low level of confidence in large companies. The public is catching on that any company's performance over the years can be made to appear favorable by a hired company historian, and the sumptuousness of the annual report is in inverse proportion to the profitability of that year.

- While small companies continue to enjoy a somewhat higher level of public confidence than large companies, they, too, have suffered a decline in level of public confidence since 1975. Small business is not necessarily beautiful in the public mind.
- About half of all the major institutions have experienced a decrease in the level of trust and confidence since 1975.
- Churches, banks, and the medical profession—the three most highly rated both now and in 1975—are currently less regarded.
- Congress, already ranked low in 1975, has continued to decline during recent years.

In line with their lack of trust in large companies, people continue to regard the ethical and moral practices of corporate executives less favorably than those of many other professionals or leaders, including corporate board members. Morals are seen to be more than a matter of pulling down the boardroom windowshades.

Corporate directors rank fifteenth out of nineteen occupational classifications in relative public esteem. Directors do enjoy more public esteem than the "yessir-nosir-ulcer" advertising executives and are better regarded than state, local, and federal government officials or labor union leaders. In this regard, labor directors bear a striking resemblance to any other director.

The public continues to think of corporations as social entities as well as economic institutions. Two-thirds of the public believe that business is obligated to help society, even if it means making less profit. While I believe business is playing a more socially responsive role, seven people in ten still say that many of the problems facing our society have been neglected by business. Businessmen are perceived to be primarily devoted to making a profit, even at the expense of the public's needs.

As it is, many shapers of public opinion are not very enthusiastic about the way a typical board of directors carries out its social re-

sponsibilities as compared to its economic or managerial responsibilities.

Indeed, this attitude prompts support for broader representation of outside representatives on corporate boards. Interestingly, I have noted that outside directors on boards always feel sorry for boards made up mainly of inside directors. Conversely, inside directors always feel sorry for those boards made up primarily of outside directors.

The majority of public-opinion shapers believe that there should be more women represented in boardrooms. Four in ten name consumer advocates, leaders of minority groups, or individual shareholders for increased representation on boards, despite most director attitudes that such representatives are needed like a moose needs a hat rack.

The public perception of boards of directors presents a challenge to improve board conduct and to demonstrate concern for the public interest. My own belief is that most boards do their work with public interest in mind, but all boards can improve in this respect.

Boardwork

Before I became a chairman, I had a dozen theories about how a board should work. Now I have a dozen directors and no theories.

In the past, when world affairs were relatively more stable and less coupled, a corporation could easily weather the perturbations which beset it. Occasional governmental intervention, competitive threats, inflation, resource availability, and political cycles were taken in stride. There has been a significant decline in corporations' abilities to deal with the challenge of technological breakthroughs, political upsets, changes in the ecosystem, and shifting value sys-

tems, and actions of boards of directors seem particularly ineffective. Fixed boardroom ritual, set policies, single objectives, and
self-regulation of external relations are no longer adequate to
maintain a state of equanimity in the boardroom.

Let me relate a true story about boardroom dynamics in our
forty-ninth state—Alaska. The Alaska Native Claims Settlement
Act of 1971 (ANCSA), passed by Congress with native approval,
has become one of the most novel social and economic experiments
in American history. No longer are the Eskimos left out in the cold.
Thirteen regional corporations were established to operate for
profit by managing and investing the proceeds of the land claims
which are no longer governed by tribal councils or the Bureau of
Indian Affairs.

Overnight, Alaskan natives—many of whom had never employed anyone—were occupying boardrooms of multimillion-dol-
lar corporations, buying hotels and fish canneries, and contracting
with oil, mineral, and other companies, while trying to preserve the
culture and life-style of the native Alaskans, developed in six thousand years of subsistence existence in a hostile climate. My job was
to present my firm's qualifications to a twenty-four-person board of
one of these newly created regional corporations. The boardroom
was immense and as well decorated as the best of the Fortune 500
boardrooms.

The directors were ensconced around a square table, with the
chairman at one end sitting with the CEO. All directors, by law,
were at least one-third native Alaskan Indian. The Tlingit-Haida
tribe predominated in this region. At least one of the directors wore
dramatic Alaskan Indian-style garb; other outfits ranged from
sports shirts to Brooks Brothers suits. One director wore a sport
coat which reminded me of an apartment that I had once moved
from because of the wallpaper pattern.

Each director had achieved his or her position (which paid very
well in fees and expenses) through popular elections dominated by
the tribes and subunits which were scattered throughout the territory. While the board members had authorized our work, it was
apparent that they needed assurance and understanding of our
consultants' role in strategic assessment of the corporation.

I entered the room and was introduced by the chairman for the
next item on the agenda. Whereupon the chairman got up, turned
his back on me, and walked out before I could start to speak. I

asked the president if I should wait. "No, he'll be back," I was told. The purpose, I learned afterward, was to show the board that he, the chairman, was not beholden to an outsider, a consultant employed to help the corporation. The politicized nature of all boardroom deliberations became even more evident as we progressed with our study.

The experience I gained in counseling directors on these newly formed political-type boards leads me to question whether in our highly industrialized societies corporate-conflict problems of competition, bigness, insensitive conduct, inequitable gains, and trade-offs with human needs ever can be monitored by self-inflicted rituals and regulation of the ways and means of conducting board business. The jury is still out on this issue. Perhaps our legal and policy rituals can't offer the stability and political sophistication needed to preserve our corporations for this stage of world complexity, rate of change, interdependency, and interactivity.

Certainly increased government intervention in the form of regulations, statutes, and policy guidelines for conduct of corporate affairs is very much in evidence around the world. The United States is leading the parade in this regard. Much to the dismay of many of our foreign boardroom friends, our greatest U.S. export of late seems to be concepts of environmental regulation, normative corporate conduct, human rights, antitrust, federal chartering, public disclosure and other corporate stakeholder interests, consumer and investor protection, and many other areas of public policy formation. My participation in corporate governance seminars in Europe and Latin America reveals attitudes of the business communities there similar to the dismay at our previous administration's relentless pursuit of human rights as defined in the terms of U.S. culture.

Director Ploys

The word "ploy" is chiefly of Scottish origin. It implies a carefully designed action. For example, the rosier the news, the higher the rank of the official who announces it. Ploys are chiefly of a frolic, escapade, sport, merrymaking, or pastime nature.

In good humor, directors are not above such an occasional affair, including an *affaire de coeur*, given a mixed boardroom. A ploy is essayed chiefly for impact on fellow directors and mainly to create impressions. Female directors sometimes dress to attract attention but are observed to be missing in action. In less than good humor, ploys are used as one-upmanship or to distract—even detract from other board members. Some examples to watch for:*

THE PARAPHERNALIA PLOY

Extra or unusual trappings include Ben Franklin reading glasses, paper-thin hand calculators, symbolic ties, and pocket dictating devices. I know one director who carried an abacus! Unusually shaped or numerous pipes are used and constantly refilled and cleaned. A chairman I know unpacks eight pipes from his briefcase before meetings and spends the entire time reaming, filling, and puffing—perhaps a physical analogy to his style of handling the matters at hand.

* Reprinted by permission of the publisher from Robert Kirk Mueller, *The Incompleat Board: The Unfolding of Corporate Governance* (Lexington, Mass.: Lexington Books/D. C. Heath and Company, copyright © 1981, D. C. Heath and Company).

THE MUCH-IN-DEMAND-DIRECTOR PLOY

One distinguished corporation lawyer from a well-known New York firm was a fellow director of a large corporation with me for seven years. Not one of the regular monthly meetings went by without his office—or someone—calling him out of the board meeting, usually at a critical voting time, to take a long-distance call. Messages were never sent in to him—he always had to step out.

Another director friend frequently arranges for special-delivery mail or telegrams to appear while the board is in session.

This much-in-demand director occasionally advises the chair openly at the end of the meeting that he must miss the next session as he will be in some other—usually exotic—location on an important mission.

THE "INTELLECTUAL" WORLDLY-AFFAIRS PLOY

This type of director

—has always read the latest *Forbes, Barron's, Wall Street Journal, Economist,* and *Financial Times of London* before each meeting and quotes from them frequently before others have caught up with the news.

—carries at least one of the latest avant-garde books, in hardback, in his briefcase and casually displays it while seeking the board meeting papers.

—bones up on some complicated topic that is germane or peripheral to the board discussion and expounds at the appropriate time to evidence erudition and one-up his peers. Occasionally gets off base or is found to have superficial knowledge if another director proves to be a hidden expert.

THE NAME-DROPPING PLOY

This type of director knows everyone important, or gives that impression, with respect to the Washington scene, overseas business leaders, or powerful people in the financial or academic world. His quotes of distinguished persons are ostensibly based on first-hand private revelations.

THE GREAT-CORPORATE-LEADER PLOY

This is mainly practiced by some of those directors who are chief executive officers of their own firms. Their annual report messages, promotional literature, news releases on their firms' activities, and in-house employee publications (peppered with the sayings and pictures of the chief) are sent unsolicited to fellow directors on a third-party board.

One fellow director friend of mine commissioned an elaborate four-color 200-page biography of himself and his family before he retired and distributed this great reference not only to key employees but to friends outside the firm where he was a fellow director. The book must have cost the company $10,000 to produce!

THE PROPER-DIRECTOR PLOY

A director using this ploy overacts in his monitoring role in an effort to get to the bottom of things. He rags the chief executive officer on details of a policy, practice, or project in an effort to demonstrate diligence. Often a bane in the boardroom, this zealous type may effect needed changes by his unrelenting, if good-humored, pursuit of some point he is qualified to question. One director I knew was always the great energy expert, for his industrial experience was with an energy company. He persisted in asking the same energy-conservation questions about each capital project. It got to be a joke in the boardroom, but it moved the management to the point where every proposal led off by dealing with the energy aspects of the project, regardless of whether this was a significant factor.

Another director, more noted for his cunning than for his conscientiousness, always spends a few minutes in the boardroom before each meeting red-penciling papers he has not read and making sure his peers see these question marks and notes.

DAPPER DAN DIRECTOR

Fashion plates boards of directors are not. Proxy statement and annual report pictures wouldn't be fit for competitive free-market publication, although they serve a rogues'-gallery purpose per SEC requirements. I've noticed that previously all-male boards are sprucing up when lady directors are elected to their midst. One ploy, or idiosyncrasy, used for years, and originating with the British, is the haberdasher rivalry. This is manifest by white-collar-and-colored-cuff shirtings, offbeat cuff links, heraldic cravats, fancy folded breast-pocket kerchiefs, and fancy check or houndstooth worsted, cavalry twill, or green thornproof suitings. Shareowners should be grateful to the feminine influence in the boardroom.

THE BOARDROOM-JESTER PLOY

Humor and diversion have long been recommended by physicians as a means of relaxation for men at the top. This probably explains the prevalence of court jesters in the Middle Ages. Educated masters preferred intelligent jesters, men who could play the fool—not simpleminded men. One example is Cardinal Richelieu's jester, the Abbé des Boisrobert, a keen wit, scandalmonger, play author, and patron of the arts. Today's boardroom jester may have a role to play in those corporations filled with a sense of their own momentum and importance. This also includes those companies with an overstructured hierarchy or those that endure strong leaders who dominate. A modern jester may help the board to achieve some detachment that provides perspective.

The use of humor in the boardroom is a risky ploy, but if well timed and well done—infrequently—may serve a worthwhile purpose. The witty director must be adroit and sensitive in his use of any humor and pick the proper time, if there ever is one, to introduce some constructive humor.

THE BIO PLOY

Directors who are on the go see to it that the frequent questionnaire pestering by *Who's Who in America, Who's Who in Peoria,* etc., are responded to religiously by their secretaries and with full, if padded, résumé references. It is an art to laden one's *Who's Who* citations with high-sounding connections, spurious or otherwise. Joining organizations whose only criterion is the membership fee is a frequent ploy if the name of the organization sounds impressive. This stuff also looks good on proxies.

THE PAGEBOY GAMBIT

One young director I know has a complicated Seiko wristwatch which includes a calculator, stopwatch, calendar, and beeper to remind the wearer of something. This director invariably has his alarm watch set for 9:14 A.M. so that it zings out after our board meeting is underway. Everyone looks around for the signal source. He hastily shuts the alarm off, explaining lamely that it is set for his own office's regular 9:15 staff meeting.

THE INSIDER-INVESTOR PLOY

This is a good way to one-up fellow directors and show an interest in investing in the company on whose board one sits. Because insider trading in company stock—buying or selling—is verboten when the company is about to make some announcement, report earnings, merge, make an acquisition, or invest in another company, company counsel must opine whether a director is not taking advantage of insider knowledge. Accordingly, the director-games-man will irregularly but scrupulously inquire in open session whether he is free to buy (he never announces intention to sell) company shares. This big-dealer image is meant to impress fellow directors and management within listening range.

So much for a few familiar director ploys. Let's see what ways and means a good chairman can use, first to arrange the boardroom for the best "ways and means" and then how to cope with ploymanship. Idiosyncratic boardroom behavior can be directed to the advantage of the shareowners.

The Steinzor Effect

Starting in the 1950s, behavioral scientists began to discover conditions which enhanced the effectiveness of groups as problem-solving and decision-making entities. These findings apply to many current boardroom situations.

Particular attention was given to the structural characteristics and the impact of both group size and group spatial arrangements upon measures of group performance and member attitudes. Member satisfaction, member consensus, leadership emergence, and group decision-making performance have all been shown to be affected by group size and spatial arrangements. Many of the findings support intuitive, commonsense expectations.* The belief that enhanced understanding will necessarily stir a board to action is one of mankind's oldest illusions.

Some of the key findings:

The impact of group size on the level of member participation and leader emergence was studied in groups ranging from two to twelve members. The findings were that as group size increases over this range, average member participation declines. This would be expected. Groups of six (board committees, for example) were found to be the most conducive to the emergence of both effective and efficient leadership. Dr. Bruce S. Old, senior vice-president (retired) of Arthur D. Little, Inc., studied committee work and concluded that the peaking of the output of a committee, versus the number of committee members, was 7/10 of a person. Obviously one must conclude that either further research is required or that people are no damned good.

* L. L. Cummings, George P. Huber, and Eugene Arendt, "Effects of Size and Spatial Arrangements of Group Decision-Making," *Academy of Management Journal*, Vol. XVII, No. 3 (September 1974), pp. 460–475.

As group size increases from five to twelve members, the degree of consensus decreases among members regarding problem solution. Maybe this was a problem with twelve disciples? This lessening of consensus is accompanied by an increasing range of individual member inputs and ideas. This is recognition of an important trade-off between ideational variety and consensus. In the fifteenth century, Nicolas of Cusa postulated that freedom among parts of a whole, and freedom that allows those parts in opposition to each other, forms a higher-order unity. This is the notion of *coincidentia oppositorum*. Within a mechanical system, or, I would suggest, in a boardroom, it is the opposition of moving parts that transmits power.

Another research project showed that as group size increases from two to six members, quality of decisions made in the larger groups tends to be more consistent than that of the smaller groups. Six-person groups also show high solidarity and tension release, and groups of four were highest in disagreement and demonstrated conflict. Maybe this explains why bridge games are the source of so many family squabbles.

In 1958 a research study concluded that to achieve member satisfaction the optimum group size is five. My experience on board committees is that five persons is indeed optimum. It reminds me of the five-piece band I played piano with during college—five pieces were all we knew. Speculation about this "fiver" finding is that the increased satisfaction associated with the intermediate-size groups may be due to the fact that members of smaller groups feel unusually exposed and, therefore, generally uncomfortable because of their high individual and personal visibility. Members of slightly larger groups—that is, six or seven members—are often unhappy because of the serious problems with communication and coordination that larger size generates.

Group speed in problem-solving on simple tasks revealed smaller groups superior or equal to larger groups. Not an unexpected finding, and it furnishes the rationale behind the numerical practice of organization of directors into standing or ad hoc committees. The obverse of this finding is that the way to control a board is to increase its size to, say, twenty-five or thirty-five persons, so that no one director or cabal can get together to challenge the chairman or CEO. One chairman of a multibillion-dollar firm boasts that his thirty-two-person board is designed that way so that he can control it—which he does to the disadvantage of the corporation, in my view.

Studies of the effects of group size on perceived interpersonal conflict within the group confirm that greater conflicts are developed in even-number groups than in odd-number groups. Greater perceived unpleasantness and alienation by members was present in the even-number groups. Four-member groups were a deceitful seatful and less inclined to compromise and cooperate than were the three-member groups.

The first major effort to investigate the impact of spatial arrangement on group interaction was carried out by Dr. Steinzor, and his findings are referred to as the Steinzor Effect (1950). He observed two ten-member discussion groups over a series of fifteen half-hour sessions, recording the amount and nature of interaction. In general, group members displayed a strong tendency to communicate with persons across the table facing them, rather than with persons directly adjacent to them. I've noticed this in our board meetings and as a consequence regularly rearrange the seating so that cross-fertilization takes place.

Steinzor concluded that the way individuals are arranged in small face-to-face groups can have a strong influence on the patterns of communication that develop between individuals within the group. His subjects were seated in a circle, and Dr. Steinzor inferred that a participant who had a greater mean seating distance from all the other participants would be likely to attain high leadership status. We are experimenting currently with a semicircular boardroom seating arrangement at our Colby-Sawyer College trustee meetings. The first two meetings have been most successful in increasing participation and managing the board meeting.

Another investigator (Hearn) found that members of discussion groups with passive leaders directed more comments to persons sitting opposite them than to those on either side of them. With a strong directive leader, members tended to interact more with their neighbors than with those sitting across from them. This suggests that leadership style has a significant influence on the impact of spatial arrangement in developing interpersonal communication patterns within groups. Manifestation of the Steinzor Effect depends on the degree of direction given by the designated leader. The greater the formal designation of leadership, the less the tendency for the Steinzor Effect to appear. It's not that the chairman is more intelligent than you, he just appears more convincing.

In a study of 467 participants in an ROTC school, observers found that persons sitting at the end position of the table rated significantly higher on the leadership scale than persons in middle positions. Study of a twelve-man jury seated at rectangular tables showed that jurors who seated themselves in end positions participated more, and were perceived as having more influence on the jury's decision, than persons sitting in middle positions. Steinzor concludes that the mean sitting distance is the determination of leadership emergence within a group. Check this out the next time you're in a board meeting. I've found this effect to be true on many occasions.

Spatial position also determines the flow of communication, which, in turn, determines leadership emergence. At a five-person decision-making group seated at a rectangular table, with three persons on one side and two on the opposite side, the two-person side greatly influenced the three persons on the other side. As predicted, members of the two-person side were shown to emerge more frequently as leaders than members of the three-person side. The rule to never arrive on time to avoid being classed as a beginner also prevails.

With respect to interpersonal relations, when the group size increases above three persons, there is a tendency for the leader to assume a position at the end of the table. In such cases the other group members normally sit as close as possible to the leader. Only rarely is the chair at the end opposite the leader used. Boardroom seating often reserves the seats adjacent to the chairman for senior directors—i.e., those who have not reached the statutory senility of bylaw retirement age.

The Steinzor and other studies have certain administrative implications for designing and participating in decision-making groups. Boardroom architecture and director dynamics are obvious implications. The following implications seem to be useful as a focus for the chairman of the board to target-model his directorate. Trade-offs have to be made to get the optimal arrangement for the board situation.

- Since the quality of board decisions is of major importance, it is useful to have a larger number of board members, say seven to twelve, so that more inputs are available to the board in making its decisions.

- A board of this size functions more effectively with a designated leader (some boards do not have chairmen). The chairman should be seated at the head of the table or at the end of the room. In less formal gatherings—committees, for example—the most acceptable leader can often be identified by seating all members equidistant from one another, for example around a circular table, and then observing the member to whom most of the useful comments are directed. This person usually is a most likely candidate for chairperson.

- If degree of consensus is of primary importance, it is useful to choose a smaller group (that is, three to five) so that each board member can have his or her concern considered and discussed.

- Director satisfaction and time to reach agreement are found to be favorably manipulated by using smaller groups. Remember that committees or boards with three members often cause one member to have low satisfaction. On the other hand, boards with four members often have high conflict and thus may not reach a quick consensus.

- Group conflict is known to be greatest on even-number boards. Ideally, a chairman should use committees of five to seven with simultaneous recognition of the need for diverse inputs and provision for coordination and control with the larger board.

- Spatial arrangements can be used to minimize conflict. Board or committee members who anticipate being antagonistic tend to sit across from one another. Members who sit across from one another also tend to have frequent and argumentative communications. A useful strategy for the chairman is to seat members with a high conflict potential beside one another. If there are two subgroups of high conflict potential, consider using alternate seating for the members.

Tips for Chairpersons

A sort of honorary glory attaches to the chairperson's role; almost everyone is pleased and proud to be made a chairperson of something. And that is three-quarters of the trouble!

It is helpful to remember that the chairperson is only the *agent* of the board when performing as chairperson. In this role (as distinct from the chief executive officer's role) he or she represents the entire board as an agent. A range of specific governance duties may be divided with others such as a vice-chairman or possibly the chief executive officer, if this spot is filled separately. Since our topic is ways and means of board operations, some pragmatic tips may help a chairperson conduct the formal sessions of the board. (Rather than emasculate the role, the term "chairman" is used by convention and for convenience in the following. The "chair," regardless of sex, is headquarters for the hindquarters.)

Tip No. 1: Why meet anyway? Determine the exact purpose of each board meeting well in advance. What is the meeting intended to achieve? Holding a routine meeting merely because the bylaws prescribe it is a waste of time. Meetings should be canceled if there is no useful purpose to be served.

Tip No. 2: Fix the formal agenda and watch for the hidden agenda. Define the objective(s) of each particular meeting in advance and arrange through the agenda to achieve those objectives. Separate informational from housekeeping and monitoring items, statutory acts from policy decisions, significant and strategic matters from less significant tactical items. Keep the board out of the executive and operations zones of management. Above all, pace the agenda to give the important matters a proper place; the early part of meetings is when persons are more alert. Two-hour meetings are long enough, and sleepiness is still the best eraser in the world.

Tip No. 3: Avoid snow jobs. Provide board members with only as much written material as is appropriate for homework. With advance skull-drudgery, meeting time can be spent on resolving issues, not exchanging information. Have duplicate sets available with the agenda for those who forget to bring theirs to the meeting.

Tip No. 4: For openers, start the agenda with a few items on which agreement is secured. This will create some resonance to help when conflict items are introduced. One of the greatest unsolved riddles of boardlife is that the board makes decisions faster when the agenda is crowded than when the agenda is skimpy. It seems that the less a board has to do, the slower it does it.

Tip No. 5: Clock the meeting. Establish and publish starting and stopping times for meetings. It will help intimidate those who may overdwell on their favorite subject if they see what's ahead on the docket.

Tip No. 6: The chairman should refrain from personal interventions in the discussions. His role is to conduct the meeting, and unless he relinquishes his chair he should seldom venture a personal opinion unless called upon to break a tie vote.

Tip No. 7: Arrange seating to take best advantage of group dynamics. This can be done by marking or placement of agenda papers, director manuals, handouts, etc. Remember seats closest to the chair are places of honor and esteem. One board I know uses nameplates (embedded in the teak board table!) to manage this practice.

Tip No. 8: Deal with pontification and rhetoric by any member in a firm but adroit way. One useful technique is to interrupt any such dress-suit language by asking someone else to comment on the garrulous one's point—*any* point in the oratory.

Tip No. 9: Draw out the quiet thinkers and the hostile or diffident types by probing with referral questions and alerting them in advance that they will be called upon. Deep thinkers and wallflowers in the boardroom need to be tested occasionally.

Tip No. 10: Occasionally put a controversial idea or proposal on the agenda to flush out dialogue and get adrenaline going. The resolution of arguments can be referred to neutral members or postponed for reflection without resorting to bayonet play.

Tip No. 11: If you have oracles, address the gurus or senior statesmen on the board last so as not to quash the input of those with less authoritative opinions. Work up the pecking order, not down.

Tip No. 12: Conclude the meeting on a positive—even happy—

note when possible. This can be done in various ways, even referring to those agenda items on which there was agreement. Close
with a reminder of the next meeting time, place, and matters at
issue, in an effort to provide a fresh start and get the board members thinking positively toward the next occasion. Or, as his biographer said to George Gershwin, "Let us beguine at the beginning."

These thoughts for board meetings are meant to reduce rather
than increase meeting necessity and duration by emphasizing how
we might design and conduct the ways and means of the board in
order to be more effective. I have employed many of these tactics
successfully in boardroom situations.

So, taking Tip. No. 12, let's conclude this chapter on ways and
means on a positive note. It is my favorite definition of an annual
general meeting—the AGM as the British term it: "An AGM is an
unnatural act performed by consenting adults in public." Given
this definition, the chore of the chairman in orchestrating this "unnatural act" is a challenging one. It would be a mistake, however,
to concentrate on the ways and means of board meetings to the ex-
clusion of their purpose and content. We must not spend so much
time building the church that we lose the creed.

6

Noetic License

The chairman of the board of directors of the Institute of Noetic Sciences (IONS) is former Apollo 14 astronaut Dr. Edgar D. Mitchell. The institute was founded in 1973 in San Francisco by this erudite cloud-hopper to study the nature of consciousness. "Noetic" means "based on the intellect," and noetic science should be of interest to all who toil in boardrooms and must deal with the subject of know-how and matters of intellectual property, that "something" in business which you can't hold in your hand, but which appears on the balance sheet as intangibles.

Earlier in this century another intellectual, the electrical wizard Charles Steinmetz, proclaimed that the greatest discovery of this century would be the discovery of spiritual power. Dr. Mitchell's more recent concept of noetic science—a contemporary version of Steinmetz's prediction—is apparently a notion whose time has come. There is wide current interest in the advanced ideas of IONS on human potential and inner awareness as a guide to self-directed growth. These notions also help us learn how to get the best out of our boards of directors.

Pioneering work by IONS is underway in electronic information exchange systems, mind research, holistic medicine, human connections and relationships, maximum executive performance, and limits of human educability. What goes on between directors in boardroom encounters is relevant to the profound transformation going on in the society. Such is the context in which our institutions function and pursue their missions. A cartoon caption expresses it well for the business world. The chairman says to one of his officers, "We've got a dummy corporation here; what we need is a smarty corporation."

How to get the board to think long and hard about the fundamentals of directing a corporation is the challenge from the public. Directors tend to avoid tackling the knotty issues in favor of peripheral matters. The *Olympic,* predecessor sister ship of the *Titanic,* was designed by the Right Honorable Alexander Carlisle, who remembered a board meeting where lifeboat capacity was discussed "for five or ten minutes," whereas the time allotted for the discussion of decorations for the liners ran up to five hours.

The web of societal problems facing directors is vast and complex. The turbulent environment in which a corporation must function is in a constant state of disequilibrium and transformation. The role of the board is a trying one in that awareness and understanding of the issues and dilemmas require a sense of history as well as judgment, analysis, and intuition to guide the corporation in the future. External interconnectedness and levels of problems, the driving forces, and the power centers provide complex manifestations which affect governance of institutions. This eternal triangle is right tangled.

My experience with the fuzzy set of conditions that can exist between the roles of chairman and chief executive officer when they are not the same person is a typical example of this complexity. This satyrlike biformity in corporate governance raises the questions of servant or master, board agent or team leader, guide or whip, moderator or task advocate. This tends to test the conflict-resolution mechanisms of organizations as well as the personal relationships of the individuals involved. The noetic license of the actors is further complicated by the politics of the situation.

Intellection

Understanding how to get a board to think about its significant problems requires understanding the noetic license of the board. The root word for "noetic" is the Greek word *nous,* meaning "reason." It concerns more than the minds of people who read each other's books, the so-called intelligentsia. In technical and commercial matters, this reasoning involves proprietary knowledge and trade secrets that are intellectual properties to be audited and monitored by a board of directors.

Intellectual property of a board of directors concerns the composite wisdom, savvy, know-how, and mind of the board. Know-how, a key component of intellectual property, is simply knowledge that you can't get from books. It covers knowing your way around, knowing how to survive, how to identify, how to grow, how to behave, and what not to do.

In a world dominated by specialists and experts, I am reminded of the old German story of the five members of a corporate planning committee, related by the *Vorstand*—the German version of our American executive committee of the board. The five planners, faced with the problem of milking a cow, decided that one of them should hold her dugs while the other four lifted the cow and moved it up and down. But the Germans are not alone in their different ways of going about things. All nations have problems getting their boards of directors to think about and tackle the real problems.

In fact, every one of us has his own form of *nous*. The literal Germans call it *Mutterwiss* ("mother wit," i.e., common sense). This active intellect, according to Aristotle, is the impersonal intellect that has created the world. The passive—or patient—intellect is that which belongs to the individual and perishes with him. Impersonal intellect is captured in modern times as "intellectual property," or "incorporeal property," under the modern juridical doctrine of the trust concept.

Intellection, *nous*, or noetic science in the boardroom is definitely a driving force in corporate governance (or should be). Thus some background on this vital property of a board of directors is relevant to understanding the noetic license of a directorate. Bear with me as I walk us through a little reportage plus hindsight. As Yogi Berra once remarked, "Ninety percent of this game is half mental."

In an industrial democracy, organized society sanctions, through charter or licenses, the operation or the development of new business. Western private enterprise receives its primary sanction or noetic license through the right of private property, which includes both real and intellectual or incorporeal property. This is the right of individuals to hold and use private property rights. The debate over ownership of the Nixon tapes focused on this particular concept. When the state acquires complete control over property, it makes little difference who holds title to it.

Certain incorporeal property rights involve financial, commercial, legal, and political considerations. These are the primary domains of the board of directors. They are somewhat fuzzy notions requiring subjective judgment as to value. This cluster of intangible business assets includes goodwill, reputation, managerial skill, monopolies, franchises, going-concern value, and capitalized expenses when dealing in the modern corporate format and language. In addition, there are the rights related to certain legalistic and accounting practices, such as recording or recognizing of income and expense (that is, generally accepted accounting conventions) for leasing versus purchase of start-up expenses. Asset value is often attributed to the intangible advantage of a government tax, credit exemption, or subsidy situations.

The fundamentals of governing a corporation dictate that the directors understand and accept the fact that the license given the corporation, when society charters its activity, requires the board of directors to think deeply and constructively about proper use of the rights granted. *Noetic license calls for a thinking board, not a token board of directors.*

The Board-Brain

Among his other posts and consultancies, Stafford Beer is visiting business school professor of cybernetics at Manchester University. His thesis about large and complicated systems hypothesizes that animals, computers, economics, and corporate enterprises each have their own "brain," or noetic center, with a control and communication system. And, of course, his study of automatic control as a coherent science is known in its own right as cybernetics.*

Certain fundamental principles of knowing and controlling apply to all large systems. In addition, there is a split in the board-brain which is important to the system of corporate governance. Split-brain research has recently revealed that "two minds" co-

---

* Stafford Beer, *Brain of the Firm: The Managerial Cybernetics of Organization* (London: Allan Lane/Penguin, 1972).

habit in our brain. The left side and the right side of our brains perform different functions. The mind-splitters note verbal and analytic capabilities come from the left side, while intuitive, nonverbal, holistic thinking is associated with the right hemisphere of the human brain.

A board of directors, in one sense, can function as a cybernetic (controlling) and noetic (thinking) center in its role of professional governancy. Here, governance is understood as the continuous exercise of authority and decision over, and the performance of, political functions of policymaking and resource allocation. That's fancy language for overseeing and monitoring a company's conduct, i.e., bugging the management to get with it.

Given the notion of a two-minded enterprise brain and its split-brain directorate as an automatic control center, we can muse over possible avenues and propose new vocabulary to better understand the profession of governance. With better understanding of these notions, our boards of directors can perhaps improve their effectiveness. Or as *Pygmalion*'s Eliza said about brains, "What you all just got to use when you ain't got an education."

I visited Yugoslavia about a year after the major political shakeup of the ruling League of Communists of Yugoslavia (LCY) to try to fathom the contradictory trends in economic reform and to judge the attractiveness of the country for foreign investment. At that time, there occurred a striking example of the left-brain style of a leader in dealing with the matter of respective roles and mutual trust as we know them in Western industrial countries. The group of European, American, and Asian businessmen with whom I was associated in the Business International-sponsored visit were deeply impressed with our off-record discussions with the late President Tito, his ministers, and leading figures in the financial, government, and business communities. Their complex—to us— concept of free enterprise with state-owned facilities bugged our group for almost a week of freewheeling interrogation and exchange of views.

The authority of the management to reserve funds for growth, for example, rather than raise the year-end bonus always bowed officially to a workers' council, which, it appeared, attempted to act as a board of directors on the one hand and a union group on the other hand. In questioning one of the industrial leaders, we were unable to get to the nub of how he made basic business decisions, in particular those involving options favoring shareowners (the people) versus employees (the workers). The chief manager of one of the largest state-owned enterprises said (with the translator's tailoring this into three languages) what may be paraphrased as "I just tell the council that's the way it's got to be!" This was reminiscent of several strong-minded CEOs I know and how they deal with their boards.

In the case of this 230-pound impressive straight-shooter Yugoslavian type of executive leader, it was obvious his dynamic personality and personal prestige transcended any right-brained ideological network of constraints. He did not permit these abstract constraints to inhibit clear left-brain resolution of an action in the best interest of the enterprise, as we would judge it in our Western value system. Even a two-minded enterprise requires that the leader make a decision for some action that reconciles thinking from both sides of the brain.

Much of the resistance to changes in human affairs seems to come from a lack of thinking on a high enough level of concern about human problems. We are more comfortable enhancing old, proven concepts and technology. Embracing novelty and change is emotionally difficult. In a business such innovativeness means not improving the enterprise one has known and dedicated oneself to, but devising a new business or activity which appears alien and possesses unknown characteristics. This resistance to change shows itself in more mundane ways than in combating strategic business innovations.

One chairman of a board on which I served for many years had a hang-up on retaining old-style furnishings and large portraits of previous chairmen which dominated the dark mahogany-paneled boardroom. More significant, however, was the large mahogany table, around which twenty-five directors could gather to do their directing. The communications were poor, as the seating put directors at one end about twenty-four feet from those at the other end. We tolerated this United Nations-like setup for five years during his chairmanship. As soon as he retired, the new chairman threw out the overgrown table, redecorated the boardroom, installed a display-screen arrangement, and clustered the swivel seats so communications were effective. The old portraits are relegated

to some seldom-used corridors. The "logic" behind this redecoration had deeply emotional origins—the new chairman not only wanted change, he wanted change to be manifest. But the old regime's fixation on the past was also emotional rather than strictly "logical."

The Boardroom Issues

One of my favorite books is Paul Tabori's *The Natural Science of Stupidity.* His theme: The greatest enemy of mankind is man's

* Paul Tabori (Philadelphia: Chilton Company, 1959).

own stupidity. As the world's bane, stupidity of greed, of doubt, of red tape, of the law, of myth and wish-dream is evident in every walk of life. The boardroom, I suggest, is no exception, despite its role as keeper of the corporate intellect. As holder of the corporation's noetic license to practice governance, the board of directors can make the damnedest mistakes of commission or omission.

We often find ourselves in today's critical circumstances, like the allies at the Congress of Vienna, where Talleyrand commented they were "too frightened to fight each other; too stupid to agree." This comment made over 160 years ago certainly fits the plight in which we find ourselves in several world areas. Some right-brained thinking is needed alongside our left-brained foreign policy. Certainly this is true of boards of directors of multinational corporations operating in these sensitive areas. The noetic license of a board assumes directors are capable of right- and left-brain trade-off decisions. Before going on to the laughed-over lighter side of the boardworld, we need to briefly acknowledge the serious issues which a board must cope with in the eighties.

A few of these issues in the complex corporate strategic context occur in a time frame of the next three to five years. Directors must find ways to govern in the face of uncertainty by reducing as much of it as possible to a measurable portfolio of business risks. We need to be serious about these issues.

To do this, boards must search for patterns. There are some general patterns which connect and show either a step function, feedback loops, slow change, accelerating change, stabilization, emergence, peaks, discontinuities, gaps, repressions, or novelties— to use those buzzwords of the management scientists.

Given this boardroom agenda for pattern search, here are some problems, not necessarily in order of importance, a corporation faces in responding effectively to key issues in the eighties. The horizons of corporate competence/incompetence are changing. Boardroom *nous* is at a premium. Responsive stupidity cannot be tolerated in corporate affairs.

1. Many events which impact corporations are outside their conventional cognizance and experience. The old nine-to-five approach doesn't give sufficient odds.

One of the most obvious in a series of recent events which illustrate this situation was the failure of many chemical companies to adequately dispose of their waste products in years past, when it

was considered safe to bury or otherwise dispose of toxic substances. The recent Super Fund legislation in which the chemical
industry contributes to a central fund which is used to clean up and
destroy residual toxic chemicals in various locations around the nation is a remedial measure made necessary when companies' conventional disposal practices proved to be unsafe.

The unwitting use of dioxin-contaminated material for road
treatment is another example of lack of cognizance and experience
with these materials.

In 1962, Rachel Carson drew public attention to twelve pesti-
cides that might be potentially hazardous to animals and humans—
DDT, malathion, parathion, dieldrin, aldrin, endrin, chlordane,
heptachlor, toxaphene, lindane, benzene hexachloride, and 2,4-D.
Since then the use of each has been regulated and some have been
phased out.

All of these events were outside the conventional cognizance and
experience of the corporations making and distributing the products.

2. These events are also often outside the organized managerial or
    governance focus of the corporation in terms of style, momen-
    tum, and continuity and, therefore, usually outside corporate
    control.

The pricing decisions of major oil companies affect more than
their own profit-and-loss statements. In our free-market economy
the effect of investment decisions or pricing decisions on many
commodities ripples through the economy of our nation and affects
our international economic and political relationships.

There is a basic incongruity between the multinational corporation (MNC) and the various nation-states in which it operates. For
example, the MNC's allocation of resources or pricing policies
around the world effectively result in a private foreign policy
which can meet with support or resistance from internal and external public policies of host and home countries.

Nations encounter challenges to their sovereignty as MNCs and
other nonstate entities (e.g., professional organizations, news
media) cross national boundaries in complicated patterns. These
activities are often incongruent with national standards, ethics, beliefs, cultural modes, and legal frameworks.

Some of the larger U.S. companies make great efforts to extend
their managerial and governance focus to be alert to those world-

wide conditions which are outside corporate control. United Technologies Corporation, for example, has its own computer-based program for measuring foreign risks in the many countries in which it does business. Ratings are made of sixty-five countries on ninety-six different factors ranging from labor unrest to economic health. Monsanto Company has a similar country-risk-rating scheme.

The need for boards of directors of MNCs to extend their concern and knowlege around the globe has spawned one of the fastest-growing professional service areas in the form of consulting firms offering international risk assessments. Some well-established services are PRISM (primary risk investment matrix), BERI (business environmental risk index), WPRF (world political risk forecasts), and Project Link (a National Science Foundation-funded series of economic models of twenty-five countries maintained by the Wharton School of Business of the University of Pennsylvania).

3. The reality of the environment may differ from the corporate perception of the environment.

American directors sometimes delude themselves about the relative riskiness of doing business in the United States, confusing actual risk with the level of comfort with risk. Risk in one form seems to be more bearable than risk in another form, although the substance may be the same.

Looking at the risk of a forced sale of a multinational company's property in an overseas location brings to mind a classic case of substance versus form. IT&T was forced to divest its American subsidiary, Hartford Fire Insurance; in Chile, the company was forced to sell Chiltelco. As far as substance of risk was concerned, there was no real difference between these two events. IT&T's board of directors may have felt more able to cope with the American form (antitrust laws) than with the Chilean form (a socialist philosophy), but the substantive effect of government action in both countries was identical: no more Hartford and no more Chiltelco in IT&T's portfolio of businesses.

4. Often corporations have an attitude or an approach which must be altered, mentalities that must be broken—e.g., symmetry breaks about growth trajectories and rates of change.

Until recent years the economic, social, political, and technological environment in which companies carried out their activities was relatively stable. Changes were gradual. Past steady-state, evolutionary trends and the ways and means of governing a corporation have been interrupted during the last decade by legalistic and regulatory intervention, and by the increased business and political uncertainties, by transformations of companies through merger, acquisition, and divestment, and by industry restructuring (e.g., financial intermediaries such as brokerage firms, investment bankers, and insurance and credit establishments have invaded each other's prior domain).

As a result there has been what the systems experts call a symmetry break. This breaking of past symmetries or patterns of corporate conduct generates variety and leads to increasing complexity. The variety of conventional board functions and board processes has yet to fully match the uncertainties, variables, and complexities of the corporate context in which directors must now govern corporations. As one result, boards are creating more special committees to delve into matters requiring attention.

A recent Conference Board study revealed that principal board committees usually total five (executive, salary and bonus, stock option, audit, and finance). However, there were seventeen other types of committees in 512 manufacturing companies surveyed in the United States. Boards are experimenting with standing committees on public policy, acquisitions, investments, strategy, corporate development, environmental affairs, marketing, and technology, to name just a few of the variety of specialized areas being focused on at board level.

The purpose of this increased board activity is to allow the board of directors to cope with the increased velocity of change in these areas and to deal with the new opportunities and problems which result when past patterns of growth and development no longer indicate what future conditions will be. Discontinuities prevail when new technologies or surprise political happenings make products obsolete or upset markets.

5. One must separate issues from problems. Often the corporation focuses on the latter rather than the former. No matter how trivial the problem, it's always possible to build it up to a major issue.

In a boardroom context I use the term "issue" to mean a matter in dispute on which there are responsible differences of opinion. Thus, an issue is debated until a decision is reached. A problem, on the other hand, is a question which is raised (or arises) for inquiry.

Some investigation or additional consideration is called for to clarify the unsettled questions. The confusion may be due to lack of facts, inaccurate facts, or an uncertain situation causing perplexity, distress, or vexation among board members.

In consulting with boards of directors help is sometimes needed in identifying the problem(s) faced by the directors so that alternate solutions or options can be presented. If there are differences of opinion on the proper solution, an issue is raised between the parties which can then be debated before the entire board. Then a choice can be made as to official action taken by the corporation.

During 1977 and 1978, under the auspices of the American Law Institute–American Bar Association, invitational conferences on corporate structure and governance were held with an invited group of corporate executives, lawyers, academics, and critics. The events were caused by the proliferation of criticisms of corporations during the 1970s, provoked, in part, by exposure of corporate wrongdoing in connection with political contributions. The primary issues were the same issues we face in the 1980s.

The proceedings did not clarify all the problems to be addressed. However, some inquiry was on whether there was "too low" a level of standard of care and loyalty of directors, on excessive social costs when corporations shut down operations in communities or polluted the environment, and on the problem of fear of power concentrated in the hands of corporate management. Interestingly, little concern was expressed about the need for structural or corporate law reform to improve the economic efficiency of corporations. The lengthy conferences were necessary to sort out and clarify problems and to develop enough information to identify and debate the issues involved. The three main issues flowing from this effort can be capsulized in the following: (a) Does the goal of long-term profit maximization continue to serve as an accurate description of corporate objectives? (b) Should corporations be further regulated? (c) Do present laws relating to the structure and governance of corporations satisfy the objectives as currently conceived (i.e., the effectiveness of boards with regard to standards of fiduciary responsibility, standards of care, and regulation of challenges to management from shareholders or corporate outsiders)?

6. There are many signals of change. It is important to reduce the noise by concentrating on those signals that are relevant.

Boards of directors tend to draw boundaries around their domain

with more certainty than experience or good conduct warrants—
for example, boundaries between the board and management or
between the corporation and its environment. As a result, many
changes outside the boundaries go unheeded. Boards tend to perform mostly as a closed system. Only with the increasing complexity have many boards begun to dig into management's domain to
ensure adequate management development and succession programs, strategic planning, adequate monitoring of overseas business
conduct, attention to consumer interests, and other activities.

In 1978, Allied Corporation (then Allied Chemical Corporation)
created a board-level committee on environmental affairs. Outside
directors made up the committee, which employs an outside consulting firm to regularly audit environmental compliance of various
operations of the company. The boundary of this board's concern
now reaches into what is normally a separate management domain.

Growing interest in overseas markets and investment opportunities is reflected in the increased number of chairmen and CEOs of
foreign companies being elected to Fortune 100 boards of directors. A 1981 survey by Deloitte, Haskins & Sells reveals one in five
of these one hundred companies now have international directors.
Boardroom compass of concern has become more global.

The International Telephone and Telegraph board reaches out
into social and other external domains through its board-level "corporate public policy committee." This group of directors concerns
itself with interpreting the signals of change which may affect
IT&T's corporate position and policy on all major public issues.
Signals of change are identified outside the normal scan of the
board's network.

7. The process is discovering what uncertainties can be converted
   to manageable risk. This is the job of the management on behalf
   of the board.

There are important distinctions between certainty, risk, and uncertainty. Risk, where the probabilities of events or courses are
known, is a special case of uncertainty. The set of risk variables that
a director must deal with may be viewed as a continuum from
complete determination on one end to the complete unknown situation at the other end. Unfortunately the scope of board action is
greatest when our knowledge is the least complete. The scope of

board action is the least when the scope of the directors' knowledge is the greatest.

One interesting technique used in strategic thinking about the murky view of the future is the use of alternative-futures scenarios. In a recent study by Arthur D. Little, Inc., for a large multinational financial institution we characterized two dominant driving forces of primary interest to the U.S.-based firm. The first was the relative level of world interactivity, and the second was the character of U.S. government intervention in the private sector. Alternative scenarios were developed given the present world condition, with increasing intensity of international interactions. Major trading nations would develop more multilateral tariff and nontariff arrangements to facilitate trade and investment. New international monetary and judicial systems would evolve, as would international codes of conduct under such a scenario of events.

Alternatively, if a protectionist scenario evolved in the 1980s with a lower global level of interaction, breakdown of some international institutions such as the International Monetary Fund (IMF) could be threatened. Such an autarkic world is inherently one of recession or depression, with currency instability, trade restrictions, and quotas. Internal industries would be restructured to reduce reliance on outsiders. Investment flows would weaken, trade barriers would rise, and so on as each nation attempted to follow a policy of self-sufficiency.

Another alternative could evolve by a move toward a more privatized form of government interaction, similar either to that in Japan and Holland or to the more bureaucratic form experienced in the United States in depression years or after World War II.

Using these alternative scenarios, some of the uncertainties could be hypothesized as determined states or forecast conditions, i.e., reduced to probabilistic risk situations, for purposes of thinking through the consequences. In this study we identified 123 separate global trends and shifts, including twenty-four areas of technological change which could affect industries served by the company. These trends and shifts were grouped as social-cultural, regulatory, techno-economic, and international trend clusters. Eight of the broader movements called for new thinking at the multinational company board level and new abilities at the executive level. The client made a complete overhaul of its management development plans, among many, in order to develop managers for the future who will be capable of managing a wide range of probable conditions.

8. Institutions are faced with a high increase in interactivity and complexity without an appropriate buffer. Otherwise, it's yessir, nosir, ulcer for the management.

The context in which corporations and other institutions now exist is undergoing profound worldwide transformation. Restructuring of most elements of our society is taking place with the political, technological, and economic shifts. The trends are apparent in the U.S. demographic shifts from north to south. Two halves of our country are undergoing different sets of experiences in economic activity.

Our mass industrial society is shifting to an information society. With 55 percent of society working in the information sector today, compared to 17 percent of the population in 1950, the strategic resource of knowledge and data—both renewable and self-generating—must be considered in addition to monetary capital.

More decentralization than centralization is taking place for the first time in history. In the political scene, power is shifting not only from the president to the Congress but, less obviously, from the Congress to the states and localities. General-interest contexts are on the wane. During the same period of time that *Life, Look,* and the *Saturday Evening Post* went out of business, over 300 special-purpose magazines were created and publishing interactivity between the separate interests multiplied.

The impact of this turmoil is illustrated by the proliferation of shareholder resolutions and activist movements on corporate activities abroad and on the use of nuclear power at home—which issue dominated last year's crop of resolutions. Corporate activity in South America, particularly Bolivia, Guatemala, and Nicaragua, was the subject of the most resolutions from church groups. Companies were asked to establish policies on promotion and distribution of proprietary drugs in the Third World and to reduce the promotion of cigarette sales in the less-developed areas of the globe. Most of the South African resolutions were also proposed by church groups, but the biggest increase in shareholder activity in 1981 was in the area of trade with Communist countries.

Sales of infant formula food, on community investment, as well as an attack on U.S. companies' labor practices, filled out the agenda of many annual meetings of the board of directors and its shareholders.

One of the buffers developed to deal with the matter of U.S. companies' activity in South Africa has been the creation of the Sullivan Principles of Equal Opportunity. This code of conduct was developed by a clergyman who was a member of the board of directors of General Motors. GM adopted these principles for conducting its South African subsidiaries in order to improve working conditions for all employees. The Sullivan Principles have since been adopted by most major firms doing business in South Africa. An independent assessment of compliance with these principles is regularly made by Arthur D. Little, Inc., for public information and policy guidance of the companies involved.

In May 1983 the Milan firm of Montedison S.A. and Hercules Incorporated of Wilmington, Delaware, announced the formation of a fifty-fifty worldwide joint venture to combine their respective assets and interests in research, development, manufacturing, and marketing of polypropylene resin, establishing an international corporate mechanism to strengthen both companies' investments in this polymer business. It provided a buffer against formidable competition in the commodity plastic worldwide industry.

9. The overall issue is the appropriate corporate strategy, corporate style, and corporate culture thriving in an uncertain environment. These issues identify and separate major boardroom problems, issues, and opportunities for the eighties. There is also opportunity for a split-brain board approach. A Swiss friend of mine recently lamented to me, "Yesterday opportunity knocked on my door, but by the time I pushed back the bolt, turned two locks, unlocked the chain, and shut off the burglar alarm, it was gone!"

Given turbulent times, an early-warning system and a strategic "do" line are needed for every boardroom. In order for boards to preserve the noetic license granted them in the scheme of things, we must recognize public opinion triggers, and this requires heavy thinking in the boardroom. Not, according to William James, what a great many people think they are doing when they are merely rearranging their prejudices.

7

Boardroom
Buzzwords

Guru-ese is the buzzword for the language of experts and learned persons. Business communication has become a corporate public relations problem because of this pros' prose. Because of such inside jargon, accountability and conduct of corporate directors is obscured. In proxy contests, corporate counsel deny the allegations that directors fail to discharge legal responsibilities and the "alligators" are defied in legalistic buzzword statements.

The public perception that the boardroom decision process is secretive, tightly controlled, and unresponsive to points of reference outside the boardroom itself doesn't help the understanding of boardroom affairs. I believe this problem is as much a lack of public understanding of what goes on behind the boardroom door, and the opacity of corporate pronouncements, as it is actual director or corporate conduct. You have to be an insider these days to really comprehend boardroom antics.

Corporations have responded to this transmission problem in some understandably self-serving ways. These include hectic institutional advertising, generous financial support for socially or culturally significant public television programs, a torrent of words in annual and quarterly reports and security analyst literature, and stilted public interviews of top executives. Despite yeoman efforts, this public educational process has only begun. Part of the challenge is in the buzzword content of the typical corporate voice.

High-Low-Variety Languages

Some interesting work on high-variety language at Queens University in Ontario helps us position buzzwords in the continuum of languages.* Variations of national language make up the center part of the continuum. Special-purpose languages, which are usually mathematically bound, tend to be more precise. Nonverbal forms of communication such as art and music are more ambiguous but can communicate emotions and notions which cannot be verbalized.

Managers and directors tend to use high-variety forms of communication and resist quantified lower-variety—more precise—support systems because high-variety language can transmit insightful information about highly complex human systems. The chairman's diary of penned-up emotions is on one end of the scale, and the chief financial officer's desktop computer terminal is on the other end.

The following language hierarchy of ambiguity and preciseness is adapted from the Daft and Wiginton continuum:

HIGH-VARIETY, AMBIGUOUS LANGUAGES

Nonverbal	Art (music, painting)
	Nonverbal expression (body language)
	Poetry
Natural language	General verbal expression
	Jargon, slang, argot, buzzwords
	Linguistic variables (semantic differentials, Likert scale)
Special-purpose language	Computer language
	Probability theory
	Analytical mathematics

LOW-VARIETY, PRECISE LANGUAGES

We can see that buzzwords, while still a "natural" language for the in-group, borders on the special-purpose-language cluster of more precise, low-variety languages. The boardroom problem this

* Richard L. Daft and John C. Wiginton, "Language and Organization," *Academy of Management Review,* Vol. 4, No. 2 (1979), pp. 178–191.

presents is that the publics who are trying to understand corporate communications are at least one level higher on the language continuum scale, i.e., nearer the higher-variety general verbal expression level. Maybe the recent interest of corporations in financially supporting the arts, symphonies, and dance (body language) is a more sophisticated effort to communicate with the public than we give the corporations credit for.

Insider Vocab

In the rapidly changing professions of today's society, buzzwords seem to be the best solution to language distress, which has become especially acute. Technically, the term "buzzword" refers to the verbal, intellectual one-upmanship of the slang, jargon, argot, and pseudo-tribal language developed by relatively small, specialized groups for their own benefit in response to their individual needs. Buzzwords consequently serve as a mechanism of self-reference, isolating the in-group from hoi polloi.

The value of this new and proliferating language practice is its adaptability to change—to convey new ideas, to explain complicated new activities and concepts. Although buzzwords are capable of injecting humor into an otherwise humorless situation (and this is their fun aspect), their primary purpose is to furnish an effective professional shorthand that sharpens communication. When buzzwords are used only for impressive effect, rather than for transmission of a new idea, or to confuse and mystify rather than enlighten or clarify, or when buzzwords overwhelm you into believing you know what you are talking about when you really don't, then discrimination and elimination are required. Language must be sufficiently comfortable and comprehensible to both user and receiver for each to benefit.

The inside vocabulary of leaders in nearly every area of professional endeavor—industry, education, government, economics, politics, aerospace, science and technology, behavioral and social science, operations research, and computer science—has proliferated like drosophilae. While the mortality rate of buzzwords is high, some flash phrases flourish as a real help to communication outside the limited sphere for which they were intended.

These phrases find their way into everyday vocabulary, and a few finally appear in conventional dictionaries. The newer words in the strategic planner's vernacular: diversification, synergistic effect; those new words in the computer and operations research words; words in systems analysis, input/output statistics, heuristics, model building, management information systems; and the new words in the social science words: affluent society, hard-core, lifestyle, have all made the grade from the buzzword stage to acceptable zipvocab. You find them in dictionaries.

Much of the bureaucratic and Madison Avenue talk, on the other hand, fades and passes away without having been helpful. However, government and advertising have by no means cornered the market on gobbledygook. Alan Simpson, president of Vassar College, when a professor at my alma mater, Washington University, put the Twenty-third Psalm into what *Time* called "educanto": "The Lord is my external-internal integrative mechanism. I shall not be deprived of gratification for my viscerogenic hungers or my need-dispositions. He motivates me to orient myself towards a non-social object with effective significance. He positions me in a non-decisional situation. He maximizes my adjustment."

Buzzwords in the Boardroom

One of the key manifestations of boardroom activity is communication. As the issues facing board members become increasingly complex, directors need to develop a new attitude toward language and sometimes a new vocabulary to deal with the multiplicity of contemporary pressures. The director's role requires that he react intelligently to the impact of specialized words that bombard him from management scientists and the business elite, as well as peripheral fields of activity. It is unrealistic to ignore the development of new words and phrases simply because a particular vocabulary is outside one's area of interest. Since most innovation in business language comes up from management rather than down from the board, and because new concepts are usually expressed in buzzwords, the director needs to learn at least some of these in order to understand and respond to those who may be a flair ahead of him in verbalistics.

The following are some of the newer buzzwords of current "boardspeak":

arbs Arbitrageurs, in corporate takeover terminology. These are stock market professionals who buy up huge quantities of a target company's shares of stock at prices below the takeover bid. The offense, hoping to shift the target's ownership from long-term investors to short-term speculators, tries to panic the target's stockholders into selling as many shares as possible into the arbs' hands. The arbs then become natural allies of the acquirer. This accumulation of stock can sometimes turn a takeover proposal into a virtual fait accompli.

asanas, boardroom Refers to use of yoga posture while in a board meeting to relax jaded director nerves. Hatha, one of the four basic kinds of yoga mental discipline, breaks down into two parts—pranayama, or breathing routines, and asanas, or various postures. These postures are used to get your body in tune with your spirit and are not exercises. Postures are less strenuous and more cerebral. At one time there were reportedly 84,000 asanas; now there are closer to eighty-four. Boardroom asanas are recommended in dull boardroom sessions in order to carve out a little piece of nirvana for yourself.

asbull A pronunciation of the acronym ASBL, *association sans but lucratif*, which translates "association without lucrative purpose." These are nonprofit organizations originally set up for Belgian schools and churches. One of the problems facing American multinational companies is the administration of their foreign pension funds. Many American firms operating in Belgium are switching these pension assets to ASBLs. This allows U.S. corporations to manage their pension funds independently, seemingly free of any investment restrictions.

auction agreement Joint venture contract term for a provision in the agreement to cope with withdrawal of a partner. Under an auction agreement, either partner might offer to buy out the other. The party receiving the offer has two options at that time: either to accept the offer or to buy out the offerer at the offerer's own terms. This type of agreement helps keep both partners honest and guards against efforts to cut losses.

baby robin education Harvard Business School professor Theodore Levitt's term for the popular "baby robin" theory of education, considered more congenial and easier to teach than the case method. Newly hatched birds thrive from the mother robin's assorted gatherings stuffed down their eagerly opened gullets. The student is supposed to listen to and learn the professional *Hoch-*

sprache similarly stuffed. It is presumed that what's said is relevant, what's relevant is heard, what's heard is understood, what's understood is retained, and what's retained is usable and used. Chairmen-CEOs who dominate their boards of directors often use the baby robin educational technique to deal with their directors, particularly if the directors are employee inside directors.

barberpole language Linguist's term for the simplest type of communication system. In advertising and public and shareholder relations, barberpole language provides only a single message through association of a single meaning with a single symbol. The familiar red-white-and-blue pole is a symbol meaning "place where a man can get a shave and a haircut" and is just one message through the association of the meaning and the symbol. The symbol "sh" associated with the meaning "quiet" constitutes an entire message meaning something like "Be quiet!"

basketry An age-old craft term used in acquisition negotiations to deal with indemnification of directors and others involved. In this the seller is entitled to a "basket," or "cushion," provision. This is a clause which says in effect that only if the damage to the purchaser exceeds a certain amount will he be entitled to collect indemnification.

bear hug An unnegotiated takeover proposal (of a corporation) made either publicly or privately to a board of directors. Object of the maneuver is to force the board into acting quickly by reminding the directors of their fiduciary responsibilities.

bisexual offer Investment bankerese for an offer to buy shares of a target company when the overture is neither an unfriendly proposal nor a friendly one. Stating that the board of directors takes no position on the offer and suggesting that each stockholder make up his or her own mind, the prospective acquiree's management may transmit a "bisexual offer" on the buyer's behalf. Target management thus exhibits an inclination in both directions. As the offered price escalates, target management's position, having started at "unfriendly," very frequently moves across the situation to "neutral," and then to "friendly." This may occur particularly if the buyer's representatives give generous assurances that titles, corner offices, salaries, club memberships, and similar perquisites will be retained.

black-suit report Flip description of audit committee's report to a board of directors. Done in somewhat funereal style by dark-suited (with vest) certified public accountants, the "black-suit report" is usually in anything but barberpole language.

body rain Sardonic reference to the suicides which occurred on Wall Street during the big depression when there were despondents plunging out office windows, constituting a body rain during those troubled times. Used now to indicate a flushout of those "bodies" in financial or other business distress who are forced out of business because of failure or impending collapse of the business. Such a body rain occurred in the real estate development sector in the 1973–1974 period when the REITs (real estate investment trusts) got into so much trouble because of illiquidity, high mortgage rates, inflation, and inadequate management and experience. Merger, bankruptcy, retraction, and failure to produce adequate returns caused a symbolic "body rain" in that industry. Reaganomics also caused symbolic body rain in several other business areas. Directors should be aware of the extra costs of the practice of targeted firms in an acquisition in providing "golden parachutes," or special compensation contracts, for key officers who may be part of the body rain after a takeover.

briarpatch society Part of the counterculture community of people who are trying to build a network of new business and work environments that relate to the values of our generation—values that are significantly different from those of our parents. These briarpatch society values have to do with learning, sharing, and a belief in the "right livelihood." Every board should have a briarpatch-sensitive director to help interpret this network's impact on the company.

brontosaurus principle Organizations grow faster than their brains can manage them in relation to their environment and to their own physiology. When this occurs they are an endangered species.

butterfly years That short period in a company's growth period between the caterpillar stage of a young entrepreneurial venture and the aging period of a mature enterprise, including extinction. The chemical and plastics industries went through their butterfly years in the fifties and sixties and since have topped out in terms of relative growth. Parts of the electronics industry and the genetic engineering business are currently in their butterfly years.

buzzard's luck Texas expression of frustration because of lack of achievement: "I didn't kill nothin', and nothin' died."

chicken switch Space jargon meaning an abort button in a man-operated missile. In a boardroom sense it refers to a decision point (or node on a decision tree) where the plan is switched to abandon the project in favor of a safer venture.

competent failure Sophisticated talk referring to the notion in a value system that to fail because of incompetence is intolerable, whereas failure after a competent effort is excusable and understandable. The phrase is used in venture capital, preventure capital, and innovative management circles when dealing with a high-risk venture or enterprise. It concerns performance evaluation of those in responsible charge of a task, a company, a function, or a project which did not succeed in spite of competent professional or managerial effort. It means that failure is not the fault of the competent individual who tried to succeed, but of countervailing forces outside his control.

corporate flagellant The SEC staff has indicated that most of the new, important undertakings in consent decrees were initiated by the defendants. The mission of the corporate flagellant is to devise innovative ways to scourge and mortify the corporation in public without seriously damaging it.

custard communication A flip pedagogical term used for annual reports and chairman's messages to shareholders, where the content goes down easily but leaves little for rumination or quotation. Contrasts with "cud communication," which leaves phrases and notions in the memory for think-back and slow assimilation.

dependencia syndrome A foreign investment policy under which foreign and domestic elites collude against the national interests of host countries. This syndrome, one of many under attack in connection with the role of the multinational corporation and its board of directors, is rapidly disappearing.

due diligence determiners The SEC provides that underwriters participating in a securities issue may rely for their "due diligence" defense on the managing underwriter's investigation, if the participatory underwriter makes a check of the manager's performance. In practice, this responsibility is being subcontracted to "due diligence determiners"—often accountants by trade who determine that the manager has been duly diligent.

endofacultatively reorientational normoprofessionism Cultivated ability to make social concessions to people in roles where they can be on your side and help you achieve success. They include bosses, public relations persons, press, distinguished fellow directors, and radio and TV personalities.

executive boutique Wall Streetese for a small broker who does no stock market or investment research, but merely executes orders. On May 1, 1975, American stockbrokers abandoned their schedules of fixed commission rates for the buying and selling of shares, whatever the size of the transaction.

financial gigolo British term introduced in the early 1930s to describe those company directors whose function is twofold. Their names act as a bait by which the public is induced to buy shares of the company and after the company is formed as a means of preserving confidence. This practice of the aristocracy in England created a "market" for titled gentlemen willing to serve as financial gigolos or corporate directors. There is a "Rent-a-Peer" service in London!

gray knight Takeover terminology in the field of corporate acquisitions for an opportunistic second bidder, not solicited by the target, who tries to take advantage of the difficulties between the target company and the first bidding company. The target company usually remains neutral in a "gray knight" gambit.

groupthink A pathological condition in boardroom decision-making with special dynamics. The concept of groupthink pinpoints an entirely different source of trouble, residing neither in the individual nor in the organizational setting. Over and beyond all the familiar sources of human error is a powerful source of defective judgment that arises in all cohesive groups—the concurrence-seeking tendency, which fosters excessive optimism, lack of vigilance, and sloganistic thinking about the weakness and morality of out-groups. Individual directors, for example, become committed to board decisions, and as a result their own personal attitudes and models of reality shift to reflect that of the entire board, in an attempt to maintain inner consistency.

haircut, to Slang for trimming budgets and development programs. To take a haircut means to cut back "nicely" on some excessive activity or expenditures to improve appearance cosmetically without jeopardizing the main body of the activity.

high-crotch functional organization A business organizational structure with only two "long legs," such as manufacturing and marketing, which communicate with each other only at lofty levels.

infallibalistic omnipotentiality (IO) Experts cannot be seen to make mistakes and avoid such on the personal level by saying things in a way that can be later interpreted to mean whatever suits the circumstances. Techniques used are implicatory suggestionism, juxtapositionary implicationism.

interstitial men Identification of a new role for linking and correlating interorganizational transactions. Independent directors of corporations are one example of a role for correlating activities of a corporation with another sector of society in which the director is otherwise identified and occupied.

Jell-O principle An image used in applied behavioral science when dealing with organization change and surviving an intervention. The Jell-O principle describes the effects of organizational change interventions in the system as similar to putting one's hand into a bowl of Jell-O. When the hand is in the Jell-O, it moves the Jell-O away, but once the hand is removed the Jell-O flows back again. Social systems are so resilient and surprisingly flexible that they survive major interventions.

joint venture space An interesting concept of dealing with the attributes of joint ventures by an international firm—a multinational—with respect to the critical needs and forces at work in the host country. The joint venture space has dimensions according to the key variables of control, risk, and skills transfer. A firm's position in this three-dimensional space captures its activity at a point in time. The MNC and host nations traditionally hold differing perceptions of joint venture space. The host nation perceives it on a simple control/skills transfer plane. A MNC views its activity usually on a risk/control plane. If both parties understand the critical dimensions of the model, more beneficial arrangements are more likely.

kangaroo strategy The more empty the pocket, the greater the leap. A Swiss buzzword for the dubious practice of companies on the acquisition kick when they leverage and pyramid their balance sheet by taking on an asset without having adequate capital to do so prudently.

literary counterattack Refers to tactics of a target company opposing a takeover attempt. The target company engages in a blitz of "literary" effort in the form of communications to shareholders, citing reasons for opposition to the takeover. This can take many forms: letters to shareowners, newspaper advertisements, speeches by corporate executives, etc.

liveware Refers to intangible management techniques such as training, organizational development, and evaluation of planning functions. Opposite of tangible techniques or methods which refer to "hardware" such as equipment, devices, and buildings.

Marco Polo syndrome A corporate planner's phenomenon which translates into "I've been there, so I know." Of course, if you're the only one who's been there, you're the only one who could know. This syndrome gets more complex when you realize that everyone in the business has it and that those who are addicted feed the habit with large injections.

mouse-milking Phrase used to imply undue effort expended to accomplish a small result. Milking a mother mouse yields little milk in return for the efforts expended. Buzzword used to describe a project where the yield is not worth the expenditure of resources.

nakoda Japanese term that translates roughly into "marriage broker." This is a professional who belongs to neither family entering into a prospective marriage, but whose duty it is to see to it that all facets of the impending union are compatible and congenial. In present-day Japan the term has been extended to cover the services of a business broker who arranges joint ventures or other joint operations between Japanese firms.

New Year's Eve parties Accountingese for the bunched major transactions corporations engage in at the end of a quarter or fiscal year. With the pressure on outside certified public accountants to audit firms more carefully as a result of management deceptions and frauds and director laxity, the courts, the SEC, and CPAs are giving extra scrutiny to all material transactions, especially those that would affect the income of the corporation or division by 5 percent or more. A New Year's Eve party, of course, is a year-end bash when things become relaxed and a lot goes on which in normal practice is not condoned.

Nob—"not on brainpower" An artificially coined acronym for that which is measured by net profit per employee on an annual basis.

Nonglomerate A peeled-back conglomerate, an operating company, not a holding company. This buzzword takes a poke at the frail ties and failures in many instances of the organization concept of a conglomerate structure for an enterprise in which many unrelated businesses are hooked together through a parent holding company organization. Management of the holding company does not rely on synergy of the component businesses in the conglomerate, but deals with each asset block on a separate nonoperating financial process basis.

one-tool viewpoint Psychologist Abraham Maslow once said: "If the only tool you have is a hammer, you tend to treat everything as if it were a nail." Such a one-tool viewpoint has been all too evident for many years in psychology, management, and governance.

outplacement consultant A specialist who, for a fee, advises companies on how to handle the firing and also tutors the fired executive on how to find another job.

PhDeities A clique of intellectuals, all possessing Ph.D. degrees in something, who perceive themselves as gods with divine rights to guide others in intellectual and cultural matters. A cynical categorization of eggheads whose intellectual arrogance shows too much for their own good.

prophet center Research and development lingo for an organizational unit whose function is to predict, review, evaluate, and analyze new technology flowing from universities, government, and industrial research laboratories.

quango Means "quasi-autonomous national governmental organization." A British acronym springing out of the nationalized-industry policies which pervade the United Kingdom. The form of quango policy councils is one device attempting to cope with the basic problems by adding another layer of nonauthority for controlling the nationalized industries.

queen bee syndrome In the sexist jungle of today's world a successful and powerful woman may strictly limit the development of her female subordinates. Drawn from the parallel in the insect world when the queen bee kills her rivals, this syndrome is being increasingly observed in the business world as the women's movement makes its way. In one insurance company, the president gathered together the few (but all) female insurance agents to discuss how to solve the corporate problem of attracting and developing more female agents. The ensconced female agents were not interested in bringing more women into their own agencies, apparently because of the threat to their queen bee status. I have observed flickers of this phenomenon on several boards of directors and trustees, where there is one woman director already aboard.

red flag study Consultantese for a type of sensitivity analysis that will alert a client as to what elements of the situation warrant special consideration for the success of the endeavor. Such a study will identify with "red flags" the potential trouble spots or points to ponder carefully.

retrospectoscope A mythical instrument with which a chairman of the board is reputed to achieve 20/20 hindsight in identifying the errors and omissions of the management and the board, including the corporate Gok's disease (God only knows).

rumortism A chronic inflammation of the body politic. Occurs frequently in hierarchies of corporations, and in boardrooms, about competitive activity.

Rumpelstiltskin effect The idea that if you can give a symptom or a problem a name it will disappear. Rumpelstiltskin was a dwarf who helped a miller's daughter weave her flax into gold and claimed her firstborn child after she was queen. The miller's daughter wanted to renege and the dwarf said, "You don't even know my name, and if you can learn it by midnight on the third day you can keep the child." When the queen asked the dwarf on the third day if his name was Rumpelstiltskin, he disappeared into thin air.

Witch doctors, physicians, and board chairmen with their aura of authority often have the same effect in diagnosing and curing diseases or troubles of the mind or firm. Naming a condition or symptom authoritatively is often part of the solution. Examples in the boardworld: the chairman's annual report message phrases on countercyclical adverse industry sector trends, extraordinary tax and accounting adjustments to comply with new regulations, the influx of petrocabbage (petrodollars) from the Middle East, or technological obsolescence.

share One of the hottest buzzwords in today's management and boardroom lexicon. No longer does one send, tell, announce, divulge, signify, disclose, proclaim, or disclose. "Share" is the verb which replaces all those, as in the chairman's message: "I would like to share with you the fact that your company lost money during the last quarter because of circumstances beyond our control." Or the CEO to a vice-president: "I would like to share with you the fact that you are fired!"

sheepdip treatment Refers to the use of peer pressure to achieve some group behavior such as in a board of directors. When sheep are herded into a chute leading through a sheep-dipping bath, individuals have no alternative to following the crowd moving through the barriers to the dip tank. Setting up a group situation in which little if any real option exists not to follow the crowd is cynically referred to as the sheepdip treatment. Directors often find themselves being given this treatment when the management seeks approval to start on a policy or capital-intensive program without giving the board of directors full implications of the resources required to be successful in the long run.

SOB Not what you think! Initials of an organization known as Sons of Bosses founded in Boston in 1969 by Gerald D. Slavin, who got together with some like-minded friends who had the common problem of working with and for their fathers. With chapters in over twelve states, the group is made up mostly of young men who have taken over control of the family business or are in line one day to get the job. Daughters of bosses (DOBs), sons-in-laws (SLOBs), and other family members headed for the top slot are also admitted as SOB members. With more maturity the organization has begun to delve into more mature problems such as estate and tax planning, purchase and sale agreements, hiring and firing, and family boardroom issues.

statutory senility Retirement by virtue of bylaws that require, for example, automatic retirement for a member of the board when he or she reaches age sixty-eight or seventy. The phrase is a somewhat sarcastic reference to retirement by physiological age rather than mental age or the age at which effectiveness is diminished.

techni-plosion Refers to the exponential growth of technology generally preceding social change. From a director's view of a high-tech company, the need for "high-touch" sensitivity to the social implications within and outside the firm need to be recognized as a long-term force at work. Obsolescence of traditional competition and ways of doing business and changing consumer and worker patterns are often consequences of the techni-plosion.

tuck-unders Acquisition talk for prospective firms which could be acquired and "tucked under" existing acquirer organizational units and which fit with existing businesses. Tuck-unders are related businesses, technologies, or services which are consonant with the strategy of developing existing businesses to their fullest potential.

underfoot "Overhead" is a common enough word; its counterpart, "underfoot," is less well known, but represents an essential management fact of life. Underfoot is the amount of work a person or a department needs to justify overhead. Most people in any large corporation are producing underfoot to sustain an increase in overhead.

Vermoegensbildung German for "wealth formation," a recent reform buzzword on top of *Mitbestimmung* ("co-determination"), a reform policy introduced to give employees the right to participate in a company's decision-making. The German government has now linked co-determination with *Vermoegensbildung,* which usually allows employees to acquire shares in their company at a favorable rate.

Wall Street rule This relates to the practice in the investment community under which institutional shareholders who disagree with management generally sell their shares rather than participate in corporate governance to the extent of engaging in a proxy fight.

whitemail One of two types of bribes or payoffs generally involving an elaborate system for concealing the use of large sums of corporate cash. These payments are invariably accompanied by false accounting, fictitious bookkeeping entries, and bogus documentation. The banana tax case with United Brands, the Gulf Oil shakedown to South Korean political interests, the Northrup Saudi Arabian agency, and Lockheed's commission troubles are examples of whitemail.

Xerox, to Madison Avenue barroom buzzword for "same again," meaning to duplicate (or replicate, depending on how long the customer has been on the bar stool) the round of drinks.

yogurt diplomacy Diplomatic corps buzzword meaning one nation supplies the "seed culture" such as startup aid (money, technology, trade, etc.), and the other nation(s) provide the "milk," or support, for the culture to ferment and grow.

Yokkakari cycle The cycle of dependence in the Japanese corporation. In the mid-1970s, Japanese industry was caught in a frustrating cycle. Imported technology tends to support a frozen industrial bureaucracy that sees limited value in creativity, leading to the need for more imported technology. This self-perpetuating cycle based on dependence on Yokkakari consists of three segments, each one helping to maintain the others: (a) dependence on imported technology, (b) inflexible industrial hierarchy and guaranteed promotions, and (c) lost creativity and self-motivation. In a production-oriented society, the Yokkakari cycle was the key factor for success. In a competitive world this cycle is now considered self-defeating.

It is sometimes difficult to find straightforward communication in the boardroom because an excess of ill-chosen buzzwords pervades the language and the system. These words become part of the jargon—officialese, journalese, commercialese, economese, even a reverse gobbledygook of short, terse, shirtsleeve English, which is in part a revulsion against other forms of gobbledygook.

As the director goes about his affairs he learns to recognize the various forms of buzzwords: (a) those that are associated with certain advanced management concepts, principles, and theory at one point in time, including venerable theories yet to be reduced to practice; (b) those that are the more expressive terms from specialist areas within management (marketing, finance, long-range planning, personnel) and are replacing classical terms and reflecting the dynamism of advancing concepts and therapies; and (c) those that are not so broadly known technical terms derived from management techniques such as operations research, merger and acquisition practice, investment and securities analysis, and production and statistical quality control. Too, some buzzwords are just interesting words and phrases from peripheral subject areas, such as law, mathematics, behavioral and social sciences, economics, and political science, which could have an impact in the boardroom.

Like street slang, buzzwords come and go suddenly, mysteriously. The best of them remain to enlarge and perhaps enrich the language. Our vocabulary is replete with terms that were once the buzzwords of new fields—aviation, aerospace, mass communications, data processing. Sometimes new words are coined ("aerospace"), sometimes old words are given new meanings ("broadcast"), sometimes buzzwords are merely pollutants that muddy our communication waters. But whatever their shape, whatever their source, and whatever their duration, buzzwords can help to make the boardroom hum.

The advantage of using buzzwords in the boardroom is that the communicator is roaming freely within a logical construct of a game which all of those in the boardroom, his elite group, are playing. He discerns the shape and characteristics of the intellectual game by a series of verbal forays of his own making. The communicator is free to explore a verbal sequence which appears logical to him, rather than be constrained to an arbitrary and preordained path of inquiry. The buzzword for such a pattern of interaction which evolves is low on the continuum-of-language scale and is called "multilog."

It is important in boardroom exchanges or in communications outside the boardroom to differentiate between such multilog and the many other dialogues which are often conducted simultaneously. Multilog is the organized simultaneous inquiry into some complex topic. This may be contrasted to a cocktail party, which is characterized by many simultaneous dialogues covering a broad array of disjointed subject matter.

Directors know what the drift of the communications exchange is by their use of buzzwords intelligible to each other and not to the uninitiated. The cocktailers, as Fred Allen used to say, merely gather to enable themselves to talk about themselves at the same time. And the person who remains after the liquor is gone is the host, left only with a buzz because he was not keeping up with the buzzwords.

8

A Pound of Flesh

Dull-reading 10K corporate "paperbacks," those annual reports required by the Securities and Exchange Commission, soared in readership during 1981. Even United Kingdom circulation of U.S.-based multinationals' 10Ks is said to exceed the British best-seller from Her Majesty's Printing Publication Services, a report entitled *Population of Great Britain: Broken Down by Age and Sex.*

For fiscal years ending December 18, 1980, and later, the SEC requires that a majority of directors sign a company's annual 10K report to the commission. In the past, usually only top officers signed the documents. The new requirement is more than a signing of the times or mere pulp and circumstance.

Not to be outdone, the *Wall Street Journal* trumpeted in Second Coming type, "Job of Corporate Director Becomes More Susceptible to Legal Assault."* The implication is that the SEC will start bringing charges against corporate directors if it finds false information in the reports. The requirement that directors sign the 10K means that they have to take a meaningful interest and hand in the operation of the business. Further, it means that individual directors will be held accountable if things go wrong.

* *Wall Street Journal*, March 3, 1981, Section 2, p. 33.

The very nature of the corporation is at the root of this board-room problem. Accountability is the mother of caution. The apparition of shadowy director accountability appearing and disappearing in corporate governance matters is, however, in part due to one of Dartmouth College's more famous competitive battles. In 1819 the United States Supreme Court declared (*Dartmouth v. Woodward*) that "a corporation is an artificial being—invisible, intangible and existing only in contemplation of law." As an artificial being the corporation then took on some mysterious characteristics, strange at least to those who would direct this figment from a director's position in the boardroom—sort of an out-of-body experience, to use parapsychologists' terminology. Directors must direct an intangible being existing only in a contemplative sense.

With the Supreme Court decision, the out-of-body phenomenon was moved from the occult domain of astral projection into the corporate domain of governance. The recent SEC form forces individual directors to materialize long enough to sign a detailed 10K report of the corporation on whose board they serve. Directors are now forced to emerge from their past state of relative anonymity as members of an artificial being, the corporation, to present some accountable flesh to the federal government and to have final judgment passed on them.

Literatim et Verbatim

The whole bargain, the exact terms of the SEC agreement, whereby directors must be accountable, has some of the same limitations Portia pointed out to Shylock, who was claiming a pound of Antonio's flesh. The exact quantity of director diligence—all flesh, no blood—is difficult to obtain because of the inherent nature of the role of a corporate director. Legal and policy detachment from the executive activities of the company on whose board a director serves makes personal knowledge by a director of all the details required by the SEC somewhat unrealistic as far as individual accountability is concerned.

The chief executive officer is in responsible charge, and directors must work through his office, or that of the chief financial officer, and not around him; otherwise, confusion will result. There is no way a director can keep up with the detail assumed in the SEC approach. About all a director can do is ensure that an adequate checkup process is in place and use common sense about what he observes in his limited exposure to company activity.

Directors are thus caught up in a Scylla-and-Charybdis version of the accountability equation. On the one hand, the government, via the SEC, forces the director to show evidence to the owners and public of diligent oversight by signing the 10K. On the other hand, the director is also looked toward by management and employees for proper and astute governance. This entails legitimatizing the corporation, directing the nature and course of corporate existence and relevance, and auditing performance of the management and the company.

This Shylock bargain which a director accepts when he is elected to a board is a vexatious problem. So far there is no easy or accepted way to evaluate or account for the role and effectiveness of either an individual director or a board of directors as a collective body.

This accountability problem in corporate governance is reminiscent of a now strange nineteenth-century navigation practice. In those early days, when Britain ruled the seas, navigation was undertaken by officers of a special branch, their ranks being preceded by the word "staff"—for example, "staff-commander." To illustrate: In 1893 the staff-captain on H.M.S. *Ramillies* ranked in command after the most junior naval cadet on board. Staff-officer duties were limited to navigation with no executive responsibilities. Staff-officers normally could not rise to a position of command. Provided with these experts, the captains of British warships relied entirely on the staff-officers to conduct their mystic art of navigation for the ship. And just as a captain did not consider himself responsible if his ship grounded through faulty navigation, so did an admiral divest himself of responsibility if his fleet's safety was hazarded.

I fear some of our twentieth-century boards of directors are not without nineteenth-century organization concepts. So part of the problem is an antiquated notion about accountable flesh. This is not surprising. Mastery of the governance process often overlooks the internal strategic management of the organization itself and the fixing of "accountable flesh" for specific tasks or development. The government is taking action to force accountability for directorship from an external view of the corporation.

Few Fiduciaries Have Fun

Robert Benchley's "The Treasurer's Report," in 1930, was a droll probe at the director's fiduciary function. Benchley recognized his own irresponsibility in financial matters better than anyone else. And he enjoyed fame and fortune mainly for the fun of it. Benchley once applied for a loan at his local bank and, to his shock, was granted the money with no questions asked. The next day he reportedly withdrew all his savings, explaining, "I don't trust a bank that would lend money to such a poor risk."

While the bankers, those men of principal, normally perform their fiduciary role with probity and rectitude, corporate directors also are required by statute to be responsible fiduciaries. This requirement of trust goes along with directors' evaluative, participative, resource, and agent-of-change roles. But in trusting anybody, both bankers and directors must still cut the cards in a detached manner.

Curiously, this detachment often breeds an uptight and somber mien in the boardroom. Perhaps it should, given the unlaughable liabilities directors face nowadays in our litigious land. But the human problems are deeper than the legalistics. They concern equanimity and perspective. This means the ability to be light-hearted about the serious side of being a director. It also means the ability to be serious about being lighthearted.

Too few businessmen, and hardly any directors, have the ability to laugh at themselves. The importance of being earnest takes all the play out of directorship and trusteeship. This is a sad situation. Good governance needs a balance and some freeboard between the seriously formal and the relaxed, informal processes of management.

Above all, directors need the ability to perceive themselves as others perceive them. Such objectivity is vital if the boardroom is to attract qualified directors, particularly those who possess sensitivity toward the real world wherein they govern the social franchise given the institutions served. Not surprisingly the conditions of this social franchise differ radically by country and culture. Those privy to governance guidelines around the globe will perceive trends that would rattle the cage of most any American directorate, were the practices exported to the United States.

Norway's plan to make mandatory the presence of local officials on boards in certain sectors could raise our conflict-of-interest levels to those approaching a New England town selectman's.

Japan's novel version of inside directors not legally being employees allows firing without violating the lifetime employment system. If the company wants to indicate to a senior manager that he will not make it to the top, he's given percussive sublimation treatment by being appointed a director!

India, from our anti-public-intervention perspective, makes a convoluted contribution to trendy corporate governance. Financial institutions which make large loans (in part convertible to equity) seat their representative on the boards of grateful corporate recipients. But the 500-rupee ceiling on director fees is so low it cools off most outsiders because of the bureaucratic hassle over reasonable compensation.

Iran has (or had) a shah-stopper scheme on director compensation. Outside directors are permitted to become compensated with up to 5 percent of distributed profit in a public joint stock company; this could come up to 10 percent in a private joint stock company.

Topping the Netherlands' worker participation in corporate decision-making, the latest Dutch disease may be the parliament's guilder complex, which requires salary disclosure on all corporate levels, including honoraria paid to directors.

Sweden's Democracy at Work Act of 1976 gives labor an effective veto over all corporate decisions. Swedish women have the highest percentage of board representation in any industrialized country. It's 10 percent now and expected to rise.

So much for a semiserious sampler of foreign governance guidelines. They may seem trendy to those preoccupied with their own national perspectives. The ability to perceive ourselves as others do goes a long way toward understanding the statutory and fiduciary differences confronting the multinational company director. These thumb rules may also help:

- In Britain, you can do it provided it's not forbidden.
- In Germany, you can do it if it's allowed.
- In France, you can do it even if it's forbidden.
- In Russia, you can't do it even if it's allowed.
- In Switzerland, if it isn't forbidden, it's compulsory.

Effective corporate leadership anywhere in the world can use such grace notes of subtle humor and feeling to alleviate the not readily perceivable pathos or absurdness of situations, characters, and consequence. But, alas, few fiduciaries have any mental fun while they "fiduce."

Subtle humor clearly serves as a leading edge of social consciousness. Witness the increasing number of caricatures and cartoons about boards of directors, governance, and top management in general. Too few directorates press their institutions to appropriately address relevant social issues in a pro-active rather than defensive role.

Structure, hierarchy, boardroom ritual, social stratification, solemnity of meetings, and legal and regulatory constraints beget defensiveness and take most of the fun out of serving on a board. Ho-ho-ho humor is certainly out of order. But a mood of humility and hospitality for a dignified sense of humor are essential nutrients in a healthy corporate diet.

Thurber defined humor as chaos remembered in tranquillity. A tranquil boardroom is a desirable state and can be a place for some appropriate humor. Unfortunately, these days many boardrooms are unsettled, even anxious, because of the profound changes taking place which impact their function. Such troubled conditions add to the grim business of business.

One of my favorite *New Yorker* cartoons depicted two convicts talking in a Sing Sing cell. The caption read: "I would like to think this is a better world because we are here." Because directors are there—in the boardroom—we should, indeed, have a better world. But I suggest corporate governance could use a little refreshing detachment and perspective to help give us this better world. Such aloofness can come at proper times through occasional constructive satire, some whimsy, fantasy, and relaxing mental play. A bit of wit and philosophy similar to George Burns's advice to senior citizens (and directors?) may even help. George said, "I'll never retire because there isn't a thing I can't do now that I couldn't do at eighteen—which gives you an idea of how pathetic I was at eighteen!"

If directors and trustees don't attain a more relaxed perspective from which to cope with the turbulent world about us, they may come out of the next annual stockholders' meeting muttering my favorite motto: "Peacock today, feather duster tomorrow!"

The Grim Business of Business*

*Man could direct his ways by plain reason, and support his
life by tasteless foods; but God has given us wit, and flavour,
and brightness, and laughter, and performers, to enliven the
days of man's pilgrimage, and to "charm his pained steps over
the burning marle."*

SIDNEY SMITH, *Dangers and Advantages of Wit*

Days of thorn and thistle for business will test the equanimity
and sense of humor of directors and executives during the uncertain
eighties, if not forever. The image of grimness in the business community generally stems from the Protestant ethic of hard work and
dedication to the job combined with the Victorian emphasis on the
worship of success and money. Laughter is particularly rare in the
boardroom lately.

This uptight corporate mien has attracted what Peter Drucker
calls business gadflies who buzz but do not sting with their best-
selling books. But C. Northcote Parkinson, Stephen Potter, Laur-
ence Peter, Robert Townsend, and the rest never seem to tackle the
main point for directors: the value of detachment and distance
from self.

As he struggles to do his best in the competitive business world,
the serious, dedicated chief executive officer needs to be able to
detach himself intellectually and emotionally from fickle Dow
Jones averages, consumerism, outside director pressures, corporate
politics, conflicts of interest, insider problems, mergers and acquisitions, and earnings slippage. Such detachment allows him to gain
a perspective on the critical issues that underlie the social, economic, and political realities of every situation. The outside directors cannot detach themselves, legally, from their fiduciary and
trusteeship roles, but they ought to learn to be more lighthearted
about the serious side of being a director.

Detachment also has value because it allows a director to be un-
emotional in the face of criticism and above all to laugh at himself.
Laughter is always somewhat humiliating for the person at whom it
is directed, but it is really a kind of leveler. Stratification is a great
field for humor, and it is an unusual director who can laugh at the
aspects of this in his own position.

* Excerpted, by permission of the publisher, from *BOARD LIFE: Realities of
Being a Corporate Director*, by Robert Kirk Mueller © 1974, AMACOM, a division of American Management Association, pp. 118, 120–128. All rights reserved.

Despite all its obvious advantages, directors are generally afraid of humor—afraid to use it and afraid to have it used. Using it entails high risk, especially for a tyro director, and is generally inadvisable until a director is well established and respected. The forces of ego, power-seeking, risk, anxiety, and pomposity combine with the huge aspiration-accomplishment gap to discourage the humorous approach. Yet humor is well recognized as a leading edge of social consciousness; political cartoons and caricatures are evidence of this.

Even with the awakening consciousness of directors to their social responsibilities, there seems to be an aversion to recognizing a sense of humor as characteristic of a healthy way of accomplishing goals in the business world. Maybe this is because directors don't know whether, how, or when to let humor be used in a management or trustee situation. Or perhaps they don't understand that humor is stratified, just as directors, officers, and employees are stratified in terms of privileges, responsibilities, and compensation. A comparison of graffiti in plant, office, and executive washrooms would quickly illuminate the differences in brands of humor. The graffiti in the TWA Ambassador editorial offices is a delightful example of letting off steam at headquarters: "Pitney-Bowes licks postage stamps." "Jim Beam drinks root beer." "Xerox never comes up with anything original." You can't think about these without mentally relaxing a bit.

Very little operating-level humor seems funny at the executive or director level, and vice versa. Too few businessmen, and hardly any directors, have the ability to laugh at themselves. Even more serious is the general atrophy of humor in the boardroom.

It sometimes seems as if the very wellsprings of humor have dried up. Derision is taken for disloyalty; political satire is almost extinct; personal caricatures can be considered libelous; parody is illegal; jokes are strictly taboo; management and labor are sacrosanct; and Huckleberry Finn has been cited as an invitation to juvenile delinquency!

The Value of Humor

There seems to be no objective evidence that a good director or chairman has a better sense of humor than a poor one, but a pertinent experiment was conducted with reference to teachers. A group of students were asked to rate their teachers according to teaching ability and amount of humor in the classroom (how often the class laughed and how often an instructor told humorous stories). In a study involving 284 teachers, the best teachers averaged 3.95 on a humor scale of 5; the poorest averaged 2.36. Thus a sense of humor certainly appeared to be a trait of a good teacher more often than a poor teacher. Inasmuch as directors project an image of a teacher by their example or by their style, a sense of humor is an important quality for effective leadership.

If chairmen of boards realized that they could save money by a proper application of humor, they would use it more. Much money is spent in trying to keep directors happy by raising fees, providing perks, and offering elaborate company entertainment. How much it would be appreciated, and how rewarding it would be to the individual directors as well as the board as a whole, if an equal amount of effort and ingenuity were directed toward relaxing the boardroom and formal meeting climate by a healthy, judicious safety valve of humor, displayed on appropriate occasion by the chairman or chief executive officer.

Seals of Approval

It can truly be said that the light touch is medically and historically approved. Humor and diversion have been recommended by physicians as a means of relaxation for those at the top. And this need and approval probably explains the prevalence of court jesters in the Middle Ages.

Wiegand von Theban, court jester to Duke Otto of Hapsburg in the fourteenth century, was a parish priest as well and evidently was successful in both roles.

A British author, Lord Dunsany, proposed in the early 1950s that a Minister of Mirth and Mockery be established in England on the thesis that a world of dangerously inflated egos needs the deflating touch of the court fool of old.

Enid Welsford, British author and lecturer, has made an interesting study of the jester. In her view, there have always been men who have a faculty for taking life in stride and gliding out of awkward situations which would baffle more serious-minded and responsibility-bearing individuals. Such characters are sources of entertainment to their fellows. Their company is welcomed. Good stories accumulate about them—especially if they seem to have little conscience and no shame. And they often manage to make a handsome profit out of their supposed irresponsibility.

Today's boardrooms could use a new type of jester—maybe only in shadow form, but one who would serve many purposes in special ways. He should fit in an institution that is filled with its own momentum and importance and has become a structured hierarchy, monarchical in the sense that it has a strong leader who gives the final go-ahead after reviewing a sophisticated drill of planning, evaluating, and strategizing. The "monarch chairman" sets the tone of solemnity, conformity, and control—or of spirited and imaginative innovation.

If history is a good guide, a modern boardroom jester-adviser could make a worthwhile contribution, even if he simply helped the board members achieve the detachment that gives perspective. But the jester-adviser could also serve as a devil's advocate in residence, helping other directors to be a little more lighthearted about their serious, sometimes grim, business and allowing constructive criticism to flourish.

The Sense of Humor in Corporate Matters

Recognizing that a sense of humor is one of the most desirable personal qualities, the board chairman might well acknowledge the importance and place of humor and its value of detachment in his conduct of certain boardroom affairs. Humor, wisely used, can be a potent input to several areas of concern to the directorate, among them the following:

• Social stratification and status. In one cartoon a man and wife are shown reading their evening papers. The wife looks up and asks, "Are we capital or labor?" In another a middle-aged director, sitting comfortably in an airliner, says to his wife, "You fail me in so many small ways, Grace, like reading a paperback when we are traveling first class." These cartoons strike at the heart of the social stratification issue, which is a principal target of anthologies of jokes and is an inherent conflict source in most business organizations. Status, income, and occupations of the extremes of the hierarchy—top and bottom, rich and poor—are the subject of a kind of humorous leveling process consistent with American values.

• Corporate public relations. The public image of business could use some humor in order to test its values and to project its true significance in society. Harvard Professor Emeritus Myles Mace once defined a conglomerate as a twelve-letter word with a four-letter meaning and thus in a wry way put a finger on a most acute corporate problem. Carnivorous aggression characterizes the public's view of the conglomerate. A sense of humor might do much to take the edge off this biting appraisal. Humor can also help to humanize business by serving as an antidote to pomposity. But it should be recognized that while humor has been found to be a satisfactory means of creating awareness and recognition of an organization or product, it does not convince or persuade in a marketing sense. Therefore, corporate use of humor had best be confined to understanding pomposity and to imparting a sense that the company (and board of directors) is realistic about its place in the scheme of things.

• Avoidance of surprise. Business thrives on risk-taking, but likes to anticipate and prepare for the risks. Surprise may be far from desirable in strategic planning, but in leadership style it can be used to relax tensions. There's a surprise element in wit that can be useful. This is the surprise of having the expected not happen, rather than having the unexpected happen. An event can be humorous when the usual result does not occur, as in this updated version of the story of the traveling salesman: A proper businessman, traveling in the British Midlands late one night, stopped at a hotel that was filled. Taking pity on him the room clerk said he could accommodate the businessman, but only if he was willing to share a double bed with a blond singer. The guest drew himself up to his full height and said, "Sir, I'll have you know I'm a gentleman," whereupon the clerk responded, "so is the singer."

• Acquiring political perspective. When we can see our own grotesqueries and droll ambitions, we become less egocentric. So it is with a governing body, whether in the boardroom or in politics. For a director gauging the executive staff, this is particularly true in acknowledging the gap between managers' aspirations and their accomplishments. Boardroom politics is not renowned for its sense of perspective.

As elsewhere in life, humor can be an asset in corporate politics, but a sense of humor may be something else again. The ho-ho-ho kind of humor emanates from the man who lives on the outer layer of consciousness; a sense of humor characterizes the man who lives

more deeply within himself. The introspective intellectual is generally considered suspect by those who prefer humor that is more
earthy than worldly. Thus wit, as opposed to jollity, is rarely encouraged by advisers to major political candidates. Indeed, many
political experts believe that the sharp wit of Adlai Stevenson contributed to his downfall. Boardroom ambiance is usually such that
wit is more in order than jollity, since it is more intellectual.

It has been said that the most valuable sense of humor is the kind
that enables a person to see instantly what isn't safe to laugh at.
This is important in the conflicts inherent in director and management activities, particularly in the somber sanctum of the boardroom.

In judging the management, directors will readily recognize the
situation typified by the blast of one president to his vice-presidents: "You fellows better start practicing human relations around
here, or I'll fire the whole damn bunch of you!" Or the often-
quoted plea of the Hollywood producer to his directors, "I want
you to tell me the truth, even if it means losing your job." These
bits of humor spotlight the survival-of-the-fittest syndrome in certain management hierarchies.

The Punch Line

Like the chairman-monarch, the chief executive officer is considered almost infallible. But a monarch can and does err; the top executive never really has the right to do so. The board has the job of
removing him if he slips too often.

Perhaps the greatest function a boardroom jester-adviser might
perform, then, if one could create such a position, would be to assume the foibles of his "master" and his cabinet and, by making
errors slightly ludicrous, make them more forgivable—perhaps
even acceptable. But even here, directors can do a great deal to
help themselves, simply by learning not to take themselves so
seriously.

As an antidote to the pressure of conflict and the rigors of survival in the executive jungle, humor needs to be better recognized
in the boardroom. This is not a new idea. Albert Rapp relates a
story of Amasis, fifth Pharaoh of the twenty-sixth Egyptian dynasty
(about 570 to 526 B.C.). Amasis rose from the ranks and appears to
have been a capable and judicious sovereign, living at the time of

Croesus and the rise of Greek art, philosophy, literature, and science. Despite this serious milieu, Amasis had a notorious routine. Every day he would rise before dawn and work like a Trojan until noonday. From then on, there would be nothing but merriment. The barley brew flowed freely, and Amasis gathered a crowd around him and swapped funny stories.

Historians relate that some of the good Pharaoh's stories were "not seemly." According to Herodotus, one day some of his closest advisers took him aside and told him that the people were saying the Pharaoh should sit upon his royal throne and be a symbol of dignity and not a humorist in the throne room. Amasis is said to have replied, "When an archer goes into battle, he strings his bow until it is taut. When the shooting is over, he unstrings it again. If he didn't unstring it, it would lose its snap and would be no good to him when he needed it."

Humor has been said to be the most philosophic of all emotions. Directors are constantly faced with problems that demand the best solution; and being only mortal, they do not always arrive at the right one. Two important qualities for successful directorship are emotional control and tact. The value of a sense of humor and a sense of detachment in gaining emotional control cannot be overemphasized.

9

Stakeholder Strategy: Missing Linkages

Men that hazard all
Do it in hope of fair advantage.
WILLIAM SHAKESPEARE, *The Merchant of Venice*, II, vii

A modern stakeholder is one who holds that which is placed at hazard. In a corporate context this goes beyond holding ownership shares in the company. It embraces those who hold contiguous land where the firm operates, those who hold jobs in the company, those who hold contracts to supply money, materials, and services. It includes neighbors affected by unemployment or employment in the community. All who have a direct or indirect interest in company activity are stakeholders. This constituency is thus greater than the conventional list of stockholders who—when things were less complex and interactive—represented the significant "holders of that which is placed at hazard."

The stakeholder theory rejects the Victorian idea of profit for the owners as the sole or primary consideration. All who have a vested interest in the continued survival and prosperity of a corporation are considered participants. How to build bridges to relate to these interests is the issue.

There has been a shift in the flow of power and information; once it was mainly from the boardroom into the organization, but now it must go outward among stakeholder groups and government in order to obtain the consent necessary to govern a corporation. This makes directorship difficult in a far-flung corporation. One chairman acquaintance solicited some director candidates thusly: "We are looking for a director who is intelligent enough to fill this role, but not so smart that he'll turn us down."

119

Enlightened directorates are examining this stakeholder concept as a more socially responsive perspective. I define the stakeholders broadly as any group whose collective behavior can directly affect the organization's future but who are not under the organization's direct control.

Given this definition, the stakeholder concept has special aspects—for example, understanding how the free economic system provides goods and services. Some stakeholders enjoy a greater share of benefits than others. In the United States and Europe there is a rising tide of political and public opinion which concerns directorship. The public believes that directors have more freedom, access to corporate assets, and social concern as individuals than they actually do or are prepared to assume. Last February, as chairman of Arthur D. Little, Inc., I received a handwritten letter from a Pittsburgh resident which went like this:

> Dear Sir:
> Please send me twelve (12) packages of pens, pads, trays, rulers, billfolds, letter openers, an Annual Report (1982), calendars, thermometers, coin purses, barber's combs, key rings, napkins, sponges, jar grippers, matches, and pencils (mechanical, colored, and regulars). We're collectors.
>
> Regards, sincerely,
> [name withheld]
> P.S. Excuse the writing due to my service injury.

The main difference in dealing with stakeholders, versus other dealings, is that stakeholder relationships are rarely a one-time event or transaction-oriented. Constituencies remain; a case in point is continued family ownership. Constructive linkages and mutual trust among interested parties, both inside and outside the owner-family circle of a closely held company, must be real and maintained. Ideally, the board of directors needs to monitor and guide this stakeholder network relationship in order that company affairs are perceived to be and are in fact conducted in a socially responsive manner. As we know, this is not always the case when the owners are the directors and managers.

The reality, of course, is that common long-term welfare depends on a successful interdependent business and social community. I believe that a systems approach to this linkage of company activities with interests of other groups is the answer to sorting out the interdependency and interactivity of all stakeholder interests "placed at hazard." Otherwise, we may find our boardroom actions are like those of the elephant that tripped in the middle of a circus performance and tore the tails out of six other elephants.

Many complex issues are involved. As an advisory director of the National Association of Corporate Directors (NACD), I participated recently in a roundup of "new" concerns for directors. These were highlighted as follows.

- Union representatives on boards—is this a good idea?
- Proxy card revisions to allow more choice—a reasonable idea?
- Board statement on internal controls—most boards neglect this.
- Shareholder Protection Act—is legislation needed?
- Liquidation proposals by shareholders—how does a board handle such?
- Board and director proxy disclosures—do they tell more than shareholders want to know?
- Corporate counsel disclosures—this seems a proper requirement.
- Corporate Democracy Act—a controversial approach which I believe is unwise at this time.

More concerns are in the pipeline of the regulatory and legislative bodies and are accreting in the data bases of opinion pollsters. One major effect of this ferment is a renewed resolve for companies to stay privately owned or for some public companies to consider going the private-ownership route.

My conviction is that there is a systemic set of issues intrinsic to the domain of corporate governance which is not being addressed sufficiently by directors. The issues have arisen as we have become a polarized have-and-have-not world. In the more industrialized, interactive, complex position, the distinction between the public sector and the private sector has become blurred. In the developing world the role of institutions, corporations, and governments calls for an entirely different perspective of governance. The shift in emphasis from the responsibility of corporations to its stockholders only to responsibility of the corporation to all of its stakeholders is the issue. As directors, we must redress this balance to fit each situation.

Bridge Building

Robert Benchley once observed, "It has always seemed to me that the most difficult part of building a bridge would be the start." And this is the problem when we think of how to build bridges with corporate constituents—the stakeholders.

Some directors are beginning to think about how to make these linkages. My position is that directors should do something about it by personal participation in various stakeholder activities—for example, local politics, professional societies, community fundraising, and adjunct teaching in schools. We cannot all be like Robert Moses, the great planner largely responsible for New York's bridges, tunnels, and parkways. He never learned to drive an automobile. A good stakeholder strategy requires the personal drive of directors.

Directors and managers are skilled at negotiation in the marketplace to improve the economic performance of a corporation. However, their skill and interest in negotiating with an increasing number of external stakeholder groups is relatively undeveloped and, in some instances, not recognized as a requirement for good governance. Failure to negotiate a constructive long-term relationship can result in significant changes in corporate future conditions of existence or strategic direction.

Where goals of the corporation may be in conflict with one or more stakeholder interests, directors need to search consciously for a win-win solution to the stakeholder "game." In an effort to teach how to do this, the Wharton School Applied Research Center recently worked with a major industrial firm to design a stakeholder negotiation game. The purpose was to provide executives and directors with simulated experience in understanding and negotiating with typical external interest groups. Each participant is assigned to a team, such as the company board, a media team, an environmental team, a government agency team, and so on. The groups are charged with negotiating a win-win solution on an issue within a twenty-four-hour period. Wharton's stakeholder game has been successful as a device to teach negotiation methods required to resolve conflicts in order for a business to survive.

A win-win solution is one in which both parties (or all parties) win. This is the not strictly competitive case of gain by each player which is greater than he would achieve by uncoordinated strategy choices predicated on self-interest alone. Examples of win-win cases involve either cooperation or coalition formation, and call for mixed strategies which function in equilibrium. If there is no cooperation involved—as exists often in business regulated by the antitrust laws—the solution need not be optimal in the sense of allowing the players collectively to realize the maximum gain possible.

The MIT Factor

Those spies of life the sociologists have a term, "malintegrative tolerance," which, in shorthand, I like to refer to as the "MIT factor." A board attempting to deal with a stakeholder strategy finds the disparate interests of these external groups difficult to place in any logical framework. The local political groups may have increased employment as their primary goal, whereas the company may be striving to automate the operations. The suppliers of new materials may be reducing their stockpiles of ready inventory at the same time the purchasing firm is planning a major production run. Some investors want dividends, others are interested in capital appreciation of their stockholdings. The differences between the goals of the various stakeholder groups and the corporation present a continuing range of issues, unclosed propositions, trade-off situations. These do not integrate neatly in any business balance sheet or profit-and-loss exhibit. Accordingly, the board must be flexible, open-minded, and adaptive over varying periods of time.

A tolerance is required for lack of closure for the benefits as well as the burdens of ambiguity and conflict. It is my thesis that a board needs a high MIT factor to proceed with its affairs. Otherwise it will get hung up because solution or nonsolution does not integrate into a logical strategy. Resolution of the conflict, closing of the gap, and integration of the interests may or may not come in time. The major comfort to directors is the recognition of the existence of the MIT factor as a fact of boardlife. It took me over ten years of directorship to be comfortable in boardrooms where all matters do not neatly and logically integrate. My engineering training did not prepare me for such situations.

The MIT factor is, of course, a normal attribute of open systems such as human and biological systems. The time constants for such system changes are themselves variable. Our complex highway systems are elegant examples of our national infrastructure; yet they can get clogged up for very simple human reasons which some transportation wags call "rushing roulette." Long delays on crowded turnpikes often are due to passing drivers' staring at an insignificant event or minor accident. However, when we finally reach this particular point we feel a desire to take part in the distraction. Thus the transport system's return to normal traffic flow becomes highly variable.

It is never certain whether a malintegrated system—highway or social—will need basic redefinition because of interaction between the system and those elements inside or outside the system. Directors—as personalities—can be effectively interactive internally but, then, can also block governance traffic. We all have the very human tendency to get involved in distractions to the main flow of the agenda. Such diversion recalls a bumper sticker I saw in New Hampshire: "God is not dead, but alive and well and working on a much less ambitious project."

As a board develops ability to conduct its affairs with responsible regard for all its stakeholders, no matter how diverse and scattered these interested or affected parties may be, the corporation will present a more human face to the public. Such a posture involves an apparent willingness to consider trade-offs of certain private corporate interests in favor of public interests.

Directors could once content themselves with keeping stockholders happy, or at least pacified. Today a large multinational corporation can be seen as having global stakeholders. This means having to function in an environment in which the classical distinction between public and private sector is virtually meaningless, because "private" decisions can have profound impact on the lives of millions. Consider what one international food company got involved in over the infant formula business in the less-developed countries; there was inadequate "bridge building" to the interested parties and insufficient understanding of the target market.

It is certain that most directors will not be able to function in the next ten years in the way Havelock Ellis described the Western world's dealing with the Pacific "with alcohol, syphilis, and the Bible." The situation is not so simple. If boards of directors fail to deal with stakeholder interests, for example, government regulators, lawmakers, and social activists will force more constraints on corporations. I believe this to be the wrong way to improve social responsibility of corporations. Directors as individuals and boards as groups must take the initiative and get down to grass roots in order to enhance corporate profitability and growth. This requires paying directors well to govern properly, and replacing them if they fail to act in a responsible way in the stakeholders' interest.

Unnatural Acts

The first class action I can remember was not of the current corporate shareholder type, and could be called capricious. It involved the near-strangling of a lawyer. This was long before I had been invited into any boardroom and even before I had read the oft-quoted priority in Shakespeare's *Henry VI:* "The first thing we do, let's kill all the lawyers."

It was October 1930, a depressing time, to put it historically. The occasion was the traditional Beginners Day in the quadrangle setting on the stately Gothic campus of Washington University in St. Louis. Engineers were, by some spurious university legend, arch-rivals of lawyers. Accordingly, freshmen engineers were pitted against first-year law students in a fierce tug-of-war, with up to sixty or seventy grunting, shouting adversaries on each end of a one-and-one-half-inch rope about one hundred feet long. The struggle for supremacy raged over a half hour of lurching, tugging, and dragging until the contestants veered up against Cupples Hall.

The legal end of the conflict got wedged into a narrow passageway extending out of the quadrangle. The engineering team somehow got positioned around a corner of the granite building to where—from our coign—we couldn't see the adversaries. This introduced some uncertainties and a near-tragedy in the battle. Neither side could assess the status of its opponent. One of the law students became wedged at neck level between the wall of Cupples Hall and the taut rope. Amid all the epithetic shouting the gargling of the unseen red-faced victim was indiscernible to those of us on the engineering end. The lawyers could see one of their own in dire straits but were reluctant to relax their end of the rope, introducing a manila-saw action, and at the same time admitting defeat. Being better educated than engineers, the lawyers were no doubt aware that a nobleman's privilege—according to English history—permitted selection of a silken rope for peer executions. The engineers were completely unaware of the hangman situation, which was around the corner and out of view.

I'm pleased to say that, albeit reluctantly, human considerations transcended professional zeal just in time for our adversaries to relieve the tensions before a tragedy occurred. The university medical staff revived the law student. True to what might have been expected from either side, the tension release, when it finally came, was unexpected and complete. Our engineering team found itself a sweaty jackstraw pile of victors but, I must admit, not really or appropriately shaken by the near-miss execution.

Five years later, in 1935, I was working my way through the University of Michigan Graduate School, employed as a "housemother" at the Sigma Phi Epsilon fraternity on Washtenaw Avenue. This occupation indoctrinated me into my first administratively ordered milieu. It now seems like a picnic compared to current regulatory climate for those who act as housemothers for corporations by serving on boards.

The board of directors of the fraternity's Detroit alumni group had responded with due diligence to University President Ruthven's call for all sororities and fraternities to "shape up." (There were over a hundred such organizations on the Ann Arbor campus then.) The alumni board's due diligence was no doubt spurred by the threat of charter revocation; over thirty charters had been withdrawn in 1935 on improper-conduct charges. Unless my memory fails me, that was the same year that the apocryphal Judge Henry Folsom looked down on an Ann Arbor student defendant and declared, "Young man, you are charged with taking hundreds of pieces of silver from a fraternity house. For your sentence I am hereby making you return every piece of that silverware to the hotels it was originally taken from."

My role was one of fraternal governance. I was employed to raise the moral tone, the fraternity's money flow, and the manpower-rushing efforts. This was critical to restore the chapter viability and reputation. The situation confronted included a five-story deteriorating fraternity house and a sixty-six-year-old, widowed Mrs. Simms as the officially required housemother. She was quartered in a basement apartment and appeared only at mealtime, at the end of a long table, to provide a symbol of respectability.

The chapter brothers were few in number but definitely entrepreneurs and free spirits in more than one sense. There was a contingent of three chemical engineering undergraduates on the second floor who, by means of drilling holes in the ceiling and floors above, had installed a tall glass fractionating column. This was part of a large Erlenmeyer flask distillation unit to clean up the denatured alcohol swiped from the school laboratory. The process involved distilling off the toxic benzene denaturant. The third-floor product wasn't bad when a little ethyl methylphenyl glycidate was available to lend a strawberry aroma, or when six parts per million of diethyl malonate was added to make a poor man's applejack.

Another attribute of the situation was an internal organizational role model problem. The president of the chapter, a senior in the business school, dwelled in a fifth-floor apartment loft with his classmate fiancée, who never showed for meals or otherwise. This cohabitation was not permissible in those days any more than the communal shower-room parties held at a nearby sorority. These latter recreations, incidentally, flamed out as the university pulled the sorority's charter.

From a governance standpoint the university administration's drive to shape up student deportment and restore more puritan conditions was moderately successful in a fairly short time. My understanding is that the Lilliputian web of fraternity house rules has since been relaxed, reflecting current social mores of our post-prohibition and post-panty-raiding periods.

These "class actions" and regulated environments experienced in the mid-thirties were tittups or natural acts of a restless college campus period after the depression. They achieved the flaunting objective of rattling the cages of those solemnly in charge of the institutions. The current rash of class action suits against directors by shareholders has some of the same perturbing effects.

According to the social norms of the day such conduct was considered perverse in the thirties and out of accord with normal feelings of behavior. What was once considered unnatural and unreasonable—I have since learned—changes dramatically along with the changing times. When we were "maturing our felonious little plans," as W. S. Gilbert sums it up in *The Pirates of Penzance*, we were unaware that throughout our life someone would be dreaming up actions which would be termed unnatural acts at the time. We had no notion, whatsoever, of the litigiousness which would prevail in the 1980s.

It has become a very litigious environment for that royal and mystic fraternal order of the corporate directorate. The incredible increase in number of statutes and regulations that a responsible director must be aware of is staggering. From all levels of our government—federal, state, and local—Americans get 150,000 new laws and 2 million new regulations each year. The necessity of interpreting conflicting laws and court decisions which pertain to the role of director has caused some directors to have their own attorneys accompany them to board meetings at corporate expense.

There is a special need in these troubled times for a fine sense of balance and understanding in socioeconomic-legal matters which reach beyond strict legal interpretation of the word of the law. One of the picturesque leaders of the legal profession was Dartmouth-trained, Boston-based Rufus Choate, who was a national figure as courtroom advocate in the mid-nineteenth century. Suffering from Bright's disease, he was urged by friends to rest that his constitution might be rebuilt. "My constitution," said Choate, "was destroyed long ago. I am now living under the bylaws."

Legislation and Regulation

Custom and social awareness dictate many laws that seem strange when times change. When change is successful we look back and call it growth. Quite often no one remembers or cares to repeal outmoded statutes. The statutes are replete with acts setting forth criteria for citizen behavior and personal conduct of affairs.

When I lived in St. Louis, an attorney who was a collector of freak laws uncovered some oddball statutes that seemed prize unnatural acts. These laws had long seen the days when their moral intent was relevant to the social scene. Some of his collection: Every male in Brainard, Minnesota, must grow a beard; a man in Lewes, Delaware, cannot wear trousers that are form-fitting around the hips; in Reading, Pennsylvania, a woman cannot hang underwear on a clothesline unless a screen is present; in Waterville, Maine, it is a violation to blow your nose in public; in Utah, daylight must be seen between a dancing couple; and in Barre, Vermont, legally, all citizens are required to take a bath every Saturday night.

The Guinness Book of Records reports that in March 1959 all the laws that were on the statute books of both federal and state governments totaled 1,156,644. Legal statisticians estimate that World War II and the depression almost doubled the number existent prior to those events. Perhaps the trend is uncontrollable. Contemporary experience would validate what Lao-Tse, founder of Taoism, observed in 604 B.C.—the greater the number of statutes, the greater the number of thieves and brigands. If stakeholders can't persuade corporations to trade off some "private" corporate interests for "public" good, they will continue to get the government to do it. Boards of directors must see that the corporations they govern take responsible action to defuse or anticipate stakeholder "irritation."

Directors' Guide to Staying Clean

Codes of ethics and codes of corporate conduct don't prevent directors from "sinning," given the many statutes, regulations, or changes in the public's expectations and perceptions of proper corporate behavior; such codes merely prevent directors from enjoying their sins to the same extent they might have in the good old days.

Social accountability—the notion of social accountability of the director as a fiduciary, a prudent person, or a trustee, and as an insider—has done the concept of directorship a great service by making such service a potential sin in many viewers' eyes. As such, being a director may be the best part of repentance. Every director's "sin" is the result of collaboration. Ovid said it properly in about 20 B.C. (before corporations): "If Jupiter hurled his thunderbolts as often as man sinned, he would soon be out of thunderbolts."

To avoid the modern equivalent of Jupiter's thunderbolts there are some "clean" ways a director can conduct himself or herself. The following guides to behavior may let God forgive you for little wanderings or transgressions in board service, even if your nervous system won't.

130

BEHIND THE BOARDROOM DOOR

1. *Never* use your board position to make a personal profit for yourself or someone else. In an unprecedented action in April 1982 the Securities and Exchange Commission had a Seattle accountant, Gary L. Martin, jailed until $1.1 million profit he made with insider information was frozen. He made the profit trading in Santa Fe International Corporation stock options soon after the Kuwaiti government announced it would purchase the oil company. Martin learned of the company takeover when he was a personal accountant of one of the company's directors. The director's loyalty to the corporation was indirectly in question because of his accountant's actions. The director's duty of loyalty did not apparently move him to oversee misuse of insider information for which he was responsible. The director, in this case, was not held personally responsible by the courts.

There is an interesting recent "reversible raincoat" twist in the matter of the director's *duty of loyalty* to a corporation—a not-for-profit corporation in this instance: "A director is a fiduciary; he cannot use his inside information or his strategic position for his own preferment. He cannot violate rules of fair play by doing indirectly through the corporation what he could not do directly...." So said our Supreme Court in *Pepper* v. *Litton*, 308 U.S. 295, 1939. But this interpretation didn't inhibit Jeffrey Ledowitz, chancellor and executive vice-president of Embry-Riddle Aeronautical University. The school was founded in 1926 and now has 6,000 students at campuses in Daytona Beach, Florida, and Prescott, Arizona. In a *Wall Street Journal* advertisement, the college offered membership on its board of trustees to anyone who donated $1 million to the school. Loyalty is not an explicit requirement. The chancellor defended this unusual recruiting device by saying that the university was merely stating publicly the same quid pro quo implied in the donor's relationships to other private colleges. The Reagan administration's reduction in federal student loans programs was cited as a precedent for this controversial seat-on-the-board offer. The National Association of Governing Boards of Universities and Colleges quickly criticized the plan, which puts in question the criteria for trusteeship and model conduct of a corporation.

In another test of a director's loyalty to his corporation, as a director I was a defendant in *Dolgow* v. *Anderson*, United States District Court of New York, 43 FRD 21, 1967. This was a class action suit brought by certain owners of Monsanto common stock, alleging that officers, directors, and other insiders had deliberately misstated prospects of the company in order to drive up the price of its shares at a time when some of the individual defendants were selling their stock. The class action was prosecuted actively, appealed, and finally disallowed "as not maintainable." The case was dismissed on merits and with prejudice in June 1972. Needless to say, my sensitivity to the vulnerability of a directorship position and the need for "loyalty" and exemplary behavior in matters of inside information were strongly branded in my mind just seventeen short years ago. The director's "duty of loyalty" is an absolute.

2. The CARE package that goes with board service is as important as the so-called duty of loyalty set forth in guide 1. It's called "duty of care."

A key principle involved is the business judgment rule. This is essentially a defensive mechanism that insulates directors from hindsight review of their decisions. A director should perform in good faith in what is believed the best interests of the company and with the due care or diligence expected of a prudent person in like position.

The first big case associated with questionable foreign payment lawsuits introduced an ingenious and innovative interpretation of the business judgment rule. Corporations targeted in lawsuits established special committees of their directors to study whether or not the best interests of the corporation mandated a stockowners' derivative action against such parties. Such a litigation committee was created in *Gall* v. *Exxon Corporation*, 418 F. Supp. 508 (S.D.N.Y., 1976). The derivative action sought $59 million from the directors for illegal payments made to Italian political parties and politicians from 1963 to 1979.

Out of this case, and many others, the business judgment

rule evolved. It presupposes that directors are not in a conflict-of-interest situation, that a board enjoys a presumption of sound business judgment, and that its decisions will not be disturbed (by a court) if they can be attributed to any rational business purpose. Directors must be able to demonstrate that they in fact made a "judgment." A "paper trail" of corporate minutes, and other documents demonstrating that reasonable diligence and care have been exercised, is very useful and perhaps essential to self-protection.

If a director performs his or her duties diligently, attends meetings regularly, and acts in good faith and with due care when making decisions, the business judgment rule is upheld as case law. Directors and managers, not the courts, best understand a corporation's need to nurture its business plans and work for the best interests of the corporation's diverse constituencies, most significantly *all* of its shareowners and employees. Back in 1903 in *Corbus* v. *Alaska Treadwell Gold Mining Co.*, 187 U.S. 455, the court wrote: "It is not a trifling thing for a stockholder to attempt to coerce the directors of a corporation to an act which their judgment does not approve, or to substitute his judgment for theirs."

The "duty of due care" essentially prohibits a director from neglecting his duties, mismanaging the corporation, exercising bad judgment, or intentionally causing the corporation to take illegal action.

3. *Control of expenditures* and transfers of corporate funds must be legitimate. No shell games with disbursements, no secret funds or secret bank accounts. This is primarily of concern to "insiders"—or very "inside" outsiders.

4. Be sure of the accuracy of corporate disclosures. While directors have a duty to protect the confidentiality of information received, the statutes and regulations require certain disclosures of corporate and personal information that is relevant to the company's activities.

In the much publicized case of *Escott* v. *Bar-Chris Construction Corporation*, 283 F. Supp. 643 (S.D.N.Y., 1968), directors who signed a registration statement for a securities offering were held liable under Section 11 of the Securities Act of 1933 for false and misleading statements about the business and financial condition of the issuer—which later went into bankruptcy. This case states in very clear terms that directors may not *blindly* rely on those who prepare a registration statement. After this case the SEC amended its Form 10K, the annual report filed by companies registered with the commission, to require that the report be signed by at least a majority of the directors.

Since September 1982 the SEC has charged at least five companies with middle-management "book-cooking" during the recession, in the form of unorthodox and sometimes illegal bookkeeping practices. Allegedly these practices evolved as companies have been pressured by difficult production aims and economic problems. AM International, Inc., Saxon Industries Inc., McCormick & Co., Doughties Foods Inc., and Ronson Corporation have been so charged, with the Saxon and AM International cases allegedly including some complicity at corporate headquarters.

5. Obedience to the unenforceable. Directors must do what their sense of fairness, ethics, values, and personal integrity tell them, even though they may not be obliged to do so by law, regulation, or custom. Neither law, regulation, nor free choice controls. Conscience, beliefs, morals, personal attitudes, and ethics must dominate. In board deliberations, ethics are concerned with clarifying what constitutes human welfare and the kind of conduct necessary to promote it.

A corporate director's code of ethics is puzzling. The board will dismiss a chief executive officer when a merger of two companies takes place, but the chairman would regard it as an unforgivable breach of honor to take the CEO's last cigarette. Such is the difference between corporate ethics and personal ethics.

The St. Louis brokerage firm Stix & Co. collapsed as a result of a stock scam by James J. Massa, an Illinois attorney, and Duane Skinner, a certified public accountant from Illinois. Both were found guilty by a federal jury of conspiring in a stock scam; the charges against them included tax evasion, mail fraud, and obstruction of justice. Stix went into receivership after Massa took control in 1979, and company officers allegedly stole at least $36 million in securities from their clients' accounts. According to the charges, the fraud was brought about through false statements to clients, laundered money, falsified tax returns, and bogus securities.

A director who serves a financial institution has some special problems of "a higher duty of performance and behavior that is expected of him than of his business corporation peer," according to the courts.

Bank directors take an oath of office, have residency and citizenship requirement, have restrictions on types of other boards they can serve as directors, and live with criminal laws which expressly prohibit certain acts by bankers, including embezzlement, making false entries, taking fees for loans, falsely certifying checks, making or granting a loan or gratuity to a bank examiner, and borrowing funds entrusted to a bank under its trust powers. *No such direct targeting of criminal laws confronts the business corporation director.*

In *Gamble* v. *Brown*, 299 F. 2d 366 (4th Cir., 1928), bank directors were held liable for failure to appoint an audit committee, as required by bylaws, to discover that a vice-president regularly made fictitious statements as to amounts in hands of other banks for collection and to check excessive and improvident loans made by the president and to prevent him from making further such loans.

The year before last the comptroller of the currency succeeded in imposing personal liability on the directors of a national bank who had knowingly allowed the bank to exceed its legal lending limits by $350,000. The court ruled that "directors of a national bank operate in an area closely regulated by federal law, and cannot maintain ignorance of the law as a defense." *Del Junco* v. *Conover*, 682 F. 2nd 1338 (9th Cir., 1982).

6. Be independent and objective. A strong group of independent directors on a board is a concept whose time has come. Board effectiveness was particularly improved dur-

ing the period when Harold M. Williams served as chairman of the Securities and Exchange Commission (1977–1981). Mr. Williams was an advocate of outside directors and campaigned strongly to increase the oversight responsibilities of corporate boards by competent outside (nonmanagement) directors, with a minimum of interlocking relationships with other corporations.

In a computer survey of 8,500 publicly held companies, compiled by Disclosure Inc., no person was found on more than eleven public boards, and only seventeen people were identified with eight or more directorships. The survey indicates that more outsiders are sitting on boards, which refutes the argument that inside directors—management, lawyers, and investment bankers serving the firm—dominate without truly "objective, unaffiliated, disinterested" views.

The country-club, crony-dominated system of directorships is on the way out with publicly held companies. A University of Chicago Graduate School of Business recent study of seventy-five directors of large companies included interviews in which each director was presented with a list of forty randomly selected directors of Fortune 500 companies and asked to indicate how many of the directors he or she knew personally. One director spotted seven acquaintances but the rest knew on the average only one or two.

A "clean" director will think, speak, and act independently with confidence and courage. He or she will resist the tendency of a board to be a self-perpetuating protectorate unresponsive to change. Such a director is willing to risk social and peer rapport and "back-scratching" with the chairman, fellow directors, and the CEO if such must be sacrificed in order to take thoughtful, independent positions. The independent director would relinquish a directorship rather than be considered captive.

These six checkpoints may help ensure "clean" director behavior, albeit they are only major reminders and may only serve to mislead or worry some tyro or aspirant directors. If that is the case, remember the old lady who had enjoyed two sermons by the new young minister. She ac-

costed him after his delivery with "I think you're won-
derful. I never really knew what sin meant until you
came."

   In addition, one ought to consider the following:

7. Stay away from political contribution or action unless the
    funds and the time involved are clearly your own, not the
    corporation's.

8. Neither a director nor any member of his or her immediate
    family should accept (or offer) favors or gifts of goods,
    money, or services from (or to) competitors, suppliers, cus-
    tomers, or anyone who does business with the company on
    whose board he or she serves. Commonsense judgment is
    to be used on token gifts, nonmonetary courtesies, or hos-
    pitality in connection with performing company business.
    The problem is that acceptance can suggest that an im-
    proper business relationship exists.

       The greatest domain of human action in the boardroom is
    the domain of "manners," or "obedience to the unenforce-
    able," so cited by Lord John Fletcher Moulton, a high
    official in the British Munitions Ministry in World War I.
    This domain is different from the domain of "positive law"
    or the domain of "free choice." The domain of obedience
    to the unenforceable is the sphere where we do what we
    should do, though not obliged to do so by law. Directors
    can be "great" if they respect this domain of good corpo-
    rate practice, which is shaped by personal conscience, eth-
    ics, values, morals, beliefs, attitudes, aspirations, vision,
    and culture. In other words, when you're in a board seat,
    you're on your own.

The Courtroom-Boardroom Duplex

   I can't recall the artist but I can remember the drollery of a
New Yorker cartoon many years ago when business travel was normally by train. Two men in business attire are entering a Pullman
diner. Handcuffs hold one to the other. It is obvious that here is
another errant soul on his way to Sing Sing. The obsequious
steward is inquiring diplomatically, "Together?" Well, the time
has come when every Argus-type corporate director realizes
that business must now be conducted with a partner. The partner is the government, backed by the courts standing at its side,

if not connected by a more formal software or hardware linkage.

In the late 1940s and mid-1950s my job was that of vice-president and general manager of the then Plastics Division of Monsanto. This included responsibility for developing a worldwide business in polymers and certain fabricated plastics. It entailed overseas licensing and establishment of manufacturing facilities in foreign lands through transfer of technology and direct investment or joint venturing with private-sector parties interested in this business. As one example, we had started building a market for our polystyrene molding compounds by supplying an injection molder in Mexico City. This business grew to a point where in 1950 Monsanto Mexicana S.A. was formed to produce the polymer for this customer and the rest of the Mexican market.

The problems of national sovereignty versus corporate sovereignty required a great deal of negotiation and compromise. The Mexican government was actively seeking foreign investment, the Mexican plastic molders needed supplies, and Monsanto was anxious to build its international network of plastics plants. The big problem was national control and influence over foreign investors to properly protect Mexican interests in all respects. Majority Mexican ownership eventually became a requirement, which raised the classical issue of how a private corporation could profitably operate its facility primarily in the interest of all its shareholders (mostly United States citizens), while accommodating the social and economic interests of the Mexican investors. The Mexican government was understandably concerned about matters of local employment and development of its self-sufficient industrial base. This situation was resolved by an arrangement whereby 50 percent of the shares were held by the U.S. parent company and less than 50 percent were held by Mexican investors; a controlling 1 percent was held by a Mexican law firm that was to act responsibly in the national interest and also in the parent Monsanto company's interest. More recent developments involving changing government attitude toward Mexicanization of all foreign investment shifted the controlling ownership to local investors as the enterprise became more self-standing. The concepts of licensing patents and continual technical support, or providing management expertise, are customary means of obtaining a return to an international business strategy where financial control of the subsidiary by foreign owners is not acceptable.

National sovereignty and corporate sovereignty require compromise and peer respect, if not some shade of togetherness. Our complex social system is basically an open system floating in a dynamic world environment. Driving forces may be termed a farrago of political, techno-economic, social, cultural, and theological energies. Advocates of each constituent force therefore need to recognize that governance involves servanthood without dominance. Peer respect for other constituent interests is necessary. As a consequence the construct in which directors govern has no single or static operational definition.

Whether an appropriate comity of courts and corporations can come to pass depends on whether lawyers, judges, politicians, directors, and managers can get their respective acts together. This entails an appropriate mode of coexistence, self-monitoring, self-evaluation, and more governance by morality rather than law. To achieve this more socially acceptable coalition, we must be more specific about board policy and action. The homicide detective's cryptic note "There were powder marks on his body before and after she shot him" is typical of the charges made against corporations and directors wherein complex motives and circumstantial evidence imply some unacceptable behavior. A vast library of books would be required to show the "powder marks" before and after a board of directors takes its action. This makes a field day for those stakeholders who would challenge the boardroom.

Thinking back over the unnatural range of this chapter's foray into the stakeholder domain, I fear I may only have added mystery to that behind the boardroom door. The very thought of a director studying all the laws and the many director-sensitive regulations flowing from them makes one shudder, scream, and quail, which, incidentally, might be a great name for a law firm.

My advice is that each director needs to stir himself or herself to become reasonably knowledgeable about this changing legal-regulatory framework in which each board serves the corporation. This takes personal initiative beyond occasionally consulting the company general counsel. It recalls an old Peter Arno cartoon in which a fond mother is explaining to a friend, "My son has his law degree and a small furnished office. It's just a question now of getting him out of bed."

10

Attentional Warps

In nautical terms, "to warp" means to shift the position of a vessel. This is done by means of a rope called a warp. Shifting a corporate course of action is more difficult because the board of directors holds both ends of the rope.

The effort necessary to significantly change director attention, even in troubled waters, usually requires more than public opinion polls or a few unhappy shareholder letters. Unfortunately, regulatory pressures or class action suits are often more effective than social concerns or internal board initiatives. Individual director legal liability and poor economic performance of the corporation are the basic forces that seem to work best in getting attention in the boardroom. Sometimes such forces may even lead judgment astray, as in Tennyson's "Cursed be the social lies that warp us from the living truth!"

How to shift the attention of the board to the important issues before it requires means of measuring and improving effectiveness, plus an understanding of how to cope with uncertainty.

Board Effectiveness

Regardless of any poetical, political, or economic warp of a board of directors, the effectiveness or "woof" of the board remains as the dependent variable to be achieved. This means other things have to come about or be "warped" to equip the board for duty.

The degree to which a board realizes its goals is a reflection of its

effectiveness. Interaction with the surroundings and changes in internal dynamics which shift organizational targets are the major sources of goal change. Goal changes sometime require board member changes too. I am reminded of the chairman of the board introducing a newly elected member. "Gentlemen, welcome Dave Merrill, Harvard M.B.A., 1956. We now have a perfectly balanced board of three Harvards, three Princetons, and three Yalies."

Another aspect of corporate effectiveness concerns resources. The so-called resource acquisition model simply refers to the ability of an organization to exploit its environment by the acquisition of scarce and valued resources to sustain its functioning. For a business enterprise this involves materials, technology, management, money, labor, supplies, customers, and community support. This model also requires realistic organizing for shortages, i.e., planning—as in using veal instead of chicken in the turkey sandwiches.

The resource acquisition model also provides clear linkages to environmental orientations that more general theories provide. My experience with improving boardworthiness indicates, above all, that intuition and instinct, plus common sense about personalities, are the best guide to improving relationships with environmental or "stakeholder" constituencies. You often need to acquire new directors who are capable of seeing beyond the boardroom door to the troublesome real world.

In the late 1950s and early 1960s I was actively engaged in helping Monsanto Chemicals Ltd. of London, Badische Anilin Soda Fabrik (BASF) of Ludwigshafen, and Monsanto Company, St. Louis, jointly develop a research, engineering, and development tripartite agreement in the field of high-density linear polyethylene plastic. This was a complicated resource acquisition model in the sense that competing business entities (Monsanto in the U.K. was publicly owned, as was BASF in Germany and, of course, Monsanto in the U.S.) legally pooled their scientific and technological programs with a pact to share patent license rights and know-how. The purpose of the tripartite agreement was to avoid duplicate expense R&D efforts in a highly competitive field. The boards of those three entities approved the pooling of resources as a means of increasing technical achievement against competition. Understandably, this pooling was carefully guided by the antitrust lawyers.

The ultimate criterion of effectiveness is survival of the enterprise over long time periods. One of the board's primary functions is to ensure continuity, if such is warranted for the role fulfilled by the corporation. When a chairman perceives that his board or company needs vital help, remember Erma Bombeck's rule of medicine—"Never go to a doctor whose office plants have died." Strengthen the board or management internally with some experienced, credible professionals who can focus attention on the key survival and development issues.

The most useful criteria for organizational effectiveness are the attributes of stability, growth in value, depth and maturity of directors and management, strategic nature, identity, and integrity of the organization and its directorate. These are all definable characteristics, albeit somewhat subjective.

These traditional approaches to improving effectiveness suggest that decisions of a board of directors are guided by either goal or resource acquisition considerations. Beyond this, there are uncontrollable contingencies and internally or externally imposed mandates which are central to the realities of governing a corporation. Such mandates may become attentional warps. Most theory does not deal with issues which these mandates raise. The corporate ship of state is often pulled astray by such warps which strike the attention (or fancy) of individual directors or the board as a whole.

In the 1960s when I served on the board of the Fome-Core Corporation of Indian Orchard, Massachusetts, a venture company manufacturing a combination paper-foamed polystyrene laminate for construction, packaging, and display uses, the four-man board of directors was strongly warped by two market-oriented members. Their concern over public relations, advertising, and promotion dominated the boardroom to a point where we neglected certain research work which was needed to get the product accepted in the marketplace. This "warp" was belatedly corrected. This experience brings to mind what our British director friends were fond of reminding us, that in Lancashire, "warping" means laying eggs— something an effective board of directors tries not to do.

Another attentional warp high on the list in the boardroom is how to deal with uncertainties, including how to cope with events beyond boardroom control. This calls for an understanding of the phenomenon of uncertainty and how to raise the consciousness of your board of directors in the face of an equivocal outlook.

Knowledge Levels

There are important distinctions between certainty, risk, uncertainty, and ignorance. And there is nothing more frightening than ignorance in action in the boardroom. In fact, the worst thing about ignorance is the conviction of the ignorant.

Risk, on the other hand, is where the probabilities of events or causes are known. Risk is a special case of uncertainty. It involves cause-and-effect relationships. The set of risk variables which a board must deal with may be perceived as a continuum from complete determinism on one end to the complete unknown situation at the other end. An arrow of uncertainty runs through this continuum of knowledge levels behind the boardroom door. They can be ordered as follows:

1. Known situations. Characteristics: No uncertainties prevail. No unknowns are apparent. What you don't know doesn't normally hurt you. What you may suspect causes all the trouble and is described in subsequent knowledge levels. All elements at this level are identified, are considered static, and are understood as the existing condition. This is an easy level with which to deal. Directors making corporate decisions in a government-controlled market or an oligarchy, monopoly, or cartel are real-life examples where the business condition is well known. The practice of "first come take all" is the usual scenario.

2. Certain situations. Characteristics: Present state and outlook are considered fixed, relatively static, settled, and free from doubt. Past business conditions have been more or less characterized by this relative steady state. Uncertainties existed but they did not dominate the outlook. Mature, established key industrial sectors in politically stable nations with steady growth and no new technology used to be prime examples of certain situations. However, in recent years what were formerly certain conditions have become less so with the impact of inflation, unemployment, political tension, and social activist movements. As a result, years spent in the boardroom may be no guarantee of adequate experience. One caveat: Eric Hoffer points out that we can be *absolutely* certain only about things we do not understand.

   A bit of advice for CEOs presenting a forecast to the board: Give them a number or give them a date, but never both.

3. Probabilistic risk. Consequences are measurable as to their expected occurrence with known levels of riskiness. Something is likely to happen. This is like the paradox that it's probable many things will happen contrary to probability.

   Quantitative management science techniques are especially useful at this level. The logical approach to risk management has been useful for normal (past) business conditions in stabilized sectors of the economy. Selection and development of highly qualified directors has assumed this stable context of the past. But now the businessman's attitude toward boardroom risk, given the increased uncertainties, seems to be if you have to travel on a *Titanic,* why not go first-class.

4. Uncertainty. Characteristics: lack of sureness on consequences of a decision. The intelligent person always seems so uncertain and the ignorant seems so certain. Quantification of outcomes is impossible at this knowledge level and, in some cases, indeterminable. The situation is in a state of flux.

    Operations in politically unstable countries, or where technology is changing rapidly, are examples where a systems approach to governing in the face of uncertainty can be helpful. The systems approach offers perceptive, intuitive, simultaneous, and qualitative thinking in the boardroom in dealing with contextual uncertainty. Such a more right-brained approach complements the left-brained logical, rational, sequential, quantitative approach to board problems.

5. Ignorance. This level is characterized by lack of knowledge of the variables involved, either present, future, or both, or even whether they exist. (Some determinists like Einstein would say that no ignorance is necessary, given enough time and manpower to resolve it.) Practically, however, there will always be some "necessary ignorance" in governance and management matters. Directors should never underestimate the power of a platitude or plain malarkey offered impressively by a fellow director unaware of his or her ignorance of the topic under discussion.

    The role of a director requires that he or she often make decisions in this "arrow of uncertainty," despite the high level of uncertainty or ignorance. The hazard is that it takes a lot of things to prove you are smart but only one thing to prove you are ignorant. This knowledge/uncertainty level may be represented by a situation in which, without adequate preparation, a company diversifies into

a business sector while having no experience or understanding of the criteria for success in that sector. The *Wall
Street Journal* daily reports divestments of businesses by
companies that acquired them only to find they could not
successfully develop them.

It is difficult to teach boards of directors to cope with ignorance. The answer undoubtedly lies in more critical
strategic assessment of business ventures before plunging
into unknown areas. As Will Rogers said, "Everybody is ignorant, only on different subjects."

6. Unk-unks. Characteristics: This is a space-jargon term. By
unk-unks we mean those unknown unknowns that are not
even suspected. A sophisticated governance process should
acknowledge these strategically upsetting possibilities,
even if control is impossible. An attitude of alertness and
flexibility in the boardroom is obviously required.

The attentional warp needed in the boardroom is the realization that we have to govern our corporations in a
world in which we understand only a small portion of its
risks and hazards. Perhaps we have to adopt a different attitude in the boardroom about the fateful future that faces
directors. There is a misery of choice, as the psychologists
phrase it, when a board makes decisions in the face of uncertainty. The Arab world offers one approach:

An Arab returned to his tent in the desert late one night
very hungry. He lit a candle and searched until he found
four dates. He took out his long curved knife and cut one
date open. It was wormy, so he tossed it aside. He took another date and cut it open, but it, too, was wormy. He took
the third and it was also wormy. Then he sighed, blew out
the candle, and ate the fourth date!

Consciousness Warps

Psychotherapists experiment with all sorts of consciousness-rais-
ing techniques and notions. These concepts can be employed to
create positive attentional warps, only provided that if there's a
skeleton in your closet, you make no bones about it.

Consciousness of the world about us is an obvious requirement
for an effective director in order to best serve the corporation. Another type of consciousness is also important: the consciousness of

the board itself and how it functions and the behavioral patterns that persist. This consciousness of fellow board members can become an interesting game to play when board agendas are dull. Try watching your peers and the performers at the next board meeting. Body language in the boardroom can be revealing.

Have you noticed that when the chief financial officer, general counsel, or chief engineer of a company gets up to make his report, say, to the board of directors, his eyes will typically glance to his right?

In contrast, the vice-president of personnel or the advertising or public relations officer or director with such background is more likely to glance to his or her left when preparing to present a position before the board of directors.

Brain research has revealed some interesting hemisphere specialization of the two sides of the human brain which is the basis for such behavioral tendency. Biofeedback instruments which register the degree of electrical discharge from brain cells show increased alpha rhythms in whichever hemisphere is resting. Ask someone a verbal or mathematical problem and the left hemisphere "fires." Present a visual-spatial or ambiguous problem and the right hemisphere begins to "fire."

Eye movements also correlate with hemisphere specialization. Our eyes will typically move away from the side of the more engaged brain hemisphere. With the left or logical side of the brain controlling the right side of our bodies, we can understand why a lawyer-trained director rising to present a logical brief will glance to his or her right.

The right hemisphere processes information or "thinks" holistically, synthetically, visual-spatially, intuitively, diffusely, and recognizes patterns and faces. It processes inputs simultaneously and in a timeless fashion. The creative thinkers' right hemisphere controls the left side of the body and eye movements. The vice-president of public relations tends to look left.

The left hemisphere processes information in contrasting modes which are verbal, analytic, reductive into parts, discrete, sequential, rational, time-oriented, discontinuous, and linear, and are often involved in language and mathematics. The chief financial officers' left-brain orientation is manifest by right eye and body movements.

According to the neuro-linguistic programming (NLP) model of communication, you can detect such aspects of external behavior while exploring the complexities of internal experience itself. Through some such perceptions, a chairman may better understand his directors and learn how to motivate them and how to effect change. This "gift of consciousness" technique is drawn from the disciplines of linguistics, psychology, and neurophysiology. NLP practitioners infer internal states and mental processes by reading the outward forms of behavior—content and tone of language, gestures, eye movements, changes in facial coloration, lip size, jaw placement. Effective behaviors are then coded in notation systems so that others may learn them.

At one of my recent board meetings I noticed one of our directors looking up left at the ceiling to recall or visualize a forgotten matter. Another director looked down to his right to check his kinesthetic feelings about what he remembered. After a while he stopped dropping his eyes and started raising his voice. Another muttered lightly to himself. These auditory internal dialogue sounds are coded mannerisms indicating he was debating an uncertain point. He probably was thinking that Mother said there would be days like this—but she never said there would be so many!

Some see NLP as a set of gimmicks for superficial "behavioral transplants" or for pigeonholing a person as, for example, a visual person or a feeling person. Others claim shifty eyes come only from watching tennis matches. But the meaning of mannerisms and behavior patterns can go much deeper than that.

- A right-handed person's looking to upper and horizontal left usually signifies recall of a previous experience—upper left of visual memory, horizontal left of auditory memory.
- Looking to upper and horizontal right often signifies new

processing—upper right, construction of visual images; horizontal right, putting expressions into words.
- Looking to lower left may signify attention to internal dialogue; to lower right, the accessing of feeling states.

These are called "eye accessing cues" and are only a few of the mannerisms and patterns useful in reading behavior. NLP practitioners also seek to model behaviors that reflect competence, excellence, or elegance (aesthetic economy). This may involve matching one's own patterns and rhythms to those of the listener to establish rapport. This technique is called "mirroring" and "pacing."

NLP places ultimate responsibility for clear communications on the sender. Communication can occur even without intent. Any utterance, gesture, or pause may elicit a response. Some implications of NLP may help directors understand each other and thus be more effective as a group.

The importance of expanded awareness, or mind-sweep, beyond the self-serving concerns that directors possess as humans cannot be overestimated for an effective board of directors. Expansion of awareness beyond a narrow attentional warp to the entire governance system requires director learning. Certainly a new attitude toward uncertainty is needed. Tennyson's curse on the social lies that warp us from the living truth is not enough. Directors must recognize the social perceptions of corporations that exist. Then the board should take action to correct the perceptions when they are not correct or change actual conduct of the corporation when it is not functioning in a broad social interest.

Halfism

To return to the Arab and the wormy dates, one way to deal with problems in the boardroom is to not really face up to the trade-offs required and just muddle along. As corporate governance has progressed in concept in recent years, it has been characterized and, indeed, encumbered by this less courageous manner in which key issues have been addressed (or not addressed) in the boardroom. When the importance of a particularly troublesome social/economic/legal issue emerges, it invariably has led to the development of polarized opinion, each opinion as extreme as the other in its absolute conviction.

As a director of the Society of the Plastics Industry (SPI), New York, in 1957–1959, I was impressed by the polarization of director policy positions into two groups: those directors who represented the plastic material manufacturers—the large chemical companies—and those directors representing the molders and fabricators—the smaller, often privately held companies. This was often a David and Goliath standoff, especially with respect to dues structure and long-term SPI investment in industry development programs requiring funds for public relations purposes and consumer education.

More recently, it is interesting to see one gaggle of company directors appearing to have captured the day as reflected in public seminars and conferences of the National Association of Corporate Directors, or the Conference Board, only to be later superseded by another group of company directors performing at workshops at the Harvard Business School, or speaking with opposite views for the Business Round Table, or performing on a New York McGraw-Hill conference panel, talking about the proper attitudes and policies for boards of directors.

The irony of this public contest with opposite views reached a crescendo at the fifty-ninth annual meeting of the American Law Institute (ALI) in May 1982 in Philadelphia. The principles of corporate governance and structure proposed by the ALI caused such a corporate reform furor between lawyers and businessmen that no action was taken on the proposals. They were sent back for extended further study until 1986.

The truth of the matter seems to lie somewhere between the two positions, usually halfway between the two extremes of views on director liability, the monitoring role, the organizational structure of large publicly held corporations, and the fiduciary duties of directors.

An entirely new approach to extricate present matters from tiresome polemics, and to avoid useless boardroom argumentation in the future, might follow the approach of "Halfism." This has been offered satirically to the scientific community in an article in the *Journal of Irreproducible Results* by a biologist and a psychiatrist.* This approach recognizes that all truth generally lies somewhere in

---

* Kevin Kelly and Anton J. Reiner, "Science and Halfism," *Journal of Irreproducible Results*, Vol. 24, No. 4 (1978), pp. 3–4.

the middle and seeks to arrive at that middle ground from a simplistic statistical viewpoint. It is generally agreed that most aspects of reality are distributed according to a frequency distribution resembling a bell or Gaussian curve. It follows that the ends of the curve simplify those examples of the reality that are least characteristic of the reality as a whole.

In the ALI case in point, the "pure" lawyer proposals and the "pure" businessman proposals for corporate reform are not realistic, given the actual conditions of corporate governance. Thus the truth lies in the middle with the problem being how to arrive at this middle ground.

Two traditional approaches that generate nothing but cries of "foul" may be described as the reductionistic and the holistic approaches. Each has a characteristic perspective and, therefore, suffers from the constraints of that scope. A reductionist approach often invites the loss of overview to an issue and results in a narrow point of view, whereas a holistic approach loses the illumination that detail can provide but often leads to a fuzzy position that is vague and overgeneralized.

According to the "halfway" doctrine, a solution is simple—one needs only to employ a much-maligned process of thought, thinking something halfway through. This ironic system of thought for directors might be called "halfism."

To extend this, an issue of importance in the boardroom can be attacked "halfistically." It is apparent that a halfistic approach can become neither lost in detail nor smug in assuming that it understands the entire breadth of an exhaustive board committee inquiry.

In doing his homework, a director thinking halfistically has every halfway measure at his disposal. According to this waggish doctrine, a study performed with brilliant insight to the midpoint of the issue is far better than a study performed with drudgery to completion. The director also has the option of reporting half, the positive half, of his deliberation. After all, if the proposal data are poor to begin with, analyzing the better half of poor data will generate results that are much better than if all the information were interpreted. Ideally, in the culmination of halfistic boardmanship, conclusions and discussions would be rigorously detailed to the halfway point, and terminated before you appear in the boardroom to debate and vote. This approach allows for modesty of your director input, with the added reward of being assured that you could have been twice as incorrect and misleading if you had offered the entire range of conclusions to the plenary session of the board.

Too, in open boardroom discussion, a well-done, half-done opinion can only promote deeper curiosity and avid questioning from your fellow directors. Such an exchange would be likely characterized by half-asked questions and halfistic replies with the understandable argument that your thinking on the matter is only partially complete.

If such a halfistic trend in corporate governance were adopted, even as boardplay, it might lead to the elimination of all vestiges of the obstructive controversies plaguing boardrooms. If more directors move forward halfistically, they will inevitably come to middling opinions and conclusions which, as pointed out previously, are far more likely to be correct than more extreme positions. Perhaps a new equanimity will reign in the boardworld. Halcyon days will be here again as boardroom conduct is half planned, half executed, and half exposed to public view through SEC reports, shareholder meetings, and the annual reports. Directors will no longer be criticized for lack of professionalism, thoroughness, or lack of care and diligence, since such qualities are inimical to the pursuit of halfism.

Quarterly earnings reports, long-range strategic plans, and corporate litigation problems will not be judged for inclusiveness, but rather for partial synthesis and limited explanations. In this way, laws and regulations, once susceptible to toppling by contraindicative conferences, restatements, and recommendations by opposite parties, will be immune to challenge, since no law is considered absolute.

In short, halfism in the boardroom has much to recommend it, as long as you don't take it too seriously. I hope my director friends will lend at least half an ear to this fey argument on how to be more effective behind the boardroom door.

One consequence of halfism may lead to what my friend Dr. Benjamin J. Luberoff, editor of *Chemical Technology*, calls Decisions of the Third Kind. Computers—and Aristotle—recognize only two diametrically opposed decisions, yes and no. The hole is punched or it's not, we will or we won't, the switch is open or closed. But life is not Boolean, so the Decision of the Third Kind was invented. It says: Let's Not Decide.

11

Perks and Pastimes

The tempter saw his time; the work he plied;
Stocks and subscriptions pour on every side,
Till all the demon makes his full descent
In one abundant shower of cent, percent,
Sinks deep within him, and possesses whole,
Then dubs Director, and secures his soul.
                          ALEXANDER POPE, *Moral Essays*, Epistle iii

Paraphrasing Upton Sinclair, it is difficult to get a director to understand something when his fees depend upon his not understanding it. A case in point: Each year since retirement from the Monsanto Europe S.A. board of directors in 1968 I have received a fee of 965 Belgian francs ($21.04, last time I converted it). The fee is for service as a nonresident former member of that company's board. This is part of the incredible social security wrappings for any and all of us who labored in the boardrooms of Brussels many years ago. The reward about measures the level of service given.

Modern Meed

A better meed, or fitting return for services rendered as a director, was typified by my recent pilgrimage to the industrial zone of Arzew, Algeria. The occasion was the inauguration of LNG-1, the nation's first national gas liquefaction plant. The invitation from SONATRACH, Algeria's Ministry of Energy and Industry, was to 250 guests from Europe and the United States, transported by chartered Pan Am 707 planes. I was fortunate to be invited in my chairman role.

Our flight—New York to Washington to Paris to Oran-Algeria—

was fogbound for five hours, so we missed now-deceased President Boumedienne's speech to a banner-bedecked grandstand audience. They were sitting, incongruously, in the desert where the grandstand had been erected, not far from the loading dock where a specially built LNG tanker was being loaded for its maiden voyage. The destination was the El Paso Company's unloading terminal in Maryland with pipeline connections to Georgia.

As a solatium—a solace payment—for missing the president's speech, thirty of us were selected to meet privately (apart from guards and interpeters) with the president for an off-the-record discussion. The exchange was candid and thoughtful and dwelled on the governance problems of our respective nations. Most of the visitors were bankers, oilmen, and engineering construction company directors. For example, Bechtel Engineering Company, which had a major role in LNG-1, had its entire board in Paris for a board meeting, from which their chairman and president took the side trip to Arzew to enjoy the perquisite pilgrimage.

In English law a perquisite is "casual income from heriots, escheats, reliefs, etc., accruing to the lord of the manor (from his tenants) and in addition to the regular revenue." In the British scene the tax imposed on direct income is so onerous that an incredible if understandable attitude pervades the boardroom (and the nation) with regard to the pickings, emoluments, totin' privileges, and supplementary benefits from a pastiche of "perks." The *Manchester Evening News* reported on September 9, 1981, that plenty of perks are available even to shareholders now, if you buy the right shares. A free funeral, a decent discount on a *QE2* cruise, and a half-price stay at the Savoy are listed in "Proprietors' Discounts," an invaluable yearly guide drawn up by brokers Seymour Pierce. The All England Tennis Club £50 Debentures go for £5,750, which entitles one person to a Centre Court seat and use of the private lounge. Dundonian will still bury you free—as long as it's a £250 funeral—but you'll need 500 shares. Buy some of Barclays Unicorn unit trusts and you get a 19 percent discount on a *QE2* cruise. With 1,000 shares in Barratt Developments, you can get between £500 and £2,500 off the price of a new house.

Continental European directorships generally differ somewhat in nature from the conventional United States version of a corporate director. The reason is that much of the capital is in private hands. Many European directors represent family or closely held

capital constituencies. In Europe, financial institutions hold much of the ownership and directors often represent their interests.

This situation leads to a slightly different attitude toward directors, and the matter of director status and renumeration, than we usually find in the States. Status consciousness is manifest in many ways. For example, it is not uncommon for registration numbers on British directors' automobiles (company-provided) to command a surprising price for transfer of ownership, since vehicles are assigned a permanent number. A few years ago the London *Times* listed JJ24 registration plates for sale for £500. This price was for the status symbol attached to the automobile: the cost of the car was additional. The JJ24 plate is based on prior owner; the local celebrity or titled status allegedly rubs off on the new owner of the vanity plates.

The provision of company automobiles with chauffeurs for directors when they are on "company business" is standard practice in the United States as well as in most countries in Europe, Latin America, and the Far East. One study in 1972 by the Kienbaum Management Consulters, an executive placement and industrial advisory company, revealed that 80 percent of all German company board members rate an official conveyance (plus chauffeur for those in the DM 100,000-and-above per annum category) for business and private use. U.S. practice on this score in industry and government may be less overt than it is elsewhere, but nevertheless it is more frequent than one might expect with the IRS looking over chauffeurs' shoulders. Radiotelephones, TV, dictating machines, and bar supplies are not uncommon extras in some director vehicles.

During one period in my career I received and enjoyed these executive and director perks that went with a large multinational company position. This was before government and public attention cooled off some of the flagrant indirect-income practices. One benefit I still enjoy from the good old days is a tailored Acrilan checkered, red-lined sports jacket given me as a Monsanto director when we visited the Chemstrand Corporation's Decatur, Alabama, acrylonitrile synthetic fiber plant in 1964. The zeal to please the directors went to the extreme of finding out each director's tailor and supplying him with a bolt of Acrilan woven cloth, with instructions to make a jacket in two months to meet the board meeting deadline. This was close, as my tailor was in London.

I also remember when my British tailor, whom I had known for twenty years, bought out a three-person bespoke tailoring business from the previous owner. With the status implied by the title of director, many sole proprietors in the United Kingdom are able to use the title legitimately and enjoy the psychic reward which ensues. Mr. O'Brien lost no time in getting calling cards and stationery out to all his clients to proudly exhibit his new title—Director of Lesley and Roberts (Tailors) Ltd. Incidentally, he was the misguided adviser who told me to wear inconspicuous blue to my first British board meeting where everyone else showed up in classy haberdashery and striped Oxford gray. This incident was not unlike my first speech, in July 1966, before a Brazilian Chamber of Commerce luncheon, when I wore an unseasonable light-colored suit and everyone else wore blue in accord with Brazil's winter season, the reverse of ours.

But back to director titles rather than director wear. In the United Kingdom, magistrates became so tired of having offenders parade before them describing themselves as directors that one brouhaha which began in 1963 was kept alive by the activist press until 1972. The incident involved a peddler by the name of Charley Smith, Director of International Whelk Stall Ltd. Charley was actually a barrow boy, peddling his whelks on the streets of London. A whelk is a spiral-shelled mollusk sold as food in England and is often peddled from a small two-wheeled cart, or barrow, in the streets. Charley bought himself a company "off the peg" for £25 and thereafter identified himself as a director. Troubles began when Charley found himself in court for obstruction of traffic. Charley paid a modest fine and went back to his fish peddling—unmoved.

Chapter 33 of the U.K. Company Act states: "A director includes any person occupying the position of director by whatever name called." Thus, Charley was legally able to enjoy the status title of director. In trying Charley's case, the Old Street magistrate, E. S. McElligott, became so irritated that his statement from the bench became a cause célèbre in the press, evoking a series of editorials and scattered newspaper coverage. His Honor merely fumed, "Today, if you own a whelk stall, you call yourself a director." The whole flap was rekindled in September 1972 when Edward Crowley, a pipefitter who also ran a whelk stall, followed Charley's example and described himself as a company director, when he stood bail (£1,000) for a friend.

The same magistrate, McElligott, happened to be handling the case. When the accused failed to appear at the Old Bailey, Mr. Crowley admitted before the court that he didn't have the bail money, and he was jailed for six months. The magistrate was again quoted widely in the press: "You get a man running a whelk stall describing himself as a company director and with all the solemnity that attaches to it, he enters into a recognizance when one knows in one's heart of hearts there isn't ten pence to support it. Nothing in the law prevents anyone, whether he be a whelk stall proprietor or engaged in an even less glamorous profession, from calling himself a company director if he is a director of a limited company."*

So much for the title of director and its benefits to the title holder in the eyes of the beholder. Directors are a separate breed in many ways. Those who qualify by legal criteria, or, more important, by professional attributes, do enjoy privileges beyond title

* Excerpted, by permission of the publisher, from *Board Life: Realities of Being a Corporate Director* by Robert Kirk Mueller © 1974, AMACOM, a division of American Management Association, New York, p. 38. All rights reserved.

recognition. Those who are directors in Britain belong in a separate class or "club" of directors which dominates this stewardship function. In the United States, the composition of the board seems relatively more open to professional director candidates, to inputs by directors from separate disciplines or professions, and to directors with outside interests. This emphasis on independence and professional qualifications for directorship is beginning to pervade the boardworld slowly in many other countries.

The British Institute of Directors represents the establishment in that country. The institute keeps tab on all matters affecting United Kingdom directors, including perks and pastimes. A recent survey of directors' renumeration, under the title "Directors' Rewards," was published in 1981 with the support of the institute. It examined all facets of current boardroom rewards and provides the most detailed information yet available.*

One interesting aspect of this survey of salaries and total remuneration, of partially executive and nonexecutive directors, includes cars, pensions, and other off-payroll benefits. A concept included in the survey has a different perspective showing "director's required income." This notion involves showing "the gross income required by directors, which net of all appropriate taxes relevant at the time, would have allowed them to support the life-styles" that are presumed fitting for anyone having director status. The rationale seems to be that it is more blessed for a corporation to give than receive, and it's tax-deductible.

Two examples of director life-styles reflect the "modern meed" which is considered as perks and pastimes by this British directors survey. For example, Style D is a relatively modest life-style. It assumes a director has recently changed houses (no doubt to be suitably located for his status), and his mortgage is based on the percentage shown for a house at current market value. Note that while the survey watches six life-styles, A through F, the survey considers categories A through C as inappropriate for director-level incomes. Style D, a minimum "requirement," affords the director a four-bedroom detached house at a 65 percent mortgage, 129 meals out per year, a 1,500-c.c. private car, telephone, and gas central heating.

Style F provides a director with a five- or six-bedroom detached

* "Directors' Rewards," Reward Regional Surveys, 1 Mill Street, Stone, Staffs, ST15-8BA, as reported in *The Director*, February 1981, p. 31.

house with three reception rooms and large garden. The house may be bought on a 58 percent mortgage. The director is allowed 150 meals out per year, a 2,500-c.c. private car, telephone, golf club, domestic help for 182 hours per year, school fees (day school), and gas central heating.

"Required income" and "required annual increase" for modest Style D were £7,560 and 25.0 percent in 1975 compared to £15,-690 and 23.2 percent in 1980. Regional income and required annual increase for the super Style F were £22,456 and 53.0 percent in 1975 but changed to £39,265 and 28.5 percent by 1980.

Clearly more attention is paid publicly to the perks and pastimes of a director in the U.K. than in the U.S. The increased responsibilities of the 1980 Companies Act show—in the view of the British boardworld—that remuneration of their directors "seems hardly adequate fee for the time and knowledge most contribute."

But lest we show any bias toward a less perky United States boardworld, perks and pastimes abound here too, if not so evident at times. A recent exception: According to a 1981 proxy statement, Steven J. Ross, chairman and chief executive officer of Warner Communications, Inc., New York, received an unusual perk for pastime and private screening of motion pictures in his Manhattan apartment. According to the proxy statement, the screening room will cost the company $450,000. However, the company noted, "Mr. Ross will bear all costs for the space and maintenance. All furnishings and equipment will be owned by the Company." While the practice of providing heads of movie companies with private screening rooms isn't new, the elaborate facility provided by Warner Communications to enhance the convenience of Mr. Ross's home screenings offers a target for hostile shareowner questions at the annual general meeting.

It is helpful to remember that there are three general classes of director compensation: real income, psychic income, and perquisites commonly referred to as perks. One of the best perks I know of is formally recognized in a union contract from which directors are, of course, excluded: the brewing industry's traditional practice of allowing brewery workers to "tap a line" for periodic beer breaks during their shifts. This may seem to be an insignificant fringe benefit, yet Philip Morris, owner of the Miller Brewing Company, calculates that at its Milwaukee plant alone during two fifteen-minute breaks a day employees down 2,000 barrels a year! Beer may constitute a perk for employees, but directors are more likely to be plied with champagne and spirits.

Aside from the thirst-quenching compensation, it has been said that directors in general are the most underpaid and underutilized people in modern organizations. Surveys by the business press, trade groups, professional associations, and consulting organizations abound on the subject of real income through director fees, retainers, expenses, emoluments, honoraria, and other hard-dollar means of director compensation.

Executive directors (insiders) are normally not eligible for this hard-dollar director compensation, since their salary and bonus are considered to suffice. The fees commonly paid out for meetings are only part of the income most directors earn. The growing trend is to provide an annual retainer, supplemented by per diem fees for meetings attended, plus out-of-pocket expenses in getting to and from the meeting place.

The psychic income benefits of directorship obviously vary with the prestige of the institution, the stature of the other directors, and the public recognition, value, and popularity of the services or products produced by the corporation. The larger tranquillities of freedom, noninvolvement in mundane operations, and little responsibility for the plight of the far-off, troubled remainder of the system, combined with the stability and status of directorship, are heady psychic benefits to some persons. It's somewhat like the religious bumper sticker I saw near the Andover-Newton Theological School: "Work for the Lord—the pay is terrible but the fringe benefits are out of this world!"

This psychic motivation reminds me of a former public relations professional, Emily Boxer, who became a producer on the NBC *Today Show* and who had a candid critique of work style and role model perceptions. She was reminiscing to her former female boss about her previous job and the disincentives involved.

She observed: "Who would want to move up to your job? When we came to work in the morning, you were already there . . . when we left at night you were still around. If you would come to the office about ten A.M. or even noon, arrive in your chauffeur-driven limo, after a stop-off at Bergdorf's, be taken out for lunch, return at three, and then be driven to a cocktail reception about four-thirty

P.M.—working for you might have its incentives." Most executives and directors alike enjoy and expect perquisites that go with the job.

Aurum Reginae

Blackstone once intoned, "The queen . . . is entitled to an ancient perquisite called queen-gold, or *aurum reginae.*" He was referring to a royal practice of possessive relations which the crown enjoyed to afford the queen earned rewards or fitting returns for favors and privileges granted certain lesser mortals. This exacting of gratuities has persisted as a way of life for those in power.

The rationale for attempting to compensate by the indirect route has, at least, nine contemporary arguments. Many of these are highly debatable. Companies give perks for many reasons.

- Private ownership. When companies are privately owned, the owner's attitude toward and expectancies of indirect compensation through use of company-owned facilities and support service systems are entirely different than in public companies, since the assets are the owner's property.
- Paternalism. The company undertakes to supply needs and regulates conduct of those under its control—a vestige of former sole-owner attitudes.
- Business effectiveness. Time off at vacation-spot meetings or special trips may renew effectiveness of a director. This has the same rationale as the sabbatical practice for preachers or faculty members.
- The competitive norm. Other companies provide perks.
- Motivation of lesser mortals. The visible privileges or properties of the directors are supposed to stir the troops into working to achieve director and perk status. In some countries this is backfiring because active youth groups are rejecting material rewards in favor of more social values.
- Imagery. Directors driving or being driven in a Cadillac, Mercedes, or Rolls-Royce make impressions—sometimes the wrong impression if such activity takes place in an economically depressed area.
- Tax advantages. The tax systems in many countries force departure from logic to provide strange perks to directors,

rather than added salary—for example, furnishing of fitted carpets for a director's house as a company asset. Birth-control pills are deductible next year if they didn't work this year. Free access to exercise facilities owned by the company is another tax-free perk. One firm I know has an elaborate health club at its headquarters office where directors and top executives can paddle, swim, steam themselves, or get a rubdown.

- Bulk-purchase economies. Bulk purchase of life insurance and medical coverage, for example, or apartment privileges in the city, limit loss of individual choice in favor of untaxed perks. The loss of individual choice is a trade-off in favor of the economic benefits and convenience.

- Mutual advantage. Equipment, cars, or facilities furnished for use by a director or executive during off-time may escape, at some risk, certain tax levies. Free (or token-payment) access to private suites in hotels at active urban centers, which a company leases for use as living accommodations and as a director sanctum, are gaining respectability and acceptance again. The Holiday Inn in Gaithersburg, Maryland, has a presidential suite that rents for $1,000 a night. The suite has an executive boardroom, an office that sports a $5,300 desk and a box of vintage cigars, rococo-modern bedroom with a working fireplace, and built-in taps that dispense Scotch, bourbon, and martinis. The master bath has a seven-foot-square whirlpool Roman bath that "seats six." Decorated at a cost of $200,-000, the six-room-and-bath suite is available to directors, executives, government bigwigs, and diplomats from nearby Washington.

One United States multinational company I know is very sensitive about IRS scrutiny of its use of corporate aircraft. Whenever wives of the top executives or directors are aboard, the pilots carefully log the body weights of the free riders and calculate this aliquot part of the total weight of the plane and its occupants which is attributable to these nonemployee, nondirector passengers. The fuel and other direct costs are then so calculated and recorded carefully in the accounting records. This shows that the free rides given were inconsequential compared to the costs of making the trip. As a fallout of the corporate aircraft phenomenon, it's interesting to observe the pecking order of corporate hangar space at Stamford County airport in Connecticut. These "gold-plated" hangar spaces vie for prestige appearance and location and can be sold anytime for a nice profit if bad times force one of the occupants to abandon its semi-perk aircraft fleet. The rivalry between CEOs as to which has the latest jet is as prickly as whose company has best earnings per share last quarter.

The Perking Order

Perquisites—perks—constitute an interesting hierarchical dimension in director compensation. The Japanese are particularly adept at devising compensation schemes for employees and officers and for rewarding by use of perks those who hold director seats. In October 1967 the *Asahi Shimbun* ran an extended profile of a typical Japanese "salaryman," Mr. Yano, who "runs on the elite course." While not yet a director, at thirty-six he held the position of assistant branch manager in charge of loans at a well-known Tokyo bank. Living in a three-room, company-owned apartment, he paid monthly rent then equal to U.S. $12.50, a token amount in a ridiculously high-rent district. His monthly take-home pay, after taxes, amounted to U.S. $221.40, but this was supplemented by perquisites in the form of meal tickets, commuter tickets, and entertainment expenses. Mr. Yano received a substantial bonus twice a year, totaling between 15 and 30 percent of his regular annual salary.

With international business the way it is, competition forces the companies in most industrialized nations to provide a variety of meaningful perks as incentives for key employees and directors. The greatest draw on perks is undoubtedly possible in privately held institutions, and in certain forms of government service, but the perquisite factor in publicly held corporations is an important competitive force to be recognized. For example, how can you compete with Personna's practice in Glasgow, Scotland, where volunteer male personnel have long availed themselves of the opportunity to take their morning shaves on the job, serving as test panels for company products?

An interesting trend is underway in the United States as outside directors are being compensated more as if they were employees. Retainers and fees are up. Deferred compensation, consulting fees, life, medical, and travel insurance, pensions, stock options, and employee purchase privileges are becoming necessary perks in order to attract directors who are increasingly apprehensive about liability exposure. There is increasing lack of enchantment over the privilege of board service.

Current SEC rules would have required me to disclose the director gift of a mahogany poker-chip case in modern Texas motif, given to each director when many years ago we toured a Texas facility. Such an expensive perk would be out of order under today's regulations. The Securities and Exchange Commission has become quite aware of the higher order of perquisites being employed to entice and compensate directors. Government guidelines for proxy statements now stress that officers and directors must place a value on perquisites and include them in the proxy statements and SEC reports wherever disclosure of remuneration is required, "whether or not the benefits were authorized."

A problem persists in that perks and pastimes afforded directors tend to be difficult to explain and justify to the SEC and to those not enjoying such privileges. Unfortunately, the aspect of payola lurks in the minds of the uninformed. In Rome, under-the-counter payments are called *busterella,* in Hong Kong it's *hai yo,* and in Mexico it is called *mordida*—translated as "the bite." These synonyms for emoluments, benefits, pickings, totin' privileges, douceur, or other fitting return as recompense for services rendered all dwell in the minds of those who doubt the integrity of companies and their directors with regard to disclosure of total remuneration.

Perquisites have been called "arrangements designed to exploit human weakness for the benefit of the firm." Yachts and villas are still provided in some corporate setups and in certain foreign countries. My position on the matter of perks and pastimes for directors is that, properly designed and administered, they are a desirable form of payment and recognition if, in fact, they are earned by the value of directorship services rendered. The judgment on this equation must be one which will pass public and shareowner scrutiny.

An interesting closing example of perquisites concerns retirement. The French have a custom of allowing directors to remain wedded to the board until death or until voluntary separation is arranged to everyone's satisfaction. One of my Arthur D. Little director colleagues, Gerard Llewellyn, former director general, Banque Nationale de Paris, and recently deceased, used to say that as long as you stay breathing you can stay on a French board. This practice is changing slowly, but it will take some time yet to change tradition. As Sir Walter Puckey, founder-chairman of Management Selection (Group) LTD., and a savant on board matters, has said, "It is easier to let sleeping directors lie." Retired persons who fill up board seats of course get most if not all the perks of board membership. In countries or companies where the age of board members is limited, some retiring sea dogs become honorary or emeritus members, or move into other positions of influence or consulting relationship to the board and continue to enjoy some if not all of the perks.

But perks and pastimes of directors will never make up for the public exposure and personal liabilities a director faces in the boardroom. Fred Allen once remarked, "My agent gets ten percent of everything I get except my blinding headaches." That is true as far as perquisites are concerned. They don't make up for the obligations and risks of being a director—but they help make being behind the boardroom door somewhat more rewarding.

12

High-Tech and High-Touch

MAN: A creature who lives not by bread alone; but principally by catchwords.

ROBERT LOUIS STEVENSON

Five characteristics separate man from other hominids—"a large neocortex, bipedality, reduced anterior dentition with molar dominance, material culture, unique sexual and reproductive behavior."[*] Setting aside any catchwords—jogging, Polident, yachting, or sleepless struggles—the most important of these idiosyncrasies in the boardroom is, of course, man's large brain. Most directors are elected because they bring wisdom, intelligence, and perspective to a corporation. But catchwords and buzzwords do creep into board affairs and trigger the thinking of directors. Two of the latest catchwords are "high-tech" and "high-touch."

Intensive social behavior, or high-touch sensitivity, would seem the most likely single cause of the origin of human intelligence. Social and reproductive behavior embodies an adaptive strategy stemming from the human nuclear family, the earliest form of directorship attempting to govern human affairs. Recent interest in the social sciences and the adverse impact of technology has increased social reform and concern for high-touch matters in the boardroom. One chairman friend expresses the hottest question before the boardroom as "whether or not to enter an altered state of consciousness."

Man's material culture, with its tools and techniques, is perhaps more obvious as it has evolved in recent times to a culture of high-

[*] C. Owen Lovejoy, "The Origin of Man," *Science*, Vol. 211, No. 4480 (January 23, 1981), p. 341.

tech-dominated activities. Example: An MIT Sloan School of Management study of 250 firms around Boston's Route 128 revealed that one hundred high-tech companies were spin-offs from four major MIT laboratories. The rest were brainchildren of former MIT faculty who were able to take theories from four different engineering departments and "put wheels on it."

But these rococo-technology days—of so arranging the world so that we don't have to experience it—are shifting rapidly toward a better balance of hard, high-tech orientation with the softer, high-touch considerations of technology impact on the world. Boardroom and legislative chambers are where most of these trade-offs are being made, but they are not the only places where we have to make trade-offs between our technology-oriented society and the human side. We constantly face such trade-offs and choice points in school, home, factory, church, and local community. For instance, we cancel our Boy Scout hikes if the stationwagon breaks down, and our television gives us nothing to do when we aren't doing anything.

The high-tech, hard-science maiden flight of the space shuttle *Columbia* symbolized the United States' most recent political swing of techno-economic priorities in relation to the socioeconomic priorities. The soft sciences have been somewhat more prominent in previous high-touch-oriented administrations in Washington. The trick for any administration—national or corporate—is to continue high-tech imperatives without abandoning the high-touch social advances made in the last two decades.

I like the offbeat twist that Tom Lehrer, professor, piano player, and satirical lyricist, put on the high-tech issue recently. He asked, "What is it that put America in the forefront of the nuclear nations? And what is it that made it possible to spend $20 billion of your money to put some clown on the moon? It was good old American technology, that's what, as provided by good old Americans like Enrico Fermi and Werner von Braun."

Earthkeeping and Networking

The social transformers are referred to as members of the Aquarian Conspiracy by Marilyn Ferguson in her recent book.*

* Marilyn Ferguson, *The Aquarian Conspiracy* (Los Angeles: Tarcher/St. Martin's, 1980).

This revealed the subculture development, the work through networks and coalitions, nationally and at community levels, to bring about an equitable transition to more human and more ecologically sustainable societies. Resurgence of local leadership and self-reliance is apparent as people are taking back the power they once delegated to impersonal governments and large corporations.

The idea of "earthkeeping" is still experimental, personal, and intuitive. It consists of sharing of information in *heterarchical* organizations rather than hierarchies. The concept is to empower people rather than wield power over them. This takes a lot of doing to overcome the J. Paul Getty dogma "The meek shall inherit the earth but not its mineral rights."

So-called planetary networking of these concepts is the opposite of the so-called old-boy network of global exploitation and power politics. Elite university circles, royal alliances, private clubs, boards of directors, and establishment groups still dominate large numbers of people, which networks respond by weaving webs of more holistic awareness and empathetic consciousness.

SPIN, the catchword acronyn for networks, stands for "segmented polycentric integrated networks." This mouthful grew out of some anthropologist's observations in 1965 of charismatic movements in churches. Other movements—civil rights, environmental, antiwar—showed similar patterns of behavior. Channels of linkage, or the people-power lines which define such networks, are not unlike the kind that exist in some forms in the boardworld. In the boardroom this is evidenced by the connections and associations between directors. But the social transformation networks are less visible than corporate board networks. The SPIN type are flexible, vibrant organizations which often exist without boundaries, bylaws, or officers. They are lines of communications, the alternative express highways that people use to get things done in crisis and opportunity.

Seven major factors make the social transformation networks function. In part, they also make boardroom networks effective as long as conflicts of interest and insider knowledge are not abused. The major channels of linkage that define a network are:

1. Overlapping membership among different groups. This bridging is especially valuable in the corporate scene if the

different groups are in different domains of activity where a "crossover" or "hyphenate" relationship can be formed; e.g., connections in different business sectors or educational or social institutions such as hospitals, foundations, etc., where different perspectives are experienced. One director I know was such a joiner of organizations he had three slits in his lapel.

2. Linkage among network members based on friendship and personal relationships. This can be a source of cronyism with political overtones in a boardroom if allowed to dominate in a director mix. The usual way to spot potential crony candidates is that they're the ones who think the way the chairman does.

3. Exchange of leadership among groups. Often a leader in one group is a follower in another. At Arthur D. Little, Inc., the professional culture functions on the notion of leadership exchange for task force assignments. The most qualified professional leads an engagement team tailored with staff from different disciplines to fit the problem to be solved. Hierarchical rank in the company is unrelated to the case team leader selection. Professional competence and peer acceptance dominate, so a staff member may lead a group on one task and be a team member on another. The model is one of an organization of consent with commando-type units.

4. Geographic movers who travel around to different groups spreading the word and interests of the network members. In business, this means of communication is, of course, common, with so many directors and employees in travel status around the world. The old-boy network of multinational corporations is an important factor in international relations.

Social networks are sometimes fascinating and provide a rich field for sociologists' research. Ithiel de Sola Pool of MIT and Manfred Kochen of the University of Michigan published an article in *Social Networks* journal propounding that an average American adult is acquainted with about 1,000 other Americans, to the extent the party of the first part would recognize and could address by name the party of the second part, who would respond similarly, if the parties happened to meet.

The small-world phenomenon, in which you turn out to have an acquaintance in common with some total stranger you start talking to, the increased mobility and interconnectedness of our society, accounts for this. Pool and Kochen demonstrate that in a country the size of the United States, the existence of such a completely cliqueless network, combined with acquaintanceship scores of 1,000 per adult, would imply an average requirement of fewer than two intermediaries to connect any two individuals selected at random. One randomly selected American adult can generally be linked to another by two or three intermediaries, almost certainly by four.

A hermit living in Florida and another hermit in the Northwest can be so connected. Since even hermits have to buy food, each of them knows at least one storekeeper. Each storekeeper knows assorted customers, wholesalers, inspectors, etc., at least one of whom will know the local congressman. The congressmen from Florida and the Northwest may know each other, but even if they don't they have a congressional aide or member in common. This example means that the maximum plausible minimum chain between any two Americans involves only seven intermediaries in the network.

5. Large conferences, seminars, colloquia, and other joint activities of networkers who have a common interest. Learned and professional societies and trade conventions and associations provide happenings at which networkers gather to promote their common interests. Unfortunately, most such conferences are where people talk about what they should be doing.

6. Grapevine communication through different media—newsletters, periodicals, books, flyers, telephone calls—and by word-of-mouth at gatherings. This is perhaps the fastest network means of spreading tidings. Remember, if it's good it goes away; if it's bad it happens.

7. A split-level ideology that forms the glue of networks with a few common themes and a wild array of variations. This

split-level ideology explains the fission/fusion aspect of political and social networks—the continual splitting and
fusing or shifting around because of internal strife within a
movement. This internal tension is often as great as the
conflict between a network movement and the so-called
establishment or opposition.

Anthropologist Virginia Hine calls a network a change-directed
structure. "A network is built for change and the transformation of
an established unchanging structure. . . . It's becoming the para-
digm of the New Age.* Networking cuts across bureaucracy and
enables institutions to cope with complex, interrelated, interdependent issues. Organizational structures create value systems to fit
their structure. When hierarchy is bypassed, the various value systems of the different organizational structures are exposed via network messages, and understanding of social behavior is increased.

Networkers usually recruit people to support their movement by
face-to-face contact in which personal trust can be achieved and an
egalitarian relationship established. This involves some sacrifices
and risk-taking, since personal commitment is a part of networking.

The normal and sociable dimensions of ordinary human conduct
are what one scholar has called the "history of the inarticulate"—
sort of the underside of history. Sociologists make a distinction between contact and noncontact species. Those of us in a contact
culture or subculture generally touch one another more, face one
another more directly, look one another in the eye frequently, and
interact more closely than those in the noncontact group. The pri-
mal form of interaction is physical contact. As anthropologist Ash-
ley Montagu terms it, touching is in a real sense the completion of a
gesture and the object of reaching out.

Keeping the high-touch dimension in the electronic banking
business is a particular chore for bank managers, as more and more
remoteness is introduced with the advent of computerized hardware and remote terminals for conducting banking affairs. One
amusing, but serious, event took place last year in a boardroom of a
small bank where a friend of mine was a director. The issue before
the board was the soundness of a good-sized automobile loan for
several Cadillacs. The top-of-the-line white-and-yellow cars were

* Virginia Hine, "Networks Empower Social Change," *Leading Edge Bulletin,*
July 20, 1981, p. 2.

for business use. This was not so unusual in itself, but a local horologist who had a reputable jewelry shop squealed to one of the loan officers that the cars were for the use of three "ladies in waiting" at a well-established bordello in suburban Boston. This tip-off on the ultimate customers was enough for the board to reject the loan, and the corporate shield of honor and ethics was properly reestablished in the community.

Ambition versus Condition-Driven Strategy

Genetic engineering, intelligent electronics, and space technology are just three examples of the dramatic resurgence of high technology. A better balance between the driving force of such technology and the driving forces of social reform has to take place if these breakthroughs are fully realized. This is a vexing governance and management challenge. It is an art form, a synthesis of two complementary aspects:

- The management of human systems: the science and technology of management striving for productivity, efficient performance, and technical competence through innovation which is sensitive to social impacts
- The human management of systems: the art of management, linking human beings with purposeful teams and catalyzing their full creative potential through leadership

The problem at the boardroom level is in seeing that a proper balance of these two aspects of managing comes into play to make a proper trade-off on the high-tech, high-touch equation. I remember working for years in the plastics materials business while we created a new thermoplastic polymer destined to replace glass for carbonated beverage containers. This styrene acrylonitrile material had unique vapor-transmission features and properties allowing it to be blown on special machinery, not unlike the process of blowing glass bottles. After years of development, millions of dollars of plant investment, and the building of a large organization to make and market these containers, the federal regulatory agency involved in approving new packaging for consumer food and beverage products rejected the permit. The ultimate cost in unemployment and write-off of assets was tremendous. Inadequate safety evaluation and changing standards proved to be the problem. Interestingly, over ten years later a new polymer was developed by a competitor, and testing criteria and procedures were improved to a point where plastic beverage containers have made a dramatic comeback.

Some say we have created a high-touch-oriented society operated by social reform networks. Social complexity, social pressures, and political imperatives are indeed challenging those who would manage our affairs with a single techno-economic star as reference. Certainly corporations are behaving differently with respect to their product introductions and employment practices.

A single goal of either high technology or high social transformation is inadequate given the complexity, uncertainty, and velocity of change in the world. The task before educational, governmental, and business institutions is a plural one. Multiple goals, multiple criteria, and multiple standards are now recognized by more thoughtful leaders as a natural condition to be faced. Effective strategies and contingencies are recognizing this multiplicity, uncertainty, diversity, high change velocity, and complexity as a normal state of institutional existence. As directors we have to learn to be more comfortable moving from one disequilibrium state to another state of disequilibrium.

The context in which our businesses now function is obviously an interactive, interdependent environment. One issue present in every boardroom is whether the directors can continue to govern the corporation as an ambition-driven institution. Such a notion is more attractive than the thought of managing a condition-driven company. The issue of ambition-driven versus condition-driven institutions is, of course, a national issue—indeed, an international one also.

When the world was a simpler place in which to live, the externalities and interconnectedness were less critical. Ambition-driven strategies were adequate to serve our various purposes, and, further, such were acceptable from a societal viewpoint. Ambition used to be what would get you to the top if the president had no daughter.

With a shrinking interactive world, social sensitivity to political, cultural, environmental, and social dimensions of our activities is a necessity. Evidence of this is the fact that we have at least twenty technology-based laws now on the books. These are administered by six federal agencies concerned with toxic substances in our environment. One wag director friend who worries about environmental affairs says, "Unless we clean up the atmosphere soon our national anthem's opening line will take on a new meaning."

Such high-touch sensitivity is in addition to, and often conflicting with, the techno-economic or high-tech focus. We are forced to consider condition-driven strategies in our business and in our own daily lives. A distinguished scientific researcher was participating in a panel discussion recently in a Boston suburban area with other learned scholars at a town meeting near my home. The topic was a comprehensive study of the nation's future water supply, which the researcher and his colleagues had just completed. "Ladies and gentlemen, I have some good news and some bad news for you. Our study shows that by the year 2000 everyone in New England and, in fact, in the United States will be drinking recycled sewage from his home water tap." "Great Scott!" came a cry from one of the town selectmen. "Quick, tell us the good news." "That was the good news," replied the scientist. "The bad news is that there won't be enough to go around."

The Temporal Dimension

> *Time, the greatest of all tyrants.*
>
> Russian proverb

An interesting aspect of the high-tech, high-touch challenge is the fact that long-range planning of our technological advances— and even our pesky economic cycles—has a relatively short time span when compared to either social transformation cycles or bio-sphere cycles. Examples of social movements are the changing roles of men and women, holistic health, peacekeeping, and urban and community development. Examples of "earthkeeping phenomena" are the renewing of natural resources and the increasing concentration of carbon dioxide in the atmosphere from fossil fuel combustion.

Interestingly, these social movements and natural or physical phenomena take longer than many of our technological advances. This is true even though there is a substantial lag—eight to fifteen years—between the time technical information is generated and the time it is used in a technological innovation. It is important to remember that from 60 to 80 percent of important technological innovations have been in response to market demands and social needs. The remaining 20 to 40 percent have originated in response to new scientific or technological advances and opportunities.

The recently formed New World Alliance in Washington, D.C., presents a social "transformation platform" or process for a new politics. This is based on decentralized power, personal growth, global cooperation, and ecological harmony. Lofty objectives, yes, and one of the keys is appropriate technology. This is a subject in itself and certainly of importance in our condition-driven technology strategy. In summary, socially relevant technology is now everyone's business. While our legislators also struggle with the

issues, the Congress approaches the topic very carefully. It opens
with a prayer and closes with a probe.

High-Tech/High-Touch Linkage

The total strategic process by which technology is made socially
relevant is an elusive one. There are at least three reasons for this.
First, those in specialized fields can't agree about the basic context
nor about questions which need to be examined. There is always
somebody who knows better than you what you mean by your
message. Second, a common purpose is not accepted; therefore research and attention tend to be a flight to the familiar. Saying it
another way, if we knew what we are doing it wouldn't be research. Third, the sheer pace and scope of development require a
degree of technological knowledge rarely found linked with the
tandem economic, social, and political concerns.

Economists and businessmen see technology in strategic terms.
Well-known studies of industrial innovation such as the SAPPHO
multiyear research project at the University of Sussex found few
criteria discriminated between success and failure. In fact, no innovation is ever a complete failure—it can always serve as a bad
example. The education of users, publicity, market forecasting, and
selling, plus coupling technology with market needs, were the most
significant measurements discriminating between success and failure of attempted technological innovations. Other positive criteria
were concentration of effort, specialized communications with external scientific community, and the caliber of the product champion who honcho'd the innovation.

How should universities and industry and government leaders
select areas for technological advance, given the competing claims
on budgets and the multiple goals and criteria for success and ac-
ceptability?

The criteria of choice to seek should avoid flaws of the single operational manner of conducting our technological affairs. This must
be done while meeting requirements for socially sensitive and relevant technologies. The old proverb holds: Do not throw stone at
mouse and break precious vase.

The traditional choice pattern of the successful scientist and
technologist is derived from the seventeenth through the nine-
teenth centuries. First of all, the quantitative sciences from Galileo,

Kepler, and Newton formed part of the general education of the upper class. Here, interestingly enough, women, too, occupied themselves with scientific problems, particularly those connected with physics and chemistry. This bit of history of distinguished women in science reminds me of a modern recognition of women and their accomplishments, as reported in a New Hampshire town paper. The town has a population of 2,500 if you count the cemetery. Almost unbelievable in its innocence, the news item was on a town competition and read, "Winners in the home-made claret section were Mrs. George Harris (fruity, well rounded), Mrs. Harvey Johnson (fine red color, good nose and full bodied), and Miss Sally Wiggins (slightly acid, but could improve if laid down)."

But back to early new discoveries. They were highly personalized products of creative individuals working in the semi-isolation of universities still cast in the mold of the medieval era. Isolation of the researcher from politics and most economic realities was nearly complete until long after his significant technical discovery. The scientific method emerged with a mystique about the process as a whole. Choice of problems was a personal one and there was little pressure to seek short-term utility.

Above all, social consequences of technology were of little concern to the growing group of honored elitists. Dominant criteria for choosing projects were internal—that is, arising from the community of scientists themselves. Science-related questions were removed from public discussion, from those "who do not have appropriate credentials."

The more social orientation of science and technology emerged within the twentieth century and especially since 1950. Research and development have moved out of university and industrial laboratories. Technologists and nontechnologists alike recognize the potentially profound impact, for good or evil, of the results of scientific research and technological development. Marvels of modern technology are the development of a beer can which when discarded will last forever and a $9,000 car which when properly cared for will rust out in three to five years!

But criteria are now undergoing changes toward more consumer-relevant and socially sensitive technology. These criteria have been imposed by external rather than internal sources—e.g., politicians, consumerists, environmentalists, ethicists, public opinion, and the marketplace.

Of the factors causing this blend of high-tech, high-touch criteria for technology programs, there are three that should be known to members of boards of directors as expanded criteria for development of technology and that are both operationally oriented and policy-oriented.

- Big science programs in aviation, weaponry, atomic energy, space, communications, and health require a technology endeavor in partnerships of industry, education, and government. These partnerships serve multiple social, economic, and political goals.
- Attempts to apply scientific methods from physical research to human and social issues have projected researchers into the high-touch social arena. The citizen and the politician can no longer remain indifferent to which problems are being tackled and which are being ignored. Urban blight, personal growth, communication, crime, and education are obvious examples.
- Ecological sensitivity is the third cause, with a new, still unsure, field of technology assessment struggling to make technology responsive to human concerns. The objective is to impose new criteria to direct the course of technology whenever undesirable social consequences can be foreseen. A 1979 bumper sticker expressed the New England sentiment on this issue: "May all you ecological bastards freeze to death in the dark."

An interesting example overseas occurred in the Federal Republic of Germany, in 1973, when a public parliamentary hearing reviewed a survey evaluating thirteen research areas sponsored by the government. Each area was examined for its expected contribution to eight national objectives, including "satisfaction of elementary human needs." Education, environment, housing, and town planning came out on top along with reductions in defense and nuclear energy. The conclusion was that priorities for research planning have to start from new social problem situations. Criteria for research selection have thus moved from criteria *internal* to science to criteria *external* to science.

The policy-oriented criteria for technology development are manifest in the United States' National Academy of Sciences reports. These clearly reflect the view that science and technology should respond to human needs, and that criteria for project selection take into account the welfare of society. Dr. A. M. Weinberg, former head of science administration at Oak Ridge National Laboratory, is in the thick of this debate with his two internal criteria of "ripeness" of a scientific field and competence of scientists in the field. Weinberg's three external criteria for "the relative validity and worthwhileness of various fields of science support by society" are (a) technological merit, (b) scientific merit, and (c) social merit. All three criteria are derived from values outside the scientific community. High-tech and high-touch considerations are slowly coming into better balance.

Spawning Innovative Technology

To illustrate the high-tech, high-touch New Age, some characteristics of Route 128 are of interest to those boards of directors concerned with entrepreneurial ventures or a new enterprise. The Route 128 phenomenon is an unusual example of the innovative technology process at work in a particular geographical region, while at the same time being accepted socially and politically.

In 1971, Arthur D. Little, Inc., was commissioned by the French Ministry for Industrial and Scientific Development to examine Route 128 around the Boston area and the new technological enterprises which were there. The objective was to determine the cause and impact of this so-called new technological enterprise phenomenon. I can remember at the time a friend and fellow director on Salzburg Seminars in American Studies, Pierre Aigrain (now corporate general manager, Science and Technology, Thomson Brandt, et Thomson Csf–Paris), saying, "It has been known in France for a long time that there are three ways to lose money: agriculture, women, and innovation. The first is the surest—agriculture; the second, women, is the most agreeable; and the last one is the fastest—innovation."

The purpose of the commissioned study (which has been made public in France) was to allow the French government to consider the possibility of re-creating a "Route 128" somewhere in France as part of its economic development program. In conducting this study, ADL reviewed not only Route 128 but the Research Triangle in the Carolinas and Silicon Valley on the West Coast.

In a larger sense, Route 128 is simply a metaphor for a series of unplanned but interrelated events as the result of a multiple combination of factors, direct and indirect, internal and external. The study concerned the background and development of Route 128; the characterization of the enterprises there; the initiating forces, the building forces, and the facilities forces; an examination of the local communities; the government laws and policies; and the support communities and facilities.

There are thirty-two communities surrounding Route 128 in which a measure of industrial facility growth was determined from the period 1949 through 1970. It has been growing again in 1980 and 1981. The technology-facilities-to-total-industrial-facilities proportion increased from 2.6 percent in 1949 to 34.3 percent in 1970. These high-technology facilities were from twenty basic product categories such as electronics, electric instrumentation systems, precision and special components, bio-engineering, cryogenics, lasers, nucleonics, oceanology, optics, ultrasonics, etc.

A large majority of the high-technology facilities have fewer than 250 employees. In every year but 1958, more than half of all the high-technology buildings had less than 100 employees. A total of 156 companies were identified as having been spawned by MIT laboratories and MIT academic departments.

It is interesting to note that of the *initiating forces*, the key, of course, is the entrepreneur—the man himself and his leadership ability. This coupled with the market—in many instances, the federal government market—made Route 128 possible, and the commercial market, developing more recently, and the general cultural opportunities around Route 128 were the next initiating forces.

As far as the *building forces* are concerned, the financing of technological enterprises with the sources and nature of venture capital, and assistance from other financial institutions available to those around 128, are important factors, as well as the spawning institutions—universities, government, and certain large companies.

There were certain *facilitating forces* in the opportunity for formation of real estate and industrial parks, in the local communities' attitudes, and in the cost of living and doing business in the area. The government laws were examined, including the IRS, the loan agreements, Small Business Act, SBICs, government contracting policies, funding of research and development. Support companies and facilities in the way of public utilities, gas, electricity, telephone, rental computers, laboratories, consulting firms, rental and lease agencies for sophisticated as well as conventional equipment, travel agencies, janitorial services, secretarial services, law firms, and companies with special services directed toward the new technology firms were keys. These service-oriented firms gave a considerable economic multiplier effect to Route 128 through economic growth and slowdown times. Suffice it to say, the phenomenon, as well as that of Palo Alto, and perhaps the Research Triangle, are examples of how development and growth can be accomplished, based primarily on technological innovations. In my association with Route 128, and many of its companies over the last fifteen years, I have not encountered a significant situation in which the high-touch aspects of the high-tech companies have not been dealt with adequately.

Seven Key Ingredients

There are no packaged, ready-made ways for boards of directors to deal with innovative technology and venture development and to balance the high-touch aspects with the high-tech dimensions. In the Route 128 study we found there were key ingredients in the initial mix essential to get such a phenomenon started. Another set of ingredients is needed to build the ventures to a point where they can be identified as successful entities. Not necessarily in order of importance, the initiating ingredients are:

1. The *concept*—whether the innovative technology and venture idea, that is, the product or service, is a viable, realistic one apparently serving a need. The concept is like Hindu volleyball—there is only one team. The challenge is to keep the ball in the air; the opposition is gravity.
2. The *technology*—the means, process, or skills to produce the product or provide the service.
3. Selected *resources*—in the form of financial support and time necessary to start the innovative venture (this is where the venture capital comes in).
4. The *man*—he who has the talent and commitment to lead the new enterprise (also referred to as "the champion"). A Boston MBTA subway poster entitled *Eskimo Sled* is suc-

cinct for a winning team: "In the back—steady dogs, in the middle—idiot dogs, in the front—one strong smart dog!"

5. The *market*—the next major concern in the sequence of technological venturing. A board needs to be sure that the management conducts a thorough market test beyond that inferred in the original concept, and perhaps by an un-biased tester. The actual market test comes at a time after prototypes have been developed and tried out, and this marketing event becomes the fifth ingredient.

I remember one treatment of a marketing event in a tongue-in-cheek annual report of a fictitious company. The sales chart showed a graph having an absolutely flat, very low sales level eleven months of the year. But there was a tremendous sales spike in July showing the sales curve peaking fifteen times the normal monthly level. The CEO's explanatory caption at the bottom of the sales graph: "The problem is not confined to this company alone, but is general throughout the fireworks industry."

Given these five initiating ingredients of the mixture, then the innovation begins to "cook," and two more facili-tating ingredients become increasingly important:

6. The *directors* and *management* capability and commit-ment.

7. The organizational *structure* of the innovative venture.

But sooner or later, success depends on how well all of these ingredients serve a real market, and then how well they are governed and managed over a longer time frame, and in what form or structure the new activity emerges.

The message which stems from this is that a high-tech, high-touch venture will be successful only if ambition-driven strategy is tempered by condition-driven strategy. This means that a balance of high-tech and high-touch at-titudes is required. This may require an entirely different attitude in the boardroom and acknowledgment of what has become known as Harvard's Law: "Under the most ri-gorously controlled conditions of pressure, temperature, volume, humidity, and other variables, the organism will do as it damn pleases!"

13

The Corporate Governance Peerage

O, let us have him, for his silver hairs
Will purchase us a good opinion
And buy men's voices to commend our deeds.
WILLIAM SHAKESPEARE, *Julius Caesar*, Act II, i

The pressure of shareowner appraisal through a proxy voting critique of directorship is usually ineffective; most shareowners go along with the nomination committee's recommendations. Directors themselves are not all anxious to listen either to criticism of their deportment at the annual general meeting or to peer review by a committee of boardroom companions. This is an understandable human reaction.

Eight years ago I served on a financial intermediary company board made up of eighteen male directors, mainly Midwesterners but four from the East. Three were local businessmen in the city where this company was headquartered. One was the chief executive of a small chain of family-owned retail supermarkets in the Midwest. The market chain was bought out and the scion-president found himself further enriched—but out of a job. He devoted his time to charitable organizations in the community, where he distinguished himself in lending some management expertise to not-for-profit groups. But he neglected to stay in touch with the rapidly changing business world. After three years of being out of the stream of business activity, his contributions to the financial intermediary board waned to a pitiful level, though his social presence and insight remained respectably high. The committee of the board charged with nomination and renomination of director candidates decided he should not remain on the board despite the public and personal relationships that might suffer from dropping a well-respected member of the community.

Advising him of this evaluation caused some internal fireworks, but the committee and the chairman held firm and he was not re-nominated. Social and personal ruptures in the community took place as he was dropped out of the director circuit. In the last year this local tension has abated somewhat, but the correct deed was done for the benefit of the shareowners. The replacement director is an active economist from an international banking firm who brings current insight to the board meetings. Moral: It's not what time you put in but what you put in the time.

While there was an orderly—if delicate—show of peer power, peer support is vain, political, and unpredictable. It's liable to leave you high and dry just when it's most needed. It's like the time Dudley, a fellow director and ranconteur, was regaling his adjoining colleagues at the quarterly board luncheon held in the company headquarters in Boston. These pre-meeting luncheons afford a semisocial period for the directors to exchange war stories and biases and to one-up each other as to who had the most impressive foreign travel schedule since the board met three months ago. Random conversation was humming like a magpie meeting at every spot around the twenty-place table. Conversation was at least 55 decibels—the noisy-home level—and each side of the table was sound-buffered from the other by the conflicting chatter groups, particularly from where I sat at the other end of the room from Dudley, who was in great form that noon carrying on with his down-Maine accent.

On this occasion it befell Dudley to be expansively telling a story to his listeners. For no reason at all the hubbub in the room suddenly fell silent. This noise pause was because of a fluke cessation of the several unrelated conversations which were going on—sort of like ten seconds of silence sponsored by the public library. In this calm, Dudley was heard by all as he finished his story with ". . . that's when I took my pants off!" It was hard for the conversation to get started again around the table. I learned later that Dudley was relating a fishing incident when his flycasting ritual was complicated by an embedded hook in his back trouser pocket.

The most effective peer evaluation method I have used in counseling boards of directors was an effectiveness rating scheme developed on an assignment with a century-old London-based multinational company. I had known the chairman personally for twelve years and was familiar with his board and the several industries in which the firm operated worldwide. The business, primarily European, was quite diversified: mining, electromechanical hardware, chemicals, and professional engineering and technical services. The board was made up of two Frenchmen, one Belgian, one German, two Greeks, one Austrian, three Britons, and one expatriate American.

The individual directors were judged by seven subjective attributes on a rating scale of one point for "deficient in performance or effectiveness," two points for "satisfactory on most counts," and three points for "director service of distinction."

Confidential ratings of the ten individual fellow directors were made orally to me in private interviews with each of the eleven directors. They were promised anonymity in return for their candid rating of their boardroom companions on the following generally agreed-upon criteria for a "proper director":

- Professional performance as a director over a sustained period, providing significant and useful inputs to the board
- Character and integrity above reproach, along with good judgment and perspective
- Balanced leadership contributions in an intellectual or conduct sense (including good attendance, active interest, and support to the company and its board)
- Sustained business or professional development achievement by help and suggestions with the company's strategy and marketing efforts or stakeholders' relationships
- Natural following, interpersonal rapport, and peer respect from other board members and top management
- Interest in board and management succession and staff development
- Special services, such as distinguished contributions or special insights to the company—e.g., public service recognition, recruiting of "stars," novel business ideas for corporate development considerations, etc.

These seven points were weighted on the one-to-three scale and then composited to get a consensus score (with a range indicated) for each director as confidentially judged by his boardroom mates. I then prepared a matrix display of ten fellow directors' ratings, without individual attribution of each member of the board. This veiled judgmental rating was then discussed privately with each director to let him know not how I rated his conduct, but how his fellow directors perceived his boardworthiness.

This dance of the seven veiled attributes proved to be an electric shock treatment to at least three of the directors. They were rated one and one half, less than satisfactory, on balanced leadership, business or professional development, and interpersonal rapport. The evaluations were never used except in my individual counseling session with each director and with the chairman, who was not given details on who rated whom at what level, but was given the composite standing of each of his directors as judged by their respective companions.

I conducted the first peer evaluation of this European board in July 1976. Since then I have kept track of the response of individual directors to their colleagues' appraisal by irregular but frequent discussions with the chairman, and, while I was doing some other consulting with the company, this exposed me to directors' continuing conduct, particularly that of the inside directors, who outnumbered the outsiders. With no exceptions, individual directorship has improved, in two cases dramatically. One lagging director was fortunately dropped when a business conflict developed. The board is swinging and swaying now with a sense of achievement and camaraderie not present before.

Pulling off such a confidential, intimate rating task can only be done when there is a level of trust and experience mutually shared by the counselor and the individual board members. Given that, it is a good technique for upgrading effectiveness of a board of directors. As far as the inside versus outside director aspect is concerned, I have found that when the board and the management are in harmony they share the mistaken belief that they live in the same world. When they start working actively together they acknowledge that they live in different worlds but are prepared once in a while to cross the chasm between them.

Before discussing how to deal better with lackluster or aging boardroom inhabitants, it is interesting to examine how the peer

process functions in a boardroom. To begin, let's look further at the social interactions which take place between directors as they gather as a group. The pre-meeting vamp inside the boardroom can be revealing. In the boardroom, conduct is characterized not only by adroit management of interpersonal relations but usually by some form of compromise.

The Psychic Moat

The latest wave of social scientists have rediscovered the everyday activity of self-preservation and "impression management." This phenomenon has been familiar for a long time to those in the world of the marketplace and to those few in the boardroom who make an impression different from the impression they are trying to make.

The trades of fashion, advertising, entertainment, personal products, salesmanship, and etiquette function with the premise that appearance is the true reality. It's a great factor in making money and vice versa. Managing impressions and manipulating identities require delicate diplomacy and an understanding of human behavior, such as the custom of measuring success by having your name in everything but the telephone directory.

Directorship has a key attribute in this regard, although too few directors seem to be conscious of the impact of personal appearance and interpersonal communications. Some think all you need is a good illegible signature to be a winner. Maybe the somber ambience of boardroom settings dampens sensitivity to the human side of being and behaving as a director.

I know of no boardroom architect who is also an ecological psychologist or a practitioner of Edward T. Hall's proxemics.° Proxemics is the label covering the "interrelated observations and theories of man's use of space as a specialized elaboration of culture." In teaching us how to bridge the psychic moat, the ecological psychologist would deal not only with the activity in the boardroom but also with the boardroom itself, the other board members (their number and attributes), the fee structures, the protocol, bylaws, and many other ecological phenomena that affect the consequences for subsequent behavior of the directors. It's as elusive a task as finding an imaginary cure for hypochondria.

The personal space or psychic moat surrounding individual directors is a key zone of interaction. Hall and others boiled the dimensions of this down to four interpersonal distances: intimate, personal, social, and public. Each has a close and a far phase, and an individual's style of performance in the transactions associated with each zone creates a separate situational personality.

I've watched this manifestation of style during my years of boardroom habitation. People behave differently when in a boardroom than they do when they are not. Many times a fellow director has caucused with me after a meeting to either explain the expressions or explore the interpersonal dynamics that took place in the board session. Some of the best insights flow into the open during bathroom breaks.

The spatial dimensions and the invasion of personal private space vary, of course, by group, geography, and race. I have found

° Edward T. Hall, *The Hidden Dimension* (Garden City, N.Y.: Doubleday, 1966). Also Hall, *Beyond Culture* (Garden City, N.Y.: Doubleday, 1976).

that Northern European directors are less intimate, noncontact types; high-touch cultures do not abound in Northern Europe. My German friends are sensitive to intrusions in their private sphere, compared to Americans. Middle- and upper-class Englishmen, according to my observation, are less inclined to expect a niche of their own in business or government settings. Members of Parliament have no private offices and frequently conduct their business on the terrace overlooking the Thames. This concept of territoriality is a neglected sociological dimension of directorship. No doubt this is a fallout of the early schooling patterns of shared nursery and boarding-school spaces. One of my Cambridge professional colleagues confessed as much in a performance review session he requested with me when his aloofness was jeopardizing his peer relationships on the staff.

Spatial spheres of privacy, territoriality, or "personal bubbles" as individual preserves have been popularized by science writers, including Robert Ardrey and Edward deBono, as useful metaphors to describe patterns of behavior. These are established by culture and learning in the form of zones of encounter and communication. A chairman of the board wishing to improve his board effectiveness needs to bridge the psychic moat surrounding his various board members.

Boardroom Kinemes

The tableau of territorial behavior is evident in all interactional territories—including the boardroom. Here's a typical scenario, not hypothetical but a composite of similar scenes I have observed in boardrooms these many years.

The scene begins with the early arrival of a single director. Bob, in a display of preparatory rites, takes off his Aquascutum topcoat and carefully hangs it up in the boardroom cloak closet. He places his Cross slim leather briefcase on the table by his regular seat at the board table. No one would dare take his position, which is to the left of the chairman at the end of a long oval teak table. He places his folded *London Financial Times* on the table, obviously already read from cover to cover and folded to a specially pertinent section. He removes his Ben Franklin spectacles, checks his pocket handkerchief, gets a glass of water to place at his territorial spot, and then begins the greeting ritual.

Bob's territory is safely held by his body and his possessions. A couple of directors, previously situated at the other end of the room and engaged in conversation, join Bob, forming a threesome. Bob stands about a yard away while the other two are only a few inches apart from each other, touching each other now and then by either elbows or a hand on the other's arm while gesticulating. Anthropologists watching this scene would recognize the Anglo-Saxon ancestral tendency to use about a square yard of uncrowded space when conversing casually. Bob is Irish-American with a penchant for things British and a strong sense of hierarchical relationships, spatial boundaries, and psychic tolerances.

The other board members drift into the boardroom and exchange salutations. The accompanying communicative body motions or "body politics" are called "kinesics" by Roy L. Birdwhistell, who, in 1952, introduced the notion that communication is not unidimensional, confined to a single sensory channel, but is a multichannel continuous process making use of all the sensory modalities including "body language." A single "kineme" of posture or gesture is a strategic and manipulative use of body language as part of a communication pattern. The greeting kinemes of board members when they enter the boardroom vary from the hearty type to the overly restrained greeting, stressing individualism and feigned independence supposedly required of a proper director. The formula may include maintenance of social distance, civil inattention, or mutual benign neglect. An anthropologist, disguised as a fellow director, would determine the spatial boundaries and psychic tolerances in this pre-meeting social scene by directly and willfully approaching and intruding on others until signs of stress, avoidance, or flight occur.

Michael Argyle and Janet Dean have proposed an "approach-avoidance" theory of proximity.* This theory holds that persons are both attracted to and repelled by others and accordingly tend to place themselves in an "equilibrium position" vis-à-vis those encountered. Experiments show pairs of subjects tend to lean backward when they are two feet apart and unconsciously tend to lean forward when they are ten feet apart—apparently trying to seek proper spatial balance.

As a guideline to sartorially sensitive directors, we must heed other findings about interpersonal approaches and confrontations in more open settings and the role of sensory stimulation. Some interesting research on this matter is pertinent to the clothing choice of a director. At an amusement park, "stimulus persons" wearing brightly colored clothing caused persons standing in queues waiting for rides to stand farther away from the stimulus person than from persons wearing more conservative clothes. Persons also stood farther away when stimulus persons used perfume or aftershave lotion than when they used none, even when the aromatic individual was of the opposite sex.†

A recent way out of the dilemma of whether to use or not to use perfume or lotion is available thanks to the 1979 creation by two Kansas City respiratory therapists who produced a Clone Cologne as the ideal gift for St. Valentine's Day. A lemon-scented fragrance "especially blended to be bland" comes in a thirty-millimeter serum vial with an illustrated booklet explaining cloning. ("It takes sex out of the bedroom and into the laboratory where it belongs.") All for $4.99. "Just splash on some science," the advertisement says, "and dare to be dull!"

As Bob, our hypothetical director, and others proceed with getting through the board meeting drill, they engage in a series of little standoffs and negotiated settlements of points lost or scored, of

---

* Michael Argyle, *Social Interaction* (New York: Atherton, 1969).

† Paul D. Nesbitt and Gerard Steven, "Personal Space and Stimulus Intensity at a Southern California Amusement Park," *Sociometry* 37 (1974), pp. 105–115.

confrontations met or evaded, of bargains struck, of tensions or embarrassments accommodated. One study of the silent struggles of social interaction collected at least 1,000 "specimens of embarrassment" which were classified into seventy-four categories of *faux pas* or *gaffes*. These were ultimately summarized into three clusters: "(1) inappropriate identity, (2) loss of poise, (3) disturbance of the assumptions persons make about one another in social transactions."*

These categories of embarrassment are all present in one of my favorite stories about three Englishmen getting into the compartment of a train to Liverpool. Once inside they proceeded to introduce themselves. The first gentleman said, "I am a brigadier general, retired, married with two sons, both of whom are professors." The second gentleman then spoke up and said, "I'm a brigadier general, married, with two sons, both of whom are physicians." The third man said, "I'm a sergeant, not married but have two sons, both of whom are brigadier generals."

Rent-a-Peer

Humorist Bob Orben recalls, "When I was a kid my mother always told me to wear clean underwear in case I got in an accident—and it's affected my entire life. To this day, I still have the feeling that if I'm in an accident, the first things the cops are going to ask for are my driver's license, Blue Cross card, and shorts."

This parental guidance on coping with peer pressure is only one end of the process or system of peer recognition. In an effort to overcome the modesty of wealthy British peers, Andrew Roth, Research Director of Parliamentary Profiles, a New Yorker gone Britisher as a political journalist and biographer, computed (over a decade) a comprehensive register, *Lord on the Board* (1972 edition), of the full economic context of the House of Lords. He estimates over a quarter of the 200 millionaires in Great Britain are peers! Peers of the realm consist of various orders—duke, marquess, earl, viscount, and baron. All are entitled to sit in the House of Lords. The word "peer" is from the Latin *pares* ("equals"), and in feudal times all great vassals were held in equal rank.

* Edward Gross and Gregory O. Stone, "Embarrassment and the Analysis of Role Requirements," *People in Places: The Sociology of the Familiar*, Arnold Birenbaum and Edward Saragin, eds. (New York: Praeger, 1973).

In his introduction, "Why the Boards Have a Lord," Roth comments that the use of peers to add cachet or respectability to a board has long been practiced by companies ranging from the dodgiest of speculative ventures to the most respectable of firms.

This habit is so distinctly British that visiting Americans have tried to cash in on it. One set up a sort of "rent-a-peer" outfit, Noble Directors. He would offer a list of vetted peers, in the hope of securing for them between 100 and 250 guineas per directorship, of which he would retain 30 percent as his cut.

Peer acceptance is a strange part of the process. It is full of mystique at times and strange practices. The literati are no exception. The English humor magazine *Punch* was founded in 1841 and quickly established a custom of weekly editorial meetings cum banquets. These were held around "the Mahogany Tree," a long table so called after a poem by William Makepeace Thackeray. These meetings continue to this day and are marked by witty banter, horseplay, and ribald limericks. A certain chosen few are invited to carve their initials into the table, a peer acceptance honor that has been accorded to only seventy-nine persons over the lifetime of the magazine.

The *Punch* table is not the only teak table where only peer-acceptable members of the elitist establishment have their named places. For some inexplicable reason, members of the board of directors of Monsanto have a six-by-one-inch silver engraved nameplate embedded in a magnificent teak table, marking the solemn seating spot designated for each director. Upon retirement as a director from Monsanto, I was given my silver plate as a memento. It now elaborates a chest in my den, where peer pressure is reduced to spouse relationships.

Peer Perspectives

Peer power is the subtle force behind our eagerness to send postcards to all our friends (peers) when we arrive at an exotic place. This peer force is also manifest in the well-meaning but egocentric practice of sending a mimeographed family form letter at Christmas with details of intimate family and sibling activities, telling more than anyone wants to know about your yearly situation.

Peer power is a substantial factor in academic, military, scientific, and some government spheres. I was surprised to hear of the recent abandoning of peer evaluations at the Naval Academy through some personal three-way correspondence with James F. Calvert, Vice Admiral, USN (Ret.), and Robert W. McNitt, Rear Admiral, USN (Ret.), Dean of Admissions, United States Naval Academy, Annapolis, Maryland. It was the opinion of the responsible officers that peer evaluations had some value if used only once or twice, but rapidly lost validity if continued for a long period of time. Evaluations did not change much over several years, and there was some concern that a low rating initially could become a self-fulfilling prophecy. To quote Admiral McNitt, with permission, "The elimination of peer evaluations has had no significant adverse effects and has been very popular with midshipmen. A third of the Brigade Officers felt that there was a loss of useful data, but that it was not worth the effort required to obtain it; another third felt that there was not appreciable effect. One sixth of the officers felt that there was appreciable loss of useful data from the elimination of peer evaluations and another sixth recommended a partial return to the use of peer evaluations."

Peer ratings are used both as predictors and as criterion measures, although the latter use is not very encouraging. Operational use of peer ratings as criterion measures in the Navy, Army, metropolitan police forces, and board of directors is considered somewhat premature.

Use of peer ratings as predictors of performance has had some impressive success, although it is no longer employed at the Naval Academy. I agree with the Naval Academy findings that reuse of this type of rating is not warranted. It presents other problems even beyond the potential self-fulfilling prophecy problem cited by Admiral McNitt.

Some of these complicating problems are the role of friendship, subgroup (clique) formation, stereotypes, and implicit theories of personality, which disadvantage new persons introduced to the intact group or board, and difficulty in understanding peer ratings before using them formally. Despite all these problems, perhaps the greatest untapped potential for use of peer ratings is as a source of performance feedback. This is a tricky process to use in an acceptable manner for most groups, and particularly for a board of directors.

It is now being used effectively on two boards—one college board and one chemical industry company board—that I am familiar with through the mechanism of the organization committee of the board. Annual reviews of members of the board are informally but rigorously carried out by the outside-director committee members, the chairman, and the chief executive. Some directors have been allowed to resign after negative ratings; others have shaped up their interest and/or attendance after a low peer rating.

Statutory Senility

Bylaws of many publicly held corporations provide for compulsory retirement from the board of directors at age seventy or seventy-two. Many also require employee directors to go off their own board when they retire as an employee—normally at age sixty-five. This "statutory senility" has nothing to do with mental competence or other directorship attributes, but is a good safety-valve arrangement provided by companies to force succession of directors. One New York company with which I am familiar has no compulsory retirement, but provides earphones, medical care, and special aides to assist the two more ancient members of its board.

Everyone is expected to be gracious upon being elected to a board, to behave graciously while serving, and to retire graciously, although there is certainly no education provided in any board-room I know of on how to perform in such a manner. At last count there were more than seventy books written on retirement, but none tackles the decoupling of a director from his or her boardlife. A director is supposed to know how to be gracious, even though being ungracious may be more natural and more comfortable as we get older.

Geriatric counselors, practically none of whom has reached sixty-five, have little to offer those who think it is more rewarding, and a lot more fun, to approach statutory senility somewhat ungra-ciously. To meet this growing need there are a few ploys that are already in use among some directors who are pejoratively classed as being in the ungracious, near-statutory-senility status. If you, too, would be ungracious without being destructive, try these tactics:

- Insist on always having minutes of the last meeting read before indicating your approval. Better still, ask for several minor corrections.
- Cultivate eccentricity or the appearance thereof. Pretend not to remember a fellow director you have always heartily disliked. Get your secretary or spouse to respond to in-quiries about engagements with "Please forgive old Bob—he's a bit forgetful these days." Be crotchety.
- Increase extravagance when on board duty. Run up room-service charges; travel first-class or Concorde only; ask for a certain chauffeur to meet you when arriving for board or committee meetings. Seldom will a company question director expense accounts or requests for service. Suggest using—for your next directors' meeting in California—the private limo service in Santa Barbara. It offers the "world's longest limousine," a $200,000, thirty-two-foot 1967 Cadil-lac, an estimated 450-horsepower vehicle featuring a spa, rumble seat, sunroof, microwave oven, color television, sink, and bar.
- Dress more flamboyantly at board meetings. Drop the con-servative, dark pinstripes you wore when struggling for peer recognition in favor of casual jackets, Oleg Cassini

luggage, and Hush Puppies or Gucci loafers.

- Question the year and bouquet of the board dinner wine with some arcane oenological opinions. Send a bottle back occasionally—no one will dare challenge your pleasure or palate.
- Occasionally refuse to make certain board actions or resolutions unanimous. Feature your fiduciary, disinterested, unaffiliated, independent role as an outside director by abstaining or asking for a negative vote to be minuted in your name.
- Ask the CEO who are the key minority and female persons in the top management development ranks, and when the board can be exposed to them. But retain your reluctance to seriously consider similar candidates for board membership.
- When the chairman's and CEO's annual compensation package of high salary, stock options, bonus, special expense reimbursement, or other perquisites are up for token ratification, indicate no quarrel with the proposed amounts but raise the general public relations issue of the trend toward unconscionable take-home pay of executives of large publicly held firms. Allude to the growing public, shareholder, and government dismay at the multimillion-dollar-a-year hired hands, so enriched while the shareholders get pennies per share. (Do not let this questioning interfere with any proposed increase in director fees. Use the old U.K. gag about British director compensation: "If you pay in peanuts, you must expect monkeys!")
- Occasionally request a change in a long-established board meeting date on the basis that it conflicts with Mardi Gras, Veterans Day, Martin Luther King Day, or, if you're on a multinational board, Boxing Day.
- Surprise the CEO with an unanswerable question in open board meeting and thus set in motion the damnedest preparation for the next meeting. At the subsequent meeting, indicate waning interest in the topic.
- Suggest an ad hoc committee of the board be formed to poke into management's "underwear." Sensitive topics include director and management succession, long-term strategy, capital appropriation follow-up of expected earn-

ings on past project approvals, ethics in foreign operations, executive benefits programs, and corporate aircraft justification. Remember that every outside director, and particularly a senior one, has a management scheme or suggestion that will not work.

- Avoid arguments with fellow directors. If challenged, fire a series of irrelevant questions at your antagonist and intently polish your glasses while he tries to answer. As an alternate, hum under your breath while examining your fingernails.
- Exhibit international savvy. Inquire as to the company's African–Middle East export strategy, and the impact of Eastern Bloc technology regarding the current unrest in the Democratic Republic of São Tomé and Principe, the State of Comoros, or some remote former U.K. South Pacific colony such as Tuvalu or the Kingdom of Tonga.
- Have something to say on every subject. A sign of age is when you know all the answers even though nobody asks you any questions.
- Listen while other directors wrangle. Pluck out a platitude and defend it righteously. Be a little right of where center was at the last meeting.
- Pursue the trend toward consultant retainer agreements for retired directors whose accumulated knowledge is deemed important to the company served. Twenty-nine of the nation's 500 largest corporations grant financial retirement benefits to outside members of their boards as of 1982.
- Press for spouse inclusion in board activities. Suggest exotic locations for investment or plant familiarization gambits or for shareholder relations purposes. But remember, you can never really get away from boardroom problems—you can only take the board somewhere else.
- When asked to review a draft policy paper or a sensitive set of meeting minutes, write comments with a red pen to frighten the author or secretary. More subtly, put a hazy line by the side of a paragraph and write in softest pencil in the margin, "logic?" Or, scatter the word "relevance?" in various places. Add the single word "conclusions?" on the cover letter.
- Bring up trade or clubhouse-originated rumors about com-

petitive firms, without offering details. Bug the management by asking what they think about such improbable
threats and gossip.

- Muse openly about director and officer liability insurance
  and whether it adequately covers kidnapping, ransom, and
  hijacking exposure of the outside directors and their families.
- Open up Pandora's charitable trust box by seeking an un-
  scheduled review of amount and propriety of corporate
  support of the charities, of which you take a dim view because of their bureaucracy or public policy on some issue
  dear to your heart.
- Forestall signing the 10K statement at the end of the year
  until the last minute, and until you can have your attorney
  study the implications to you as a responsible independent
  director.
- In the course of some meeting, manage to doze off early
  and later to be called out during a critical moment to answer a call from your secretary.

As Gypsy Rose Lee used to say in her later years, "I have everything I had when I was twenty-one—but it's all lower than it used
to be." The good news is that your retirement party will be all the
more appreciated if you have been somewhat ungracious before
statutory senility sets in. Finally, take solace that it's better to be an
ex-director than a former pope.

14

How to Get the Best Out of Boards of Large Companies

Now that I hope you are on board with me we can sum up seriously some seldom-cited limitations that exist behind the boardroom door. "Do Not Disturb" signs are off many boardroom doors in these United States. The corporate creature known as the board of directors is also stirring. The question is how corporate boards will transform their roles to improve their effectiveness.

The general public believes that directors represent wealth and power. Little has occurred to change this historical image. An open system is required for a board to remain relevant to the economic, political, and social environment. This is vital in these complex times if the social franchise granted the corporation is continually justified in the public perception.

One high-technology company chairman acquaintance of mine became so upset recently at a *Fortune* article about his company's lack of social responsibility that he threatened to sue the publisher. The public criticism apparently hit a tender spot which was also troubling several of the outside directors, who had been nervous, if silent, about certain corporate practices and policies. The chairman brought up the critical article at a board meeting in an emotional outburst. He threatened to take legal action, drop advertising in the magazine, and cancel all subscriptions by directors and employees. The board session calmed him down, but it was interesting to note that at the next proxy time the most outspoken of the nonexecutive directors, who had agreed with *Fortune*'s assessment, did not stand for reelection. Apparently there was a mutual agreement between the chairman and the "errant" director that his services were no longer welcome and his continued presence on the board was not going to significantly change the attitude of the board on this socially sensitive issue in the immediate future. As a sequel to this incident, the board role in related social activities is very slowly being improved, despite the first internal management and chairman reactions. The power of the press is evident.

Singular economic operational definition of a corporation (such as profit-seeking being the only goal) is a heritage reflected in the behavior of many boards. Such boards are inadequately positioned for governing in an interactive environment. However, interdependence among institutions and other public sectors abounds. Larger companies are particularly affected by these interactions with governmental, community, educational, environmental, and consumer interests (i.e., the stakeholders), and must cope with multiple forces and objectives.

In keeping with their twentieth-century role, most corporations do bear increasing responsibility to their various publics. For example, those industries that abuse the environment must correct their methods or face the consequences mandated by both government and the occasionally vengeful public it represents. One could say it's a situation in which there's nothing to fear but atmosphere itself. The ultimate responsibility to achieve this pollution cleanup

falls on the shoulders of corporate directors. In the eighteenth century, Charles James Fox, leader of the English Whigs, averred that "the right of governing is not a property, but a trust." This trust in the political world is a long-term, continuous one. It nettles business leaders, who too often focus on quarterly earnings and on a single economic criterion.

Corporate governance concepts and processes are undergoing transformation to adapt to changes in (a) the role and nature of boards, (b) the boundary or compass of board concern, (c) board structure and board processes, and (d) board renewal and development. These dynamics are for the most part evolutionary and company-specific. Changes are often subtle. How to make directors pay attention to these issues is the problem. One marketing-oriented director friend suggests the best way to get your message to your board is to advertise on swizzle sticks. More seriously, there are at least eight limitations that directors must learn to cope with.

Limitation One: Boardroom Boundaries

Boards of directors tend to draw boundaries around their domain with more dogmatism than experience or good conduct warrants— for example, boundaries between the board and management, or between the corporation and its environment. Boards are often closed systems similar to the command-and-control, closed system characteristic of the conventionally structured management system. A board is perceived to be a closed domain, but it must be open to opportunity and relations to the outside world—like the basketball coach's office with its sign on the door reading, "This office is closed, but if you can see over the transom, come in."

Open systems allow information, beliefs, intuition, attitudes, aspirations, value systems, and needs to continuously flow across any boundary which identifies the system. Such a perspective causes traditional boundaries of a board to become irregular and fuzzy. Beliefs, attitudes, and values may enter the board process and appear to be in conflict with the traditional notions of the board's internal rationality.

In 1978, Allied Corporation (then Allied Chemical Corporation) created a board-level committee on environmental affairs. Outside directors made up the committee, which employed an outside consultant regularly to audit environmental compliance of various operations of the company. The boundary of this board's concern now reaches into what was historically a separate management domain. Given the environmental cleanup situation Allied found itself in at some of its plant locations, I believe this change in board-level boundary of concern was an outstanding example of how to cope with the classical tendency of boards to draw boundaries around too narrow a compass of concern.

Growing interest in overseas markets is reflected in the increased number of chairmen and CEOs of foreign companies being elected to Fortune 100 boards. A 1981 survey by Deloitte, Haskins & Sells revealed one in five of these companies now have international directors. The boardroom's reach or compass of concern is becoming more global. Where it is not practical to have foreign nationals on boards, because of the time and travel requirements, the boundary of the parent board interest can be extended by the creation of regional advisory boards, tapping the wisdom and experience of distinguished directors locally available on a more relaxed board meeting schedule. Chase Manhattan has twenty members on a worldwide advisory board. Other firms with international advisory boards are General Motors, Westinghouse, IBM, Exxon, R. J. Reynolds Industries, Sperry Rand, Corning Glass Works, W. R. Grace, AMF, CPC International, and Merck. Swiss Banking Corporation, Volvo, and Thyssen come to mind as companies with headquarters in Europe and with international advisory directors.

The International Telephone and Telegraph board reaches out into social and other external domains through its board-level "corporate public policy committee." This group of directors concerns itself with examining IT&T's corporate position and policy on all major public issues, exemplifying a definite extension of the boundary of concern of the boardroom.

My advice to board chairmen who recognize the tendency of their board to close its boundaries around too narrow a scope of concern is to heed the ancient Chinese proverb: The shrike hunting the locust is unaware of the hawk hunting him. Public and government hawks will get the corporation that fails to fulfill its broad social responsibility.

Limitation Two: Board Nature

Many boards do not explicitly allow for the often bewildering options open to directors in decisions they face in governing a corporation. In many cases there is no one "right" answer to a problem or question requiring the board's resolution. It is often the wisest course to offer a fix that recognizes the fact that a decision will not be carved in stone, will not please anyone totally, but *will* recognize and allow for the ambiguity of a given solution. The current debate over acid rain is an example. To completely eliminate high sulfur emissions from coal-burning power plants entails a high capital cost which cannot be borne by the individual plants without unacceptable economic impact. The issue is whether consumers of the products produced from the power supplied or the owners of the power plant should pay for this remedial scrubbing of stack gases or conversion to low-sulfur fuel. The solution probably will be to gradually cut down the level of stack emissions and move progressively in the direction of an alternative energy program. A somewhat ambiguous resolution will undoubtedly be adopted. Ambiguity of decision-making may be an asset in certain instances where international relationships, political considerations, and tolerance of conflicting attitudes are important to recognize in thinking of multiple causation rather than single causes.

A study published in 1980 of ninety senior executives interviewed at General Mills, Pillsbury, Exxon, Continental Group, Xerox, Pilkington, General Motors, Chrysler, and Volvo revealed an explicit rationale for leaving strategic pronouncements in a somewhat fuzzy state.* The respondents preferred ambiguity in strategic declarations to avoid (a) undesired centralization, (b) focusing otherwise fragmented opposition, (c) rigidity which closes down options and makes explicit goals hard to change, and (d) breaches of security on sensitive plans.

An example of the positive use of ambiguity occurred in an assignment I had last year with the chairman-CEO of an East Coast industrial firm. With retirement coming in three years, the chairman-CEO was undecided about which of three internal candidates should be nominated to be his successor in the CEO position. We developed a careful rotation plan over a two-year period in which the three executives had to adjust to new roles, new power structures, and new interpersonal relationships. Before eighteen months

* James Brian Quinn, *Strategies for Change: Logical Incrementalism* (Homewood, Ill.: Richard D. Irwin, 1980).

had passed, one had blown his chances by his insensitivity to the politics of his new assignment, another had the misfortune of a health problem, and the third did well and was given the CEO position. Leaving the choice ambiguous for this period uncovered the best selection for the board to make.

Another case of ambiguous design at the board level took place when the board of a high-technology company in Massachusetts spun off three of its most promising new developments into separate organizational entities (two were freestanding divisions, one was a corporation) with separate advisory or statutory boards and an established line of credit from the parent company. Separate compensation schemes, with equity participation for those in responsible charge, added specific motivation. The chemical process venture (which was the incorporated strategic business unit), the project management services company, and the mining division unit all substantially stepped up their growth within three years. The decentralization and flexibility afforded by leaving strategic guidance by the parent company in an unclear state and relying on the decoupled, strategic options to be properly pursued at the decentralized level might be called fuzzy or ambiguous governance. However, it served the purpose of retaining multiple degrees of freedom for overall development of the parent corporation's multiple interests.

Few boards explicitly address and recognize multiple corporate objectives, multiple criteria, multiple standards, and the conflicts, tensions, and stress inherent in such pluralism. Arthur D. Little, Inc., is a unique international research and consulting organization in this respect, and the board has to deal with this multiplicity. While our core business is consulting, we do more than that. The firm undertakes research, organizes and produces information in actionable form, manages intellectual property, helps people in adversary or negotiating situations, and transfers technology. Our goals are multiple: serving clients well, building professional effectiveness, and offering fulfilling careers to members of the company staff, improving profitability to at least 5 percent of revenues, and providing a return on investment to our shareholders of better than 15 percent of equity invested in the business.

Boards generally exist as collectives. As such they are somewhat vague, inconsistent bodies in terms of a few bylaws, policies, practices, and decisions. The latter are reached by a group pondering extensively together on matters inherited or presented to them and which they can understand.

Despite the difficulty in focusing philosophies, aspirations, visions, and flexible strategies on multiple criteria, there is an increasing number of larger companies going public with their corporate aims. One of the more recent was 3M in a July 1981 annual meeting statement by chairman-CEO Lewis W. Lehr. A four-part "goals and objectives" statement covered 3M's corporate principles respecting profit and growth, products and customers, human resources and citizenship. While these aims are clear enough, the trade-offs required for major corporate decisions remain properly ambiguous to permit the corporation to use its multi-perspective board powers when a choice situation arises.

I find it interesting that most board members I know find themselves psychologically compelled to demand that responsible, full-time management present issues at a level of simplicity suited to the needs of those in the boardroom. Because a director has to demand concreteness and clarity of the management, he gives up, in his own mind, some of his right to elegance and rigor, and dispenses with the uncertainties that are generated by elegance and rigor in order to face open-ended, messy reality. Such is the role of a director.

Given the short time allowed for decision-making and the few people who can be forcefully convincing while being (perhaps spuriously) concrete in their drive to reduce uncertainty and ambiguity, an interesting consequence is set up in the boardroom. The importance of forcefulness tends to be overvalued in setting criteria for nominating and later evaluating board members. The result is that relatively few less overtly forceful, perceptive, intuitive right-brain-oriented directors wind up in boardroom seats compared to the more logical, rational, quantitative left-brain-oriented types of directors. These latter tend to be more convincing personalities. These directors sound "harder" and are more specific in their style of directorship.

I am also especially alert to the fact that boards have difficulty in coping with multiple objectives, criteria, and standards. This is true unless they have available to them (and have accepted) some version of what is known as general systems theory. This theory de-

mands explicitness about the equilibrium in a system between input and output to the system. In turn this makes it hard to avoid noticing how much strain is placed on the system when any small selection of inputs or outputs are attended to without regard for the consequences to other inputs and outputs that are also part of the overall system.

A poignant example of neglect of the total system is the recent case of a Midwestern company which decided to reduce overhead by cutting out all corporate vice-presidents. They were assigned to various subsidiary companies, and the top side of the parent corporation adopted a holding company model. This made sense to the board and top corporation executives, but was a drastic shock to the de-veeped staff sent to the "farm clubs." One executive vice-president tried to sell this defrocking to one of his previous vice-president subordinates by stressing the increased freedom, power, and stature identified with the particular service company to which he was assigned. This effort was to no avail, as the individual was so shaken that two months after the action he had not yet told his wife, who he knew couldn't socially face her peers now that her husband was no longer a corporation vice-president. A year afterward the damage to the egos involved had still not been repaired.

According to my friend Edward O. Vetter, director of Western Co. of North America, an oilfield drilling company in Dallas, this trimming of the corporate hierarchy, by putting overhead employees to work in the operating levels, is like hitching your pet bull to a plow to show him life is not all romance. John A. Fanning, president of the company, terms putting his corporate officers to work in field operations as making them "load-bearing" employees.

Limitation Three: Board Life Cycles

All boards have a life cycle of their own, and the stage in the life cycle represented by the board's condition may not be congruent with the life cycle(s) of the corporation served or the strategic business units involved in a diversified enterprise.

Board life cycle depends upon the nature and composition of board membership, the respective maturity and group experience of directors in working together. Within the boardroom, directors have either an explicit or implicit contract (or conflict) with others within the collective unit. This relationship is either a social, intellectual, or emotional contract, or a mix of these. As a consequence, directors are bound together by sharing the same fate of directing an institution as stewards, trustees, or fiduciaries in an uncertain environment. The problem with some boards is that they are in a declining state of effectiveness, and inaction is the consequence. They often act like the annual conference of clairvoyants who canceled their meeting because of unforeseen circumstances.

The maturity of the board may be classified in the conventional embryonic, growth, mature, or aging stages. These stages reflect the sophistication and capacity of the board to deal with the life cycle dynamics and conditions of the enterprise. For example, the company being governed may be in a start-up or a declining survival mode, a rapid development and growth mode, or a mature, defensive mode. The optimal situation is when the competence and attitudes of the board are tuned into the governance needs of the corporation served. Congruency of the maturity of the board and the maturity of the corporation is important.

Massachusetts Mutual Life Insurance Company, like many other large companies, has a committee on organization and operations of the board of directors. Matters of composition, organization, operations, functions, and procedures of the board and its committees are handled, along with the nomination, evaluation, and reelection of directors. Needs of the company vary at the board level, and the director succession is so planned.

IT&T has a "committee on directors" which establishes criteria for board membership and committees, determines the target number and composition of the board, recommends director compensation, annually reviews qualifications and effectiveness of incumbent directors, and reviews retirement policies and board processes. The criteria and standards are congruent with the company's needs in the boardroom.

Limitation Four: Board Renewal

Renewal, succession, and continuity of a board of directors is as vital as for key management. Unfortunately, sometimes director recruitment, education, development, evaluation, separation, and succession are neglected processes. The only practice worse than this neglect is for a board to finish things they never should have started, like mixing spouses too frequently in connection with board affairs, particularly executive staff and director cocktail parties, where the real business is either to look out for a wife, to look after a wife, or look after somebody else's wife.

The plain facts are that the role of the board is often unclear and not fully accepted in many situations. Crises, takeovers, and succession struggles are the usual exceptions. The conventional functions of governance generally described as legitimatizing, oversight, monitoring, auditing, and general strategic direction are often dominated by strong management or owner interests.

Separation of governance from management through a well-defined role for the board is yet to be universally and realistically accepted in many firms. This is particularly true of closely held corporations, small and medium-sized companies where stakeholder or commonweal interests may not yet be fully acknowledged.

One of the major causes of failure of the timely renewal of a board is dominance by a chairman who is also CEO, and who is unwilling to give up the dual role. The compensation, perquisites, prestige, and power which go with the chief executive role are understandably hard to replace or relinquish. When the chairman-CEO, with or without inside director support, dominates his or her board to the extent that outside directors do not force timely board renewal, then corporate governance suffers.

The best way I have found to handle this situation is to convince the chairman and the board that an assessment of the strategic condition of the business be made by outside, independent experts. If this assessment is done properly, the need for strategic changes and for a board and management process to implement such changes will become evident. This will call for a shift in power and a plan for succession of the CEO in order to carry out the long-term aspects of the new plan.

Closely held corporations have a special problem in this regard. Luckily for shareowners and employees, the general trend is toward more outside, independent directors. A 1981 Deloitte, Haskins & Sells survey showed 88 percent of public companies surveyed had a majority of nonmanagement directors versus 65 percent ten years ago. The next challenge is to encourage outside directors to be more independent and to fulfill their role properly by forcing timely board renewal. The SEC requirement for an audit committee of the board composed of outside directors and the general trend toward a nominating committee of outside directors are examples of this initiative.

Limitation Five: Board Process

The researcher's motto fits here: If we knew what we were doing it wouldn't be research. In the boardroom, if we knew the answers we wouldn't be governing. Governance processes do not necessarily match those processes which are most effective in resolving issues in the management realm. Board functions differ significantly from those of management. The latter are hierarchically oriented. Management decision processes are judicial and directive in nature, with allocation of power and accountability.

Governance, in contrast, is achieved in a nonhierarchical form. Political processes and peer processes are at work in the boardroom. Consensus is strived for. Differences in opinion are (or should be) encouraged. Meshing this governance process with the management process requires a "system of systems" to provide proper operational linkage of the systems for financial control and strategic decisions, power flow, and information feedback.

An important dimension of board service is the matter of ade-

quate information being available to the board to allow it to fulfill
its role in auditing, monitoring, and strategic oversight of the company. Just what boards need to know varies with the maturity of
the company, the technology, the industry, and the competitive
position or target goal of the organization.

Clearly presented, objective, pertinent information furnished
well in advance of board meetings, and on a continuous basis, is
vital in order for directors to carry out their responsibilities as
directors. A recent study of 394 corporations revealed that the
number of managements supplying their board of directors with
any advance information was increasing and is now up to 80 percent. There is general agreement that the information a director
needs to know on a regular basis includes at a minimum:

- A statement of corporate objectives which is up-to-date
- A review of historical results for perspective
- An explicit statement of strategy and alternative business
  plans
- A statement of financial strategy, current financial results
  properly analyzed, and a forecast of near-term outlook
- Management succession strategy and plans
- Significant changes in shareholdings and market price, and
  trading trends of the stock
- Litigation underway or threatened
- Legal or regulatory changes or trends potentially affecting
  the future of the company
- Important operating matters such as technology, labor relations, supply, distribution, quality, environmental assurance, production costs, and significant customer or
  competitive events which are likely to have an impact

These information needs ebb and flow in importance depending
on environmental, political, and social changes and the state of development of a company. For example, in a start-up situation the
board may need to know more details about the stage of plant construction, process demonstration, new customer prospects, cash
flow problems, competitive inroads, and many other elements of
running the business. As a company grows and develops its momentum and its survival is insured for the immediate future, other

problems of strategic direction, international markets, employee training, and management development may rise in importance from a director's viewpoint as proper areas to monitor and provide oversight. The trick is to avoid information overload and yet keep the board members well informed only on those matters they need to know to perform responsibly in their governance role.

More corporations are engaging their boards actively in strategic thinking as the restructuring of industrial and business sectors takes place during trying economic and political times. Retreats and facilities tours for the entire board to review long-range plans are becoming routine with many companies. Examples are Texas Instruments, Massachusetts Mutual, Cabot Corporation, Milton Bradley, Mead Corporation, and Monsanto. The difference between a smart board and a dumb board isn't that smart directors don't make mistakes; they just don't keep making the same mistakes over and over again. A proper board process will help avoid mistakes by aerating differences in judgment and allowing debate.

Limitation Six: The Temporal Dimension

Boards tend to be occupied with what is for the present or short-term future. Many tend to confirm the status quo. But time and tide wait for no board; the need for timely governance persists.

The values of busy and effective directors are often satisfied by the pragmatic occupation with immediate matters. These are dealt with incrementally, building on a base of the status quo. Incrementalism is, in itself, a way to ignore and thereby reduce uncertainty. The problem is that boardroom incrementalism becomes rather sheeplike in the kind of followership it induces. Sort of a "so many lemmings can't be wrong" attitude. Incrementalism is neither leadership nor true conservatism. Furthermore, it often fails to fulfill the criterion of directorship, which demands financial accountability, independent thinking, and freedom from conflict of interest— real or perceived.

I experienced a dramatic example of this incrementalism when in the mid-1960s I was on the board of Plax Canada Ltd. in Ontario. The company was jointly owned by American and Canadian companies. The board meetings were routine, enhanced by a sumptuous lunch which was always preceded by a long cocktail period at an elegant private men's club. The operations of the enterprise were primarily in the plastics-molding business, and the technical and marketing cues were transferred from U.S. experience with similar products. The Canadian directors were dominated by the American experience and followed the advice of the U.S. directors without much challenge. As a board, we dutifully introduced the same U.S. products and timed the expansion plans after the U.S. experience. This creeping response caused us to lose our leading position in the Canadian market, which had different dynamics.

Strategic planning is one antidote to incrementalism. It demands consideration of longer time spans. But many organizations act as though long-range planning were the complete answer and nonplanning were always irrational and bad. Devotion to the logical and analytical may not produce the best of all pathways. Some flexibility is needed for intuition and opportunism to be effective. Such openness coupled with plans considering alternative futures—and often some luck—can help deal with the time dimension.

The best example of flexibility and opportunism I know took place in 1950–1951 when Felix Williams, then a senior member of the Monsanto board, and I sought to establish a new subsidiary in the suburbs of São Paulo. The company was to produce vinyl chloride monomer and polymers for the booming plastics market in Brazil. We needed Brazilian partners and capital and succeeded in getting this commitment by appealing to wealthy Brazilians, the banks, and potential PVC customers. After we got the initial money deposited, we reestimated the cost of the project. Inflation rates were so high that the plant cost had doubled, and the Monsanto board rejected the project on economic grounds. I had the uncomfortable job of returning to Brazil with the bad news. We gave every investor his money back with full interest.

The surprise good news was strictly fortuitous. The land which we had purchased in Campinas for a plant site had quadrupled in value because of inflation in price of real estate and of the timber in its eucalyptus grove. We came out whole from a financial viewpoint, although our corporate commitment to Brazil suffered considerably.

Limitation Seven: Board Score

Boards do not often study or objectively examine the more elusive, ineffable, noncommensurable attributes of the domain of corporate governance. Characterizing, assessing, and evaluating board effectiveness and board gestalt is a formidable if delicate task. The limitation is that it is nobody's business to do the rating, except perhaps in those instances in which the chairman is also the CEO and an important stockholder in his or her own right. In most companies the board and the CEO are both, to an extent, creatures of the other. As a result, it is presumptuous for either to advance complicated ideas about the ineffable qualities of the board's activity.

Unfortunately, most academics, business analysts, consultants, journalists, and other board watchers are unaware, unqualified, viewed as self-interested, or without the standing necessary to tackle assessment of board effectiveness. This leaves board scoring up to the chairman and directors themselves. This, in turn, has a limitation in the nature of the learning process.

A few boards do in fact tackle the sensitive issue of individual boardworthiness and total board effectiveness. Most of such rating is subjective, informal, and seldom disclosed. One example of a more formal appraisal drill is that carried out by Adams Electric Cooperative Inc., of Gettysburg, Pennsylvania. The entire board appraises (with unsigned rating forms) the performance of each director and the board as a whole. Rather elaborate written forms are provided for describing each director's activities during the year, an analysis of board responsibilities, and a judgmental rating of how the board carried these out.

In addition, forms are provided for opinions on matters for the board to work on during the forthcoming year. This consists of a four-page, twenty-nine-item checklist, and is more than most directors would care to fill out. This system may be appropriate for this cooperative, but I would not recommend it for a corporate board.

Limitation Eight: Learning

Directors' personal mechanism of perception and cognition basically operate to limit sensory input so the individual can make sense of a data-rich world. Moreover, awareness of the experience and opinions of others also influences the director toward sensory input and meanings which are compatible with others' experience—which is what you get when you were expecting something else.

These learning processes serve a director by creating consistent frameworks from which to review the world and determine how to conduct oneself in it. Learning is involved as the organizing framework is modified to account for repeated exposure to experience not in accord with the original tenets of an individual director.

More formal learning situations are becoming fashionable for directors. Universities, colleges, professional associations, trade associations, consulting firms, publishing houses—all have jumped into the director seminar and corporate governance education field. Several New York organizations, the National Association of Corporate Directors, the Young Presidents' Association, the Conference Board, and the Cheswick Center in Boston, plus business schools across the land, are offering courses, materials, journals, books, seminars, and conferences on directorship. Corporate directors are going back to school to help bring themselves in tune with the changes underway in the boardworld.

Strangely, because of the prior seven limitations cited, boards are inclined to behave in ways that inhibit the learning process. To some extent this makes individual directors immobile—i.e., incapable of grasping, let alone grappling with, anything that is not forced on them by dramatic external events and pressures.

A board of directors of a company in Europe, which asked for help in redefining their role, given the changes taking place in the EEC, provides a recent example of immobility of a board inhibited by tradition and convention. This company was being strategically redirected in 1982 by the demands of its business, but the directors were resisting change. The firm was being governed as though it were a family-owned enterprise. What was good for the seven family owners—who originally controlled the company but who now controlled only 15 percent of outstanding shares—was considered good for the company. The board met weekly and delved into management matters far beyond a point where separate accountability could be maintained. The solution proved to be separation and definition of the respective roles of directors and managers, a reduction in meeting frequency, and a redirection of the board's attention more to externalities and linkage with outside stakeholder interests.

Boards often stand in the way of needed change. A more appropriate function of a board is of course to ease, simplify, and legitimize those change processes. Short-term demands within a hierarchy to routinize and otherwise focus on the business at hand are often in conflict with longer-term requirements for needed change.

Sometimes this board behavior sets up an unconscious and unnoticed polarization between senior management and the board. As such, each is dynamically forcing the other into positions that neither can productively nor exclusively occupy. These positions, for example, can place senior management where it believes it must contend with a status quo board. The board, in turn, gets signals that suggest the management may be inadequate or reactive. So the board gets more devoted to the status quo and those managers with vision get more frustrated.

Undoubtedly there are more than eight limitations to the current transformation of boards as they attempt to address the issues of the 1980s. The heartening aspect that I perceive is the level of consciousness about the need for changes in corporate governance, which is rising rapidly.

Some boards tend to be populated by directors having similar backgrounds, value systems, and perspectives, which exaggerate the tendency to conceptually close the board as a governance system. The worth of a board made up of directors with entirely different perspectives is improved when we introduce the governance theory of cultural propriety, as discussed in Chapter 15. Systems culture is important in all forms of human systems management. It affords a commonsense way of creating and representing knowledge about complex, interactive, interdependent, conflicting, changing, and even incommensurate conditions or situations.

Each perspective illuminates the strengths and weaknesses of others. The best performance of a board can be obtained when bridges are formed between the hard intellectual and the soft intellectual viewpoints on compounded economic-technological-social-cultural issues. The primary job of the chairman is to forge such linkages.

Perhaps better recognition of general systems theory can be a guiding beacon to help those behind the boardroom door to do a better job. Charles Dickens (in *Nicholas Nickleby*) referred to this systems notion as a "kind of universal dovetailness with regard to time and place." This approach affords an opportunity to those directors qualified to deal with system-sensitive thought patterns to work on solutions rather than being part of the problem of improving board effectiveness.

15

The God of Governance

Some thirty thousand gods on earth we find
Subjects of Zeus, and guardians of mankind.

HESIOD, i, 250

In Anglo-Saxon times, kings were elected by the witenagemot or "meeting of the wise" and, therefore, were the choice of the nation. In our high-tech, high-touch times, directors as the shareholders' sovereigns are elected by proxies at the annual general meeting. At that time the directors become the "wise" choice of the owners.

Frederick the Great's crack "They say kings are made in the image of God: I feel sorry for God if that is what he looks like" should be transposed to substitute directors for kings if we accept the growing public perception that directors are not up to their obligations in modern governance. Directors are our corporate gods of governance, whether they are up to such a godlike role or not. If this is so, then it is useful to look at boardroom culture as the garden of our gods of governance.

Divinity Fudging

The interesting thing about boards of directors is the relative absence of practical means of assessing effectiveness or any "godlike" conduct of the group. Self-assessment is as difficult for a directorate as it is for an individual. Some directors worry about this. Some fudge when they judge boardworthiness of themselves and fellow

219

directors. Others, notably professional directors, even manifest a godlike demeanor while failing to conform to the late Justice Brandeis's definition of a profession. Brandeis opined that a profession was "an occupation for which the necessary preliminary training is intellectual in character, involving knowledge and to some extent learning, as distinguished from mere skill ... which is pursued largely for others, and not merely for one's self ... and in which the financial return is not the accepted measure of success."°

° L. D. Brandeis, *Business: A Profession* (Boston: Small, Maynard, 1914), p. 2.

Given the frailties of human nature which exist in those of us chosen to be directors, we can get comfort in Cervantes's observation that "everyone is as God made him, and often a great deal worse." Hence, a little fudging now and then.

The Russians' governance god is the management scientist. No fudging is allowed in the system, which is centrally controlled and sovereign. The great gap between our and their approach to managing and to governing was brought home to me sharply at an international technical meeting in Cleveland, Ohio, in June 1969. Dr. T. J. Williams of Purdue University asked me to deliver the closing address to the International Federation of Automatic Control Symposium on Optimal Systems Planning, on the first occasion of this group's meeting on U.S. soil. The meeting was well attended by cyberneticists and systems experts from East and West Europe, the Asia-Pacific, the Soviet Union, and the Americas.

The address, which I called "The Managementality Gap," gave a top corporate viewpoint of the management science movement, focusing particularly on the problem of understanding and communications. Need for changes in attitude of scientists, executives, and directors, respect for their different value systems, the management scientist's tendency toward intellectual one-upmanship, and the executive's educational lag behind the advanced thinking of the scientist's each present challenges to the scientists and executives to manage themselves more properly before expecting to manage an organization.

These remarks were well received except by those in the Russian delegation, who made it a point after the meeting to respond that the scientists were not used to being talked to like this by a practitioner. Furthermore, they declined to accept the need to talk more simply to the mundane bureau director or manager. In essence, the Russian scientists made it clear that it was not their job to worry about the translation or application aspects to a practitioner; their charge was to forge ahead regardless of whether anyone followed. Their *system* is their god of governance.

Perhaps this response should not be confined to this situation nor to the Russian delegation's reaction. Certainly the Soviets may have a basis for this posture, considering the nature of the educational and institutional life in their social and political system. However, the sense of indignity apparent in the reaction from this sector of a sophisticated international audience may be symptomatic of a fundamental issue involved. The issue is one of the respective management and governance cultures involved.

A repertoire of perspectives is needed to appreciate the importantly different roots of good governance on the one hand and good management on the other. Governance and management each have their respective values, sanctions, norms, beliefs, articles of faith, symbols, dominant themes, and manifest behavior. This repertoire calls for a systems perspective, a holistic view of the two cultures involved.

Management Culture

Professor Charles Handy of the London Graduate School of Business Studies, now retired from his position as Warden of St. George's House in Windsor Castle, originated the notion of using Greek gods to symbolize the management culture in the mid-seventies. He shared his stimulating metaphysical thinking in his book *Gods of Management: Who They Are, How They Work and Why They Fail.*[*]

Professor Handy introduces four gods of management. The club culture was depicted by Zeus, the dynamic entrepreneur who ruled his empire on snap decisions. Apollo symbolized the realm of order and bureaucracy. Athena, the goddess of wisdom, of warfare, and of craftsmen, recognized only expertise on the basis of power and influence, and was the symbol of the skill-based culture. Dionysus was the god preferred by artists and professionals—those who owe little if any allegiance to a boss. Dionysus represented the existential culture.

These four distinctly different cultures exist in various degrees in a management system and, according to Professor Handy, are the roots of managerial and organizational difficulties.

Governance Culture

Taking Professor Handy's lead in symbolizing management culture and applying the notion to the open system domain of governance requires only a little slightly unorthodox application of the

[*] Charles Handy, London: Souvenir Press, 1978. Later edition, London: Pam Books, 1979.

Greek god metaphor. Since metaphors are based upon only partial truth, metaphor requires of its user a somewhat one-sided abstraction in which certain features are emphasized and others suppressed in a selective comparison.

One of the major metaphors in organization theory is that of the organism. The organism is used to refer to any system of mutually connected and dependent parts constituted to share a common life and focuses attention upon the nature of life activity. With main emphasis on open systems approach, the close interactive relationship between management and a board of directors, and the context in which it governs, determines continuity and survival of the entire enterprise system. While the interactive relationship between management and the board must be a close one, it must still be an independent, objective linkage to avoid group-think or lemminglike behavior. A poor role model in this regard is like the endorsement I heard in a TV testimonial: "In a recent impartial taste test among users of our products at random from employees of our advertising agency . . ."

Aristotle pointed out that every society needs a "wondrous tissue" of myth in which to develop its traditions and ideals. The boardroom society provides a rich source of "wondrous tissue" in which it develops its own governance culture. The nature of this board culture can be identified, if only a partial truth, with one of the most powerful figures in the ancient Greek imagination of their Olympian gods—Hermes.

But before relating Hermes to contemporary directorship we need to symbolize governance as a systems culture. To do this we tentatively accept some symbolism in order to conceptualize the board's open system of governance as embracing the closed management system. The systems culture represents a relatively stable datum from which directors can audit, monitor, direct, and lead an enterprise amid a galaxy of other institutions and forces.

Most of the canons and axioms of governance are elusive, ineffable, or subjective. The occult perception of directorship is further due in part to the privileged nature of board deliberations, the fuzzy criteria for boardworthiness, and the multiple roles of directors which are seldom understood by the public, or are explicitly incomplete. This makes a good dwelling place for Hermes, our governance patron.

One of the greatest of the twelve Olympian gods, Hermes was the son of Zeus and of Maia, the oldest and loveliest of the Pleiades, daughters of Atlas and Pleione. Hermes personifies the systems culture. Hermes was all things to all concerned, and his attributes were the most complex and varied of any of the major gods. As in all such sweeping contexts, there were positive and negative consequences or impacts of his all-encompassing scope of activities.

In creating the god Hermes, the Greeks endowed him with certain astrological attributes of the planet of whose influences he became the personification. I know one board chairman who blamed his company's cycling fortunes on the stars, an "excellent foppery of the world," to use King Lear's description of astrology. To continue with our patron, historians have long attributed the name of Hermes with a mystical significance implying wisdom—a primary quality of an effective director.

Hermes' scope of endeavors was vast and varied and embraced almost the entire system of Greek mythology. Hermes was responsible for a scattered array of assignments, even including increasing the animal world as a herd developer. He was the deity of wealth, of trade and travelers, of roads and commerce, of science, invention, oratory, eloquence, and even of manual skills. Patron of athletes, Hermes was also god of the wind, with the speed of which he was able to move. Representations of him in this role are symbolic of the hastener, the agent of change, with particular majesty in flight—leader, communicator, shaker, and mover. Looking the part is important for a god or a director; you can't lead the cavalry if you look funny on a horse.

Hermes was not above some conduct unbecoming a patron god of governance. On the first day of his life he stole Apollo's cattle and made a lyre and gave it to Apollo, who reciprocated by giving him the caduceus, a golden-winged staff with intertwining serpents—symbol of today's profession whose purpose is to prevent people from dying natural deaths. On the same day Hermes invented the *talaria*, or winged sandals, and then anticipated the Boy Scout movement in making fire by rubbing sticks together. This won father Zeus' approbation and a gift of that winged cap called *patasus*—the trademark of FTD Florists Transworld Delivery.

Even on the negative side, Hermes did things superbly. He was the deity of Thiene, and his son, Antolycus, became the champion thief of the world. Unfortunate for our metaphor, Hermes was further identified for his cunning, trickery, and luck in discovering treasure.

Further on the vulnerable side of his image, and despite all his talents, persuasion, and other powers, Hermes got into some socially unacceptable activities, notably theft. Happily our systems notion recognizes such transgressions and incompleteness of character as negative attributes and then must resort to the next higher level—the metalevel—for resolution of such behavior and conflict. This requires trade-offs, sacrifices, and curtailments which may be ethical, economic, social, or political, but not always emotionally acceptable to those involved in a governance system.

Such is the plight of anyone who is a director. Greek gods and corporate directors both possess weaknesses—some serious and some humorous. When I was an undergraduate I remember a question journalist Don Herold posed: "What do you suppose God thinks of a man (created in His own image) putting on his pants in an upper berth?" Alas, gone are those upper-berth days where one rose to retire and got down to get up.

Hermes could handle the most troublesome and dispersed tasks, whether competitive threat, personal development, salesmanship, or capturing the bad guys. Among these tasks was the killing of the hundred-eyed Argos and the purifying of the fifty daughters of Danaus, who murdered their bridegrooms and were doomed forever to draw water with a sieve in Hades. Hermes successfully sold superman stable cleaner Hercules as a slave to Omphale, queen of Lydia. Then with Father's help in the form of a Zeus thunderbolt, Hermes was able to tie up Ixion, king of Thessaly—celebrated sinner and the first murderer—to a revolving wheel in Hades, using serpents as lashing.

What an array of strengths and talents—and how suitable to the "patron saint" of the boardroom. Hermes was very much at home with his fellow members of the highest governing group—the gods and goddesses of Greece atop Mount Olympus. One thing is clear: Hermes had style and identified with governance, culture, and the Olympian systems view of the world and all its activities.

Governance Systems Culture

I would define systems culture in a board context as the placing together of a scattered complex of philosophies, principles, concepts, dogmas, axioms, and doctrines. These are arranged or ordered in a rational dependence to form a harmonic union or coherent whole. Some elements surface as bylaws, articles of incorporation, or policy. Other elements are implicit, transient, and personal. Some form of regular personal interaction unites the parts of a governance systems culture. A normalized pattern of relationships of people and ideas creates a structured harmony of events.

Boardroom culture can be demanding at times, depending on the style, spirit, and traits of your fellow director. At one period, while on the Monsanto board, we had three Southern-born directors whose company careers had begun, by God, in Jack Daniel's country of the former Swann Chemical Company. This company had been acquired in 1935 and became Monsanto's Phosphate Division.

As the newest Monsanto director in 1961 I found myself paced by these colleagues (Felix Williams, John Christian, and Ed O'Neal) on many an occasion of a plant visit by the board, a company party where drinks mix people, or a pre-board session of poker—that game in which it's darkest just before you've drawn. One of the things I quickly learned was to always drink standing up because it's much easier to sit down when you've had too much to drink standing up than it is to stand up.

An FBI agent friend of mine in St. Louis taught me a trick he used when he had to infiltrate an undercover situation and joining in the spirits of the occasion was likely to make him either lose his inhibitions and give exhibitions or, worse, reveal his mission. The trick was to swallow two ounces of olive oil before the sun goes over the yardarm. This lines your alimentary canal with a protective coating. Years of practice with this secret defense has kept my stomach in good shape. It wasn't until 1972 after I moved from Monsanto that I eliminated the briefcase emergency bottles of olive oil.

Given the impact of personalities on a board culture, the boundaries of the system are permeable and far-reaching. The scope may be so extensive that it is difficult for directors to get their minds around the entire sweep of the domain in which an institution must function. The compass of the board is proscribed by the interest and concerns of individuals who make up the system. Oversimplifications are necessary to be practical about the boundary of governance at most any stage of the system's maturity and competitive existence. Almost anything is easier to get into than get out of, so one of the tough problems is to prevent directors from letting the corporation wander into business or social areas in which the corporation is ill-fitted to compete.

If the directors insist on strict containment of their interests, the system is a closed one. As with a management system, the parameters then have rigid time constraints. These are very long, relative to the length of the cycles or the processes by which the board system operates, for example, investment in plant facilities may have to pay out in four or five years, but the board's horizon for strategic planning may be ten to twenty years. As Harry Walker, former

manager of the Houston Astros, said, "You gotta be planning for the future and at the same time you gotta be thinking ahead."

If the system is an open one, as we conceptualize the board's true domain, the time constraints for system change are themselves variables. This means most anything can happen, as it does in our personal lives; if in the course of several months only three worthwhile social events take place, they will all fall on the same evening. It is never certain when an open system itself will need basic redefinition. This is because of interaction between the system and the environment or between system elements and other entities inside or outside the system.

This fluid feature of an open system is discomforting to directors and managers who are not used to struggling with fuzzy situations and continual uncertainty. Lack of precision, lack of director association with many of the variables, unknowns, and conflicts in governance make an open systems notion unattractive to those who value or need structure, order, and unequivocal situations. Intuition, instinct, vision, beliefs, values, faith, and common sense are the primary recourse for directors in a board system culture. One troubled New England company chairman trying to recruit a West Coast director specified to me he needed a man to bring in a Western viewpoint and one who wasn't afraid to hear a discouraging word. The chairman was acknowledging the need for a flexible director.

Professor Handy's theory of cultural propriety helps us if we rephrase it to fit an open system culture. Our domain of the director is territory distinct from the realm of the manager to which Professor Handy applied his theory. We would reshape the theory of cultural propriety in order to make it congruent with a boardroom's fuzzy boundaries.

Thesis: A Governance Theory of Cultural Propriety

1. Ambiguity, vagueness, incompleteness, ineffectiveness, slack, and even incompetence in boardroom behavior are in a large measure due to external uncertainties. This situation is often compounded by a lack of congruence in the life and career cycles of the directors, in contrast to those of the senior management. The directors are frequently older, more experienced, sometimes dated in their perspectives and expectations, with the management made up of younger men and women of the go-go type. The reverse condition also exists when a board is younger, more aggressive, and more active than the key management with respect to visions, philosophies, and attitudes. The latter circumstance often is a matter to be addressed when a merger or takeover of one company by another presents a mixed-up set of governance and management philosophies, styles, and cultures.

   The average age of fifty-seven years for U.S. corporate directors recently surveyed has changed little over the last twenty years. Most directors earned their business or other spurs before the current flurry over corporate law reform which is a prime boardroom concern. Too, most directors had their management or professional experience during a period of rapid economic growth, relatively little government intervention, less legal and regulatory constraint in

consumer and environmental matters, surefooted international expansion, and limited conflict or interdependence
between profit, nonprofit, or government-sector institutions.

2. Board and management organizations develop their own
specific company cultures, which are a blend of the different philosophies, styles, and attitudes of the persons on the
board and in the top management.

   Beliefs, values, attitudes, and ethics are a set of complex
abstractions. When these abstractions are wrapped up in
one organization they become the culture of the institution. Culture is concerned with the integrated behavior
pattern which deals with the norms for "right" behavior in
which the values and aspirations of individuals shape the
culture.

3. Few organizations are culturally pure, as boards are
usually composed of individuals who may have very different experience, education, and perspectives, even though
they have certain things in common such as status, titles,
age, political or social background, and philosophy. A
blend of individuals is desirable to enable the board to
cope with rapid change, discontinuities, or upsets in the
growth and conduct of the company or institution they
serve as directors.

4. Individuals have preferred directorship philosophies
which may or may not be congruent with the organizational culture(s).

5. Analysis of a cultural perspective of governance is a diag-
nostic aid providing clues to the comfort and discomfort of
individuals, depending on the nature of the cultural pro-
prieties.

6. Boardlife is a set of jobs-to-be-done which are of three
types:

- Steady-state, programmable tasks which can be handled by
systems, bylaws, routines, and prescriptive rules (usually 80
percent of most organizational work and a prime domain of
management, as distinct from governance)
- Development tasks that deal with new situations or issues
requiring new systems or routines which adapt to change
(the prime domain of a directorate)

- Asterisk situations which are exceptions, emergencies, discontinuities, and symmetry breaks requiring rather polar qualities: reflection, instinct and creativity, rather than logical analysis and personal intervention
7. The lure of the boardroom is to cope with and avoid mismatch of multicultures for the three types of tasks to be carried out by the management and board organizations.
8. A monoculture is wrong for most organizations, certainly for a boardroom. Differences in personal culture are healthy and spawn creativity and change. Choice and blend of cultures should be designed and managed by the board for the best composite culture for the company, rather than haphazardly experiencing cultural changes through—for example—unprofessional criteria for boardworthiness in selection of candidates.

Introduction of new perspectives can help keep the boardroom condition consistent, even compatible with the existing maturity stage, the governance system culture, and the competitive position targeted for the enterprise. If you have a board of twelve Yalies who all married blondes from Darien and are Episcopalians, then you might get a lot of easy agreement on issues but you certainly won't get many effective solutions to real problems. Such individual directors would at least have the same "preferred directorship values and philosophies," but those values, attitudes, and philosophies might not fit with the target culture of the particular company being governed by that board.

Corporate development and boardroom development are not always in sync. Ideally, the board of directors provides leadership and a Hermes role model for directing and positioning the corporation. If all boards could possess such divinity, I fear our directors might assume the perception of themselves that Fred Allen attributed to movie stars who wear their sunglasses even in church—they're afraid that God might recognize them and ask for autographs.

Adjournment

My previous book on boards of directors provided hundreds of calls and letters—well, thirty-nine, to be honest—all asking the same thing: What's with the boardroom? What really goes on behind the boardroom door? And that question from the thirty-nine of you has prompted this book. What it all boils down to is that there are two ways to look behind the boardroom door—through the keyhole or over the transom. Both have been used to explore my smorgasboard view of boardlife, board dilemmas, and the humor of the body-board. However, neither perspective is completely satisfactory.

For instance, the keyhole view can be narrow and limited. It's sort of like the time everything went black for the fellow waiting outside his girl's apartment. She must have hung something over the doorknob.

The transom view looks down on a board. This implies a judging of the human side of board affairs. It assumes some standards of governance for individual directors, whereas such normative touchstones are far from established in our various societies. Such a transom view suggests a comparison against my own vulnerable beliefs, values, and sense of propriety. To draw any such judgment or censure of board behavior from the previous fifteen chapters would be missing the point and, more important, be insensitive to

the basic issues underlying director conduct and behavior. I am reminded of a doting mother's attitude upon receiving a letter from
the camp director informing her that her son needed discipline. She
replied, "Dear Director: Please don't slap Irving. He is very sensitive. Slap the boy next to him. That will scare Irving."

Some directors are nervous as they see litigation and conviction of board members who haven't conducted themselves properly. Perhaps this tongue-in-cheek book tour of boardroom overworld mystique will unmask the director role for what it really is—a very complicated, taxing, risky, vexatious character part in real-life drama. The challenge is to see that our corporations are managed effectively and in everyone's interest.

Being a good director these days is like trying to drink out of a fire hose—you can't really control or get on top of the situation, and you may get drenched while trying. But you must try anyway.

So, in adjourning this book about the more frivolous side of boards as well as graver matters, I find myself like the funeral director trying not to smile at a $10,000 funeral. Board meetings are indeed dignified, serious, and earnest events. But I see no reason at all not to poke a little fun at ourselves, as does the London Institute of Directors' 1971 Standard Manual:

And while the Great Ones repair to their dinner,
The Secretary stays, growing thinner and thinner.
Racking his brains to record and report
What he thinks they will think that they ought to have thought.

Our meeting is adjourned!

Index